Li-Chun Hsiao

The Indivisible Globe, the Indissoluble Nation

Universality, Postcoloniality, and Nationalism in the Age of Globalization

Li-Chun Hsiao

THE INDIVISIBLE GLOBE, THE INDISSOLUBLE NATION
Universality, Postcoloniality, and
Nationalism in the Age of Globalization

Bibliografische Information der Deutschen Nationalbibliothek

Die Deutsche Nationalbibliothek verzeichnet diese Publikation in der Deutschen Nationalbibliografie; detaillierte bibliografische Daten sind im Internet über http://dnb.d-nb.de abrufbar.

Bibliographic information published by the Deutsche Nationalbibliothek

Die Deutsche Nationalbibliothek lists this publication in the Deutsche Nationalbibliografie; detailed bibliographic data are available in the Internet at http://dnb.d-nb.de.

ISBN-13: 978-3-8382-1524-2
© *ibidem*-Verlag, Stuttgart 2021
Alle Rechte vorbehalten

Das Werk einschließlich aller seiner Teile ist urheberrechtlich geschützt. Jede Verwertung außerhalb der engen Grenzen des Urheberrechtsgesetzes ist ohne Zustimmung des Verlages unzulässig und strafbar. Dies gilt insbesondere für Vervielfältigungen, Übersetzungen, Mikroverfilmungen und elektronische Speicherformen sowie die Einspeicherung und Verarbeitung in elektronischen Systemen.

All rights reserved. No part of this publication may be reproduced, stored in or introduced into a retrieval system, or transmitted, in any form, or by any means (electronical, mechanical, photocopying, recording or otherwise) without the prior written permission of the publisher. Any person who does any unauthorized act in relation to this publication may be liable to criminal prosecution and civil claims for damages.

Printed in the EU

TABLE OF CONTENTS

Abstract 7

Introduction 9

Chapter 1
The Postcolonial Paradigm/Paradox: Theorizing between the
Universal and the Particular... 15

Chapter 2
Toussaint, Mimicry, and the Primal Scene of Postcoloniality 47

Chapter 3
In the Name of the Father: Representing Postcolonial Nationalisms 93

Chapter 4
Toussaint, Globalization, and the Postcolonial Spectacle 131

Epilogue 163

About the Author 167

Bibliography 169

Abstract

This book attempts to rethink, under the rubric of globalization, a number of key notions in postcolonial theory and writings by revisiting what it conceives of as "the primal scene of postcoloniality"—the Haitian Revolution. Theoretically, it unpacks and critiques the poststructuralist penchants and undercurrents of the postcolonial paradigm in First-World academia while not reinstating earlier Marxist stricture. Focusing on Édouard Glissant's, C. L. R. James's, and Derek Walcott's representations of Toussaint L'Ouverture and the Haitian Revolution, the textual analyses aim to approach the issues of colonial mimicry, postcolonial nationalism, and postcoloniality in light of recent reconsiderations of the universal/the particular in critical theories, and psychoanalytic conceptions of trauma, identity, and jouissance. This book argues that postcolonial intellectuals' characteristic celebration of the Particular, together with their nuanced denunciation of the postcolonial nation and the Revolution, doesn't really do away with the category of the Universal, nor twist free of the problematic of the logics of difference/equivalence that sustain the "living on" of the nation-state, despite an ever expanding globality; rather, such a postcolonial phenomenon is symptomatic of a disavowed traumatic event that mirrors and prefigures the predicament of the postcolonial experience while evoking its simulacra and further struggles centuries later.

Introduction

The Postcolonial Problematic

As with the precedents of postmodernism and poststructuralism, the expansion, together with the eventual ascent, of postcolonial studies to a paradigmatic status on the contemporary intellectual scene in recent decades doesn't seem to help clarify many of the fundamental questions about the field. There have been theoretical debates over the parameters, definition(s), methodologies or epistemological grounds, speaking positions, and the locality of postcoloniality: For example, is the postcolonial "post" in the same sense as the postmodern or the poststructuralist? When is (was) the postcolonial, or was there ever such a moment? What is postcoloniality, and how does one conceive of it vis-à-vis postcolonialism (and vice versa)? Who are the postcolonials? Who speaks as/for the postcolonial? Are the ex-colonized and ex-colonizer "postcolonial" in the same sense?[1] Like the designation "postcolonial" itself, key notions/terms in the

---

[1] One of the most important representatives of such debates can be found in the special issue of the journal *Social Text* 31/32 (1992), which some critics consider an "event" in the short history of postcolonial studies (e.g. Masao Miyoshi, 750; Grant Farred, "New Faces, Old Places"). For queries of the term "postcolonial," see, particularly, Anne MacClintock's and Ella Shohat's pieces in this issue. For the contour of the debate and the focus of these polemics, see the editors' "Introduction" to this special issue. The first question enlisted here, about the semantic vagueness of the "post" in "postcolonial," is adapted from Kwame Anthony Appiah's essay with the straightforward title, "Is the Post- in Postmodernism the Post- in Postcolonialism?" The most notable and fiercest critiques of the "careerism" of postcolonial intellectuals, their complicity with the dominant neo-colonial regime of knowledge or cultural production, and their position vis-à-vis the non-cosmopolitan postcolonial subjects they presumably represent, are levied by Aijaz Ahmad, Timothy Brennan, Arif Dirlik, Stuart Hall, and Benita Parry, though Hall is adamantly critical of what he perceives as reductionist dismissals made by more orthodox Marxists, particularly Dirlik (see Hall, 258–259). In addition, Hall conveniently reviews these contestations over the term postcolonial itself, especially on the question of its temporality, in his "When Was the Postcolonial?" For critiques from scholars who identify with and work within the field of postcolonial studies yet register discontent with the French-inspired "high theory" in much of the works of prominent postcolonial theorists, see Bart Moore-Gilbert's distinction between "postcolonial theory" and "postcolonial criticism." For fairly comprehensive documentations of the more general "postcolonial controversies," see Ania Loomba (*Colonialism* 7–19) and Vi-

field, such as "hybridity" or "diaspora," tend to lapse into loosely conceived and exuberantly celebrated buzzwords as they appear more and more frequently in and beyond postcolonial studies.

In this book, I'd like to approach, in the spirit of polemics, the postcolonial "controversies," or—as I prefer to call them—"problematics" by focusing on two of the multiple and entangled facets of the issues: 1) the spatial dimension concerning the manifestations of these problematics in the postcolonial nation and the variegated inflections of postcolonial nationalism; 2) the temporal dimension entailing the indeterminate, convoluted temporality of *post*coloniality, trauma of colonial slavery as the "remainder" of the history of colonialism, and a query of the presumed pastness of colonialism in certain discourses of postcolonialism. Against the backdrop of this "postcolonial problematic," which might as well be called the point of departure of this book, I'd like to locate another, deeper, and more latent problematic in postcolonial studies—the question of the universal/particular; this latent level of the postcolonial problematic, as well as its manifest instantiations, then, has to intersect, or even be traversed by an "Event" that encompasses these contestations by both illuminating and problematizing them: Toussaint and the Haitian Revolution.[2] Let me briefly explicate the centrality of the historical figure of Toussaint—whose emergence itself was an "event" in the history of colonialism—and the Haitian Revolution to this book before we move on to full-length explorations (in Chapter 1) of the universal/particular problematic in postcolonial criticism and theory.

---

lashini Coopan. Also see Graham Huggan for a recap of the institutional history of postcolonial studies as a field, as well as the trajectories of the postcolonial debates (228–264).

2   This capital "E" certainly cannot hide its implicit allusion to Alain Badiou's notion of Event or Truth-Event. For reasons that will become clearer to the reader in the remainder of the book, I'd say, under the rubric of Badiou's work, the legend of Toussaint and the Haitian Revolution is definitely an Event for the post-Bastille "situation" from which it sprang, and, to a certain degree, for the problematic of the "postcolonial situation" we're exploring in this book: It is an Event in the sense that it foregrounds the inherent lack or excess of the "official" situation—what the latter has to exclude in order to come into being; it produces its own Truth—a new Universal—which is not yet accountable or justifiable in the terms of the preceding situation.

Who is Toussaint?

This, no doubt, is meant to be more of a rhetorical question. Rather than supplying a biographical account or historical documentation, I'd draw attention to the historical disjunction or discontinuities in historiography through which Toussaint is largely forgotten in the Western memory of colonial slavery—a forgetfulness that is the background against which this question, in its literal sense, has to be asked, especially for those stumbling into the field of postcolonialism: no, really ... who is Toussaint?

Maybe it would be easier to reawaken the memory of Toussaint by citing a work of canonical Western literature which treats Toussaint as its subject matter. One such rare case can be found in William Wordsworth's "To Toussaint L'Ouverture":

> Toussaint, the most unhappy man of men!
> Whether the whistling Rustic tend his plough
> Within thy hearing, or thy head be now
> Pillowed in some deep dungeon's earless den;—
> O miserable chieftain! Yet die not; do thou
> Wear rather in thy bonds a cheerful brow:
> Though fallen thyself, never to rise again,
> Live, and take comfort. Thou hast left behind
> Powers that will work for thee; air, earth, and skies;
> There is not a breathing of the common wind
> That will forget thee; thou hast great allies;
> Thy friends are exultations, agonies,
> And love, and man's unconquerable mind. (*Poems* 577)

Ironically, not only had Toussaint few allies, but he has been virtually forgotten, most conspicuously in Western colonial and abolitionist discourses (Hesse 164), before C. L. R. James's ground-breaking book, *The Black Jacobins*, resuscitated it from obscurity and the brink of oblivion, stirring not only memories but also Third-World revolutions in the mid-twentieth century.[3] In his interview with C. L. R. James, Stuart Hall says of his anecdote: "I once met a Haitian intellectual who told the story of how astonished people were in Haiti to discover that *Black Jacobins* was written

---

3 To be sure, the memory of Toussaint and the Haitian Revolution had lived in local folklore, historical accounts, and official documents written by Haitian historians or fellow Caribbeans, despite the metropolitan neglect which sufficed to ensure the marginalization of this memory. It was not until after the emergence of James's book, and the political climate of the last century, that it was able to have such planetary influence and significance. See Farred ("Mapping"; "Victorian").

first by a black man, secondly by a West Indian. Because of course it had come back to them through London, through Paris" (qtd. in Farred, "Mapping" 227). Perhaps thanks to Toussaint, James's work suffered another round of neglect. For instance, Paul Gilroy, whose ground-breaking conception of the "Black Atlantic" as an alternative to Western modernity charts the trajectories of the lives and works of a few monumental black figures, curiously relegates both James and Toussaint to nearly total oblivion. Though Gilroy acknowledges the importance of James, himself a diasporic intellectual, and refers to others' writings on him (see, for example, xi, 221), his virtual omission of Toussaint and the Haitian Revolution is quite puzzling: It is particularly so when one considers how the author attempts to, rightly, recuperate the significance of the memory of slavery and elegantly elevates it to the "slave sublime" (187–223); how the Haitian Revolution emerged as the first successful slave revolt in history;[4] or the fact that Toussaint and the slaves, displaced by the Middle Passage and thrown into an unknown modern world, collectively constituted or participated in the prototypical diasporic experience, which Gilroy argues is the defining characteristic of the routed Black Atlantic (and we may add, of the "postcolonial condition").

Remembering Toussaint, Rethinking Postcolonial

Why Toussaint and the Haitian Revolution? How do they tie into the context of our postcolonial inquiry? In my view, Toussaint's Haitian Revolution, which has often been considered an imitation of its immediate historical precedent, the French Revolution, best exemplifies the inherent inconsistency/antagonism of the Western model nation-state and presents itself as a thought-provoking case of the potentialities and limits of (post)colonial mimicry, the question of postcolonial nationalisms, and the convoluted temporality of the postcolonial. It was the first successful, sustained decolonization movement against European colonialism in history, and, in some sense, the first "postcolonial" moment as well. Yet Toussaint's Haitian Revolution further complicates the temporality of postcoloniality

---

4   Eugene Genovese emphasizes that the Haitian Revolution differs from the numerous slave revolts before it mainly because of its revolutionary ideology and practices, not simply due to its much greater military success over the white colonial powers.

not only in the sense that it predated, and inspired, the mid-twentieth century anticolonial movements, against which certain paradigms of contemporary postcolonial criticism register their antagonism and identify themselves as "postcolonial"; but also that it presaged a certain "undead colonialism" after decolonization, mirroring the uncanny recurrence of violence, corruption, and dependency epitomized in the failures of the postcolonial nation-state in our historical juncture. It is, in other words, an instantiation of Édouard Glissant's well-known notion of *vision prophétique du passé* ("the prophetic vision of the past"; 227). The displaced or disavowed memories of the colonial encounter and slavery, as well as the structural impossibility of revolutionary ideals, which I shall highlight in the analyses of the case of the Haitian Revolution, constitute the traumatic kernel of the postcolonial and engender or evoke what I call "the primal scene of postcoloniality" (see Chapter 2).

Still, such "institutional forgetting" of Toussaint, the Haitian Revolution, and colonial slavery persists in our allegedly "postcolonial" present, especially in the form of "spectacle." To rehabilitate the significance of Toussaint, the exploration of which cannot be extricated from the memories of the Haitian Revolution and of colonial slavery, would require that we remember them beyond their various forms of spectacle. Years before Edward Said's well-known argument that the Orient is literally the (discursive) creation of the West,[5] Frantz Fanon had contended that it was Europe that could be considered "literally the creation of the Third World," since it was the exploitation of the material resources and labor from the colonies, "the sweat and the dead bodies of Negroes, Arabs, Indians and the yellow races" that sustained the "opulence" of Europe (*Wretched*, 76, 81). Further back in history, colonial slavery, as Hardt and Negri argue, can be *"perfectly compatible with capitalist production"* (122; emphasis in original), even though it appears that the capitalist ideology of freedom "must be antithetical to slave labor" (121). "There is no contradiction here," Hardt and Negri conclude wryly, "slave labor in the colonies made capitalism in Europe possible, and European capital had no interest in giving it up" (122). This uncovering of the material base of colonial/capitalist

---

5   It must be noted that Said, as he was to stress again and again, never discounts a "really existing" Orient outside of the West's discursive formations. In his later works, for example *Culture and Imperialism*, he points out, on the other hand, the West's dependence on its epistemological and cultural Other.

system at an increasingly global scale is not merely the reinstating of a materialist mode of analysis—which is important itself, or even a sort of economic determinism; rather, it seeks to probe, in light of a psychoanalytic approach, the traumatic effects of a colonialism that often starts with, but goes deeper than material devastation. Moreover, this book attempts to bring to the fore what has to be radically excluded from this system so that it can be constituted, or how such "constitutive exclusion" is systematically obliterated, even by means of rendering it a spectacle.

To remember Toussaint properly is therefore to confront the traumatic effects of colonial slavery, in its variegated forms, under the aegis of today's capitalist, globalizing world that feeds on the disavowal or liquidation of its memory (, Hess, 158); it also means to re-examine the West's liberal-democratic fantasy of the pastness of colonialism and its simultaneous rendering of contemporary postcolonial failures as otherworldly spectacle. In a more politically salient sense, to remember Toussaint is to come to realize that "the cruelest Haitian paradox, then, is not that its role as the nation that birthed the black postcolonial movement is forgotten. Nor is it that the country that was one of the wealthiest of the Caribbean ... is currently the poorest in its hemisphere. Rather, it is that the very model of resistance that Toussaint and the slave developed almost two hundred years ago continues to offer *unread lessons* to contemporary postcolonial societies in Haiti, Ghana, Kenya, Jamaica, and even in the newly post-apartheid South Africa" (Farred, "Mapping," 245; emphasis mine).

Apropos of the structure of this book, the centrality of Toussaint and the Haitian Revolution to this book in general will be illuminated in terms of universality/particularity; of the final moments of (formal) colonial slavery and the fine moments of revolutionary hopes; of taking place at the originary instances of the (Western) nation-state, decolonization, and postcoloniality; and of the constitutive yet disavowed role of colonial slavery in an expanding capitalist globalization. Each chapter of this book, in a sense, is structured around one of these illuminations, though interrelated points are unavoidable and may thus cut across different sections.

Chapter 1
The Postcolonial Paradigm/Paradox: Theorizing between the Universal and the Particular

Although postcolonial debates, as outlined in the preceding discussion, have resulted in more problematics than consensus, the spotlight postcolonialism is enjoying has nevertheless invited more critical and, sometimes, soberer scrutiny across disciplines in the humanities. In the following pages, I do not attempt to document or reenact in detail these contested issues, but would like to situate them in the context of the rise of anti-foundationalism and multiculturalism on the (mainly Western) contemporary intellectual scene and on one of the most quintessential debates arising from the (in)compatibility and/or tension between them: the issue of the universal and the particular. I will, furthermore, call attention to a certain internal contradiction of postcolonial discourse and examine it in light of the complicated relationship between universalism and particularism.

Universalizing the Particular or Particularizing the Universal?: Between Anti-foundationalism and Multiculturalism

It is a critical commonplace of recent decades that the Enlightenment notion of the Universal is bankrupt, or at least, theoretically specious and politically malevolent. A wary critic, however, can notice at least two undercurrents in such "universalising condemnations of the universal" (Hallward, 176). On the one hand, there are profound and influential critiques of the foundationalism of Enlightenment Reason, consummated in the postmodern/poststructuralist debunking of the transcendental, universalist Subject and the subsequent substitution of "subject positions" in its place. The "dismantling of the universal" as well as the relentless questioning of any foundationalist claim to an epistemological ground or determinate identity has no doubt been summarily regarded as the founding gesture of contemporary (Western) thought (Schor, 15), befitting the characteristic fragmentation of the social in the present-day world. In the wake of, or perhaps owing to or in response to, the "death of the subject," we witnessed, on the other hand, a proliferation of ethnic, sexual, racial, national, cultural, and other increasingly particularistic identities (e.g. age groups, women or gays within minority communities, disabilities, etc.) under the rubric of multiculturalism which, while sharing with postmodern anti-foundationalism the emphatic rejection of the Universal (as the "ethnia of the West," for example) along with the valorization of difference and particularity, nevertheless makes claims to a certain degree of authenticity and subjectivity in "identity politics." The rise of postcolonial theory and literatures can be said to have taken place in the debates over postmodern anti-foundationalism and multiculturalism, in the *simultaneous affinity and incommensurability* of the two.

As in the case of the popularization of cultural studies in Western academia,[6] the remarkable spate of general interest in postcolonial studies stemmed from a growing dissatisfaction among cultural and literary critics with the (earlier) postmodern/poststructuralist approaches—probably the most widely endorsed theoretical means available—not only for their preoccupation with deconstructing "grand narratives" primarily at the linguistic and epistemological levels, instead of directing or extending the assault to more "toxic" socio-politico-historical issues; but also for their apparently Eurocentric frame of reference—both in terms of theoretical edifice and objects of study—which appears inadequate in the face of the necessary pluralization following the breakdown of metanarratives and which runs counter to the patently postmodern imperative to always contextualize and attend to the local, the marginal. The typical postcolonial gesture against the postmodern paradigm is that "merely postmodern writing," as Peter Hallward recounts, "tends toward a certain placelessness, a disembodied abstraction uncomfortably close to an ideological reflection of prevailing modes of production in the West" (20). The "postcolonial," by con-

---

6   Huggan suggests that the rise of postcolonial studies in the 1990s be seen as "partly the offshoot of a wider institutional phenomenon—the so-called turn to cultural studies in an increasing number of English (among other humanities) departments at Western universities," or even "an analytical attempt to *globalise* the already wide scope of cultural studies" (240). Loomba's book *Colonialism/Postcolonialism* further places the recent boom of postcolonial studies under the aegis of historically situated anti-imperialist critiques produced in modern as well as contemporary socio-cultural movements and phenomena, such as the history of decolonization and the "revolution" within the "Western" intellectual tradition (Marxism, 1980s colonial discourse analysis, etc.).

trast, signals not only a temporal lapse, but also a certain spatiality, an outside, a "somewhere-else," though the accent is predominantly placed on the transient trajectories of migration (rather than the "fixed" locations themselves), on the border-crossing, boundary-effacing movements of unspecification. In short, postcolonialism sets itself against what it perceives as the failed postmodernist/poststructuralist promise to affirm the particular or the marginal and eschew any universalizing attempt by more forcefully valorizing the particular and the marginal and highlighting what heretofore has been neglected and marginalized by Enlightenment thought and Eurocentric anti-foundationalism alike. This brings postcolonialism closer to the particularism of "identity politics," one of the important players in the debates about multiculturalism.

Apropos of multiculturalism, postcolonialism is empowered by, and caught up in "the politics of authenticity": the postcolonial gains a great deal of currency in the milieu of a pluralist promotion of particularity and multiculturalist accentuations of strong identity claims from the margins; however, the particular, though born of contingency, can hardly present its particularity if it is conceived as constantly permeated by the contingent, by a flux of (subject) positions or movements of the changing, which postcolonial intellectuals believe characterize contemporary mode of existence. While recognizing the necessity to somehow vindicate a certain particularity in their distancing from the postmodern penchant of obliterating origins, of collapsing all kinds of boundaries, including the identitarian one, the postcolonial critics, like many participating in the debates on multiculturalism, are quick to avoid, locate, and even castigate any trace of ethnic or racial essentialism in the constitution of identities.[7] After "the linguistic turn" and the "cultural" or "ethnic" turn, therefore, we don't quite have yet another paradigm shift. It is easy to discern in postcolonial

---

7   A notable exception to this unanimous avoidance of the designation "essentialism" would be Spivak's proposal of "strategic essentialism," which is echoed among cultural critics and theoreticians (e.g. Laclau, *Emancipation(s)*, 50–51). However, numerous instances in Spivak's writings, ever elusive themselves, disprove the notion that she would by this term endorse the common understanding of using essentialism strategically, as a tool to reach some common political goal. Her self-reflexive, relentlessly self-deconstructing tendency in what she calls a "self-separating project" (*Postcolonial Critic*, 21) and more recently, her affirmation of some sort of ineluctable yet productive "complicity" (*Critique*, xii, 3–4, 9) in any resistance certainly mark a sharp distinction from those insisting on maintaining strong, politically salient identity claims.

writings the anti-foundationalist penchant of poststructuralism or postmodernism (for example, the overflowing glorification of hybridity and syncretism, the insistent avoidance or renunciation of essentialism); more obvious are the theoretical vocabularies and explicit or implicit references to well-known poststructuralist thinkers deployed in the work of postcolonial theoreticians.[8] Such a theoretical indebtedness to an entrenched anti-foundationalism is presumably what makes postcolonial studies inadvertently or self-consciously swing back to the other end of the debates surrounding multiculturalism and anti-foundationalism and repeat the gestures and practices it seeks to do without: its ineluctable propensity to generalize and universalize in its theoretical speculations; its alleged Eurocentric orientation in its historical frame of reference (e.g. histories of the colonized structured exclusively around European colonialization) and indifference to distinct socio-historical conditions when "applying" Western theoretical insights; its unabashed culturalism and textualism which privilege questions of culture, textuality and language over social, historical, macro-political, and economic issues.[9]

These major fronts on which postcolonial studies has been attacked signal more than its oscillating status (especially of its theoretical endeavors) between opposing camps on the contested terrain of critical engagements; it also foregrounds the *internal contradiction* or inherent tension

---

[8] A crude, sometimes caricaturing, sometimes heuristically motivated characterization which has been circulating around for quite some time has been to identify behind Bhabha, Said, and Spivak—who Robert Young calls the "Holy Trinity" of postcolonial theorists—the monumental figures of Lacan, Foucault, and Derrida, respectively. Those sympathetic to postcolonial theory and those critical of it both seem to accept this linkage to poststructuralism/postmodernism: students and those who have no prior local and historical knowledge of colonialism recognize in postcolonial discourse the familiar and paradigmatic terminology and themes of postmodernism and accept it on this ground, while on the other hand, there are others maybe equipped with the necessary socio-historical knowledge of colonialism—for example, Marxists and many Third World intellectuals not trained in Western academia—who reject postcolonial studies, especially the theory part, precisely because of its postsructuralist association. See Moore-Gilbert for a distinction between French poststructuralist theory-inspired "postcolonial theory" on the one hand, and on the other, the "wider field of postcolonial criticism" that is, generally speaking, averse to or skeptical of "theory."

[9] For a similar itemized summary of the general critiques of postcolonial studies, see Hallward, xv. For more refined marshallings of such attacks on postcolonialism and/or detailed analyses of one or more of these critiques, see Ahmad, Cooppan, Dirlik, Loomba (*Colonialism*), MacClintock, and Shohat. This list, of course, can't be exhaustive.

within postcolonial discourse, a contradiction, I argue, that is entwined with the question of *the universal and the particular* and is intrinsic to the debates about anti-foundationalism and multiculturalism, a context from which postcolonial studies cannot be detached. As Ernesto Laclau observes in his account of the increasingly visible contradiction within the theoretical edifice and politics of the aforementioned debates,

> [i]t is important, however, to realize that these two debates have not advanced along symmetrical lines, that argumentative strategies have tended to move from one to the other in unexpected ways, and that *many apparently paradoxical combinations have been shown to be possible*. Thus, the so-called postmodern approaches can be seen as weakening the imperialist foundationalism of the Western Enlightenment and opening a way to a more democratic cultural pluralism; but they can also be perceived as underpinning a notion of 'weak' identity which is incompatible with the strong cultural attachments required by a 'politics of authenticity'. And universal values can be seen as a strong assertion of the 'ethnia of the West' . . . but also as a way of fostering—at least tendentially—an attitude of respect and tolerance vis-à-vis cultural diversity. (*Emancipation(s)*, 47; emphasis mine)

Such paradoxical positions often go unheeded, that is, they have the political efficacy—at least within academic circles—to resonate among and mobilize previously incongruous groups under a radical or progressive rhetoric, especially in the days when cultural studies and postcolonial studies, as new, emerging fields, were rapidly expanding their intellectual territories.

On the terrain of postcolonial theory, critics have pointed out that Homi Bhabha, one of the elite group of theorists who in many ways personify and popularize the field, cannot help but reveal his generalizing or universalizing tendency in theorizing colonial (and anti-colonial) discourses and the colonial encounter amidst the particularist rhetoric pervasive in his work as well as in plainly anti-generalizing claims such as "I have attempted no general theory" (*Location*, 170). His preoccupation with the enunciative instability—the "cracks" or immanent *différance*—of colonial discourse as evidence of the irreducible hybridity of the colonial subject (on both sides of the colonial divide) inevitably leads one to question, as Ania Loomba does, whether this "hybridity of enunciation spills over into becoming the definitive characteristic of *all* colonial authority, everywhere, at any time" ("Overworlding," 172). One can even go as far as to say that Bhabha's employment of "enunciation" exemplifies, rightly or wrongly, his constant and "problematic shift" from "a particular act of enunciation to a theory of all utterance" (ibid.), that it ultimately equates any particular subject (dominant/dominated, colonizer/colonized) with "an instance of enunciation itself" (Hallward, 27).

In the bigger picture, as Peter Hallward remarks, "postcolonial theory often seems to present itself as a sort of general theory of the non-generalisable as such" (xi). Paradoxically, the proliferation of heterogeneity and difference, which has accompanied the rise of postcolonialism, as well as postcolonial theorists' attentiveness to even more particularistic and marginal categories, entails a purview that is "scarcely less inclusive, both historically and geographically, than that of something like the study of everything affected by modernisation and its consequences" (Hallward, xi). The most representative of such unexamined and unduly expansive postcolonial studies is probably Bhabha's wide-ranging definition, in highly abstract language, of "postcolonial criticism":[10]

> Postcolonial criticism bears witness to the unequal and uneven forces of cultural representation involved in the contest for political and social authority within the modern world order. Postcolonial perspectives emerge from the colonial testimony of Third World countries and the discourses of 'minorities' within the geopolitical divisions of East and West, North and South. They intervene in those ideological discourses of modernity that attempt to give a hegemonic 'normality' to the uneven development and the differential, often disadvantaged, histories of nations, races, communities, peoples. They formulate their critical revisions around issues of cultural difference, social authority, and political discrimination in order to reveal the antagonistic and ambivalent moments within the 'rationalizations' of modernity. (*Location*, 171)

Ironically, Bhabha's expansive reference to generic "nations, races, communities, peoples" betrays his well-meaning, legitimate attempt to valorize the particular, to recuperate the "differential, often disadvantaged, histories" of the hitherto marginalized, just as the "geopolitical divisions of East and West, North and South" not only reveals the "antagonistic" moments or divisions over issues of cultural difference, but, under the aegis of this inclusivist rhetoric, also implicitly envisages an all-encompassing globality which houses a thriving multitude—differences that make up the whole or consist of an underlying Sameness.[11] This further exemplifies how "many

---

10   This "definition" originally appeared in an article of 1992 whose title serves a clear purpose—"Postcolonial Criticism." The original passage was slightly revised and included in an essay called "The Postcolonial and the Postmodern: The Question of Agency," collected in *The Location of Culture*.

11   Here I am drawing on Slavoj Žižek's explication of Badiou's critique of multiculturalism, which often describes itself as premised on the Deleuzian "rhizomatic multitude."

writings on postcolonialism," as Loomba points out, "routinely claim to be describing '*the* postcolonial condition', or '*the* postcolonial subject'," despite their emphasis on "concepts like 'hybridity' and fragmentation and diversity" (*Colonialism*, 15; emphasis mine). Such a theoretical short-circuit or inconsistency—and the disavowal of its existence or relevance—arises, I argue, from an indifference or reluctance to engage with the inescapable problematic of the universal/particular, and is certainly not an inconsistency peculiar to Bhabha.[12]

Edward Said, the preeminent postcolonial critic/theorist who is credited with founding the field of postcolonial studies, or at least its contemporary instantiation—a mode of analysis that draws heavily on Western critical theory—is an exemplary case in which the postcolonial intellectual occupies what Said himself terms as "the counterpoint," mediating, in a somewhat facile and serene manner, "an array of opposites, negatives, oppositions" (*Culture and Imperialism*, 59–60).[13] Critics of *Orientalism* have pointed out "the profound paradoxes, even confusions, within the argument of *Orientalism*," despite the book's status as a ground-breaking study and its far-reaching influence (Moore-Gilbert 43). For instance, James Clifford, Dennis Porter, and Robert Young have all called attention to the contradictions resulting from the incompatible methodologies and epistemological positions deployed in this work: the underlying humanism and

---

In his writings on Deleuze, Badiou has characterized him as "the most radical monist in modern philosophy" (Žižek, *Totalitarianism*, 238, 269).

12   I shall return to tackle some other issues raised in Bhabha's work, specifically his appropriation of Lacanian psychoanalysis, in Chapter 2. Spivak's relentlessly particularistic and singularizing approach will also be discussed later in the book, with the emphasis on her admitted "complicity" in the totalizing/universalist schemes she sets out to deconstruct.

13   Patrick Williams and Laura Chrisman claim that Said's *Orientalism* "single-handedly inaugurated a new era of academic inquiry: colonial discourse, also referred to as colonial discourse theory" (5). Thanks to Spivak and Bhabha, the other two of the "big three," Said's status as the founding figure of the (sub)field of postcolonial theory is further consolidated in their acknowledgement of *Orientalism* as a work that "inaugurated the postcolonial field" (Bhabha, "Postcolonial Criticism," 465), or as "the source book in our discipline" (Spivak, *Outside*, 56). Before Said's intervention, there had certainly been a well-developed body of work on colonialism and postcolonial situations that was diverse disciplinarily as well as geographically (by Third World intellectuals such as Fanon and C. L. R. James besides the Western ones) yet that didn't garner as much currency as its post-*Orientalism* counterpart. For this last point, see Ahmad, Lazarus, Loomba (*Colonialism*), among others.

Said's recourse to the Italian Marxist Antonio Gramsci, on the one hand, and his anti-humanism, *à la* Foucault, on the other. The originality of *Orientalism* lies primarily in its laying bare the complicity of Western scholarship and academic productions of knowledge about the Orient *with* the material and political institutions that dominate their objects of study—hence a rejection of the liberal humanist understanding of the "disinterested" pursuit of knowledge. Cast in the language of universalism/particularism, Said's book discloses how the universalist discourse of Orientalism is implicated in its own particularity while posing as the transcendent agency which represents or speaks on behalf of the *particular* objects organized under its purview.

Yet the Foucauldian linking of "the will to knowledge" to the exercise of power also entails Foucault's conception of power as a ubiquitous and impersonal force or network of relations which operates through a multiplicity of channels and sites and which "dissipates" down into the very constitution of the subject, thereby hindering agencies or sites of resistance, if not foreclosing them. Reinstating agency and intentionality of power to his project, and envisaging a mode or strategy of resistance quite different from the particularistic, localized "guerrilla wars" at the margins inspired by a largely Foucauldian vein of thought, Said "clearly inscribes a model of agency and intentionality drawn not just from Marxism [mainly Gramsci], but from a humanist tradition to which, judging by the generous praise accorded to scholars like Erich Auerbach, he remains deeply attached" (Moore-Gilbert, 37). We recall, however, that this humanist tradition and its pretentious claim to a universal agency in the discursive formation of Orientalism is precisely what Said sets out to critique in the first place. This contradiction would seem impossible to mitigate unless one distinguishes "good" Orientalists, a prospect Said sometimes does concede in *Orientalism* (e.g. 326), from the throng of accomplices in that imperialist enterprise of cultural domination. Such a distinction would also allow for the opposition between a "good humanism" and a bad one, and, by extension, a desirable universalism and the Eurocentric one that has been rightly denounced. Unlike most postcolonial critics, Said does not demur from the rhetoric of universalism. The problem, however, is that much of Said's universalist penchant derives from his "unflinching adherence to the traditional virtues of a disinterested, broadly humanist criticism" (Hallward, 52).

This penchant still persists in his later works, and appears even more incongruous in relation to his post-*Orientalism* writings in which he increasingly favors and valorizes the inclination of "fragmenting, dissociating, dislocating, and decentering the experiential terrain covered at present by universalizing historicism" ("Orientalism Reconsidered," 102). Placing the accent on "discrepant experiences," "each with its particular agenda and pace of development . . . coexisting and interacting with each other," Said strives to *"think through and interpret together"* these experiences from a "contrapuntal perspective" (*Culture and Imperialism*, 31–32; emphasis mine).[14] Said's attempt to articulate disparate particulars or heterogeneous elements in the same breath or under the same scheme results in a curious "eclecticism, which," argues Bart Moore-Gilbert, "is perhaps both the strength and the weakness of *Culture and Imperialism*," in which Said's continuing recourse to the humanist tradition is evident. Thus T. S. Eliot is juxtaposed with Frantz Fanon, and the frequent references, "without demur," to writings by conservative critics, which coexist in the book with more left-leaning, materialist paradigms of cultural analysis, or even mentions of Deleuze, sometimes come "close to reinscribing some of the problems involved in the older humanist model of a 'common culture'—but this time on a global, not national scale" (71). It is clear, though, that Said endows the "contrapuntal critic" with some sort of privilege or "disinterestedness" that transcends his/her own particularity and that does not clearly account for the critic's interconnectedness vis-à-vis the myriad of elements he/she mediates and coordinates (Hallward, 58–60). While it would not be fair or accurate to characterize Said's appeal to a universalism as merely falling back on that (Western) humanist model he still invokes from time to time, Said's work does foreground, albeit without openly acknowledging it, the inherently contradictory tendencies necessarily opened up by, and operating in or even fueling, contemporary metropolitan postcolonial discourse—at once (patently) particularistic and (inadvertently, inevitably) universalizing. This constitutive paradox is rendered

---

14 In Said's conception, the "contrapuntal" position, in accordance with its musical connotation, connects, synthesizes, or coordinates discrete yet now related elements. Hallward comments that such contrapuntal perspective can only be "the perspective of the *whole*" (58, original emphasis), since, according to Said himself, counterpoint is the "the tying together of multiple voices in a kind of disciplined whole," as distinct from their "simple reconciliation" ("Criticism, Culture, and Performance," 26).

even more conspicuous as the field of postcolonial studies or the postcolonial mode of cultural analysis and production assumes a paradigmatic status. Before we further pursue this paradigmatic postcolonial problematic, I'd like to place it under the broader rubric of recent critical reconsiderations of the universal.

In Search of a New Universal: Horizons and Impasses

Up until 1990, Cornel West, known for his activist stance, could still celebrate the "postmodern politics of cultural difference" with unequivocal optimism and enthusiasm by pronouncing that it set out "to trash the monolithic and homogeneous in the name of diversity, multiplicity and heterogeneity; to reject the abstract, general and universal in light of the concrete, specific and particular; and to historicize, contextualize and pluralize by high-lighting the contingent, provisional, variable, tentative, shifting and changing" (3). This statement, which might as well be read as a *manifesto* of postcolonialism, represents postmodernist cultural studies at the height of its power as well as the fast-rising popularity of postcolonial studies; but if it heralds the paradigmatic status and hubris of postcolonialism since the early 1990s, it also anticipates the increasingly glaring fissures opened up by the constitutive contradiction between elements once loosely grouped under the banner of postcolonialism: Do these injunctions not point to some generalized, and universalizable principle? How can one not sense the irony of this proclamation's recourse to some sort of binarism (homogeneity/heterogeneity, the general/the specific)—postmodernism's sworn enemy? More importantly, how does one reconcile the concrete with the shifting—how does particularity, as mentioned above, manifest itself through, or in spite of, the changing? Since the early 1990s more and more scholars have begun to seriously call into question the premises of postmodernist/poststructuralist model(s) and rethink particularly, as if in a dialectical move, what had been unanimously dismissed—hence the resurgence of the question of the universal back to the top of theoretical and political agendas. In fact, as some remind us, the term/concept "universal" is not endemic to Enlightenment thought (it dates back to classical philosophy) and has *always* remained a central or ineluctable category in French feminism as well as other strains of modern and contemporary European philosophy, despite the postmodern dismissal or suspension of the universal (cf. Schor, Scott).

Naomi Schor identifies an event in late 1991 that served as the watershed for the "return of universalism within the precincts of the American academy"—a conference on "Identity in Question," co-sponsored by *October* and the Collège International de Philosophie and held at the CUNY Graduate Center in New York (28). Although the force of recent reconsiderations of universalism couldn't have been shaped out of just one single occasion, the weight of the venue of publication of the conference proceedings—a special issue of *October* 61 (1992)—and the celebrity of the panelists bespeak its benchmark status. One prime example of the effects of this turn of events, as Schor specifies, is the change of positions of Judith Butler, who had been a prominent anti-universalist yet came to recognize, shortly after *Gender Trouble*, that "identity is essential to politics and that the category of the universal cannot be done away with" (27). This "return," of course, is hardly an outright reversal of the earlier trend. The unqualified glorification of the particular as well as the unthinking denunciation of the universal may have been curbed, but that doesn't lead to reinstating Enlightenment ideals on the contemporary intellectual scene. A more plausible reading of this putative return to universalism in critical thought is that it reflects, as Linda Zerilli points out, "a growing consensus that poststructuralist political theories are incapable of generating a viable alternative to the collective fragmentation that characterizes late modernity," and that "poststructuralism is critically valuable but politically bankrupt" (3). A logical corollary following this realization of the inadequacy of the poststructuralist denunciation of the universal would be to admit the "necessity of universalism."[15] What remains to be contested in theoretical endeavors in the wake of this "reconciliation of sorts between those who refuted these [Enlightenment, universalist] ideals and those who sought to realize them" (ibid.), therefore, still concerns a vexing question,

---

15 This happens to be the title of an essay in a special issue on universalism in *difference* 7.1 (Spring 1995). The forthright message of this particularly long piece by Lazarus et al., moreover, is also indicative of the overall consensus of the articles in the same issue—a significant theoretico-politcal intervention by itself, though there are definitely nuances in the positions of individual essays.

one that has been raised time and time again in history, though with perhaps unconscious certainty: How does one conceive of the universal? Now we may have to rephrase it more subtly: How do we conceive of the universal in such a way as to bridge the gap between theory and practice, to address the challenges of our time? What is this (new or necessary) universal or what does one mean by "universal"?

The common denominator in the recently revived reconsiderations of the universal, including the still persistent and rampant poststructuralist suspicion of it, is that the "old universal" was in fact a "pseudo-universal," whose duplicity and many vices we need not recount here. This universal is also an "inflated particular"—which is why it is false—whose cover has been blown not only by exposing its particularity (white, male, European, straight, etc.)—but also by highlighting other *excluded or incommensurable* particularities. "To speak of a false universalism," however, as Schor points out, "logically implies that there is such a thing as a *true universal*, unless, that is, one simply assumes that all universalisms are by definition false" (22, emphasis mine). In other words, unless one is prepared to accept the wholesale poststructuralist dismissal of universalism, one is bound to confront the binary opposition of "true universalism" versus "false universalism," besides the already troublesome one between universal and particular. It's not that we should reject all binary oppositions in the good old spirit of poststructuralism, but the task of constructing a radically different universal requires more than substituting a new universal in the place of the old and would seem insurmountable, especially when one still clings to the idea of a false universal as an inflated particular, or the ideal of a true universal in which each particular can find its place—a universal that, as Zerilli puts it, "could someday be One" (10).

Invoking an alternative and ideal universal, Schor states that "the goal is to arrive at a new universal that would include all those who wish to be included, and that would above all afford them the opportunity to speak universal while not relinquishing their difference(s)" (42). Such an all-inclusive universal as a new, authentic universal, according to Zerilli, is also what is envisaged by many who share the renewed interests and efforts in postulating a universal (3). However, few are specific enough in delineating this all-encompassing universal beyond staking out a general direction and the widely felt need for universalism. "What form shall this new universal take? How will it differ from the old?" Schor asks. But even Schor herself cannot offer satisfactory answers to these questions, as she confesses when concluding her essay of feminist intervention: "Reinscribing universalism on the agenda of feminism is, *relatively speaking*, the easy part. Determining what might constitute a specifically feminist universal of our time . . . presents a far more daunting challenge" (43; emphasis in original). Like many other attempted returns to the universal, Schor's above-quoted statements characteristically reflect the inherent tension or contradiction in the conception of universality, new or old. Not only is there a discernible discrepancy between the "specifically feminist universal" and a non-specific, generic "universal that would include all those who wish to be included"; but the professed open-ended universal seems to amount to little more than ameliorating the enlightenment model of universality that was never truly realized (thus ending up as a way of completing the "unfinished project of modernity," as Habermas would have it). If indeed this new universal is an ever-expanding ground with no apparent boundaries or exclusions, how will it be different from the formalistic idea of abstract universality that underlies the Kantian notion of some formal a priori framework with its contingent, shifting contents? If such a universal cannot be free from exclusions, on what basis does it conceive its exclusion/inclusion without repeating the (undeclared) exclusionary logic or epistemic violence of Enlightenment thought which had been rightly renounced? How will this new universal with its inevitable exclusions live up to the billing of a universal that "would really be inclusive of all people, regardless of race, class, gender, sexuality, ethnicity, nationality, and whatever attaches to the 'embarrassing etcetera' that, as Judith Butler reminds us, inevitably accompanies such gestures of acknowledging human diversity" (Zerilli, 3–4)? Similar to Bhabha's definition of postcolonial criticism quoted earlier, the thrust of this all-encompassing universalism seems to lie, paradoxically, in an insistence on differences, particularities, and marginalities.

The theoretical impasse we seem to inescapably encounter in rethinking the universal results in part from an insistence on an ideal universality (hence the distinction between true universalism and false universalism) as well as insufficient reconsiderations of the relationship between universal and particular. Based on the strains of thought on the universal/the particular I will underscore in the following pages, this book maintains that *the universal cannot be determined solely on an empirical basis, nor deduced from a logical, teleological, or a priori epistemological principle*. To say that the universal can be deduced according to some transcendental governing principle or epistemological ground would mean that the universal can be determined in advance, or that the universal is embodied by a certain entity which is destined by nature to assume that role; to derive the universal from empirical phenomena wouldn't preclude the prospect that this universal is theoretically fallible (or fallibilistic) as soon as a case which is not taken into account, whether in the present situation or in the unforeseeable future, indicates otherwise. The former falls back on or risks repeating the Enlightenment notion of the universal because universality thus conceived either results from some underlying essence along the line of a certain unconditioned principle, or operates in the precinct of "a regulative idea" which, even if it's "empirically unreachable," has an "unequivocal teleological content" (Laclau, *Emancipation(s)*, 55). One prime example would be the classical Marxist concept of the "universal class," in which the proletariat is designated as the agent who serves this role merely by virtue of the capacity emanating from its social being.[16]

As opposed to this epistemologically regulative universality, there is another kind of regulative universality which is merely empirically generated and hence "would be better named 'regularities' or 'tendencies'" (Hallward, 179). Immanuel Wallerstein, for instance, proposes to construct "a new universalism based on a foundation of countless groups," with an empirical approach not unlike that in his construction of the "world system" ("Revolution," 231). In their opposition to the particularizing inclination in postcolonialism (along with postmodernism), Marxist critics such as Aijaz Ahmad, Arif Dirlik, or Neil Lazarus seek to identify an overriding universality in capitalism, whose ambition, scope, and historical developments seem to deserve the name. Lazarus et al. further make clear in their manifesto essay "The Necessity of Universalism" that this necessary universalism has to be firmly grounded in the *observable* historical consequences of capitalism (85; cf. Lazarus, 16–17).[17] As compelling as

---

16 One can also find a more recent case in Habermas's idea of the aseptic space of free communication which presupposes its own universal rules and whose teleological end (of unimpeded communication) ensures the participant's intelligibility to the Other (and vice versa).

17 This capital-driven universality, of course, is to be combated, not defended, and it cannot be effectively combated through the partial and particularistic struggles that postcolonialism seems to embrace. Both Dirlik and Lazarus argue that one should develop

their analyses of the universality of capitalism are, and as important as empirical knowledge is to any theorizing move, the empirical approach to the universal is, however, flawed on two fronts: It is methodologically unsound and fallible, since a universality premised on empirical examples, which can hardly be exhaustive, is likely to be undone by one single exception, whether under the rubric of present circumstances or in the unknown future. Moreover, identifying universals empirically may wind up affirming the status quo, since it can call universal that which, rightly or wrongly, is taken for granted or is already universalized (rather than envision what is universalizable but not yet universalized). The empirical universal therefore may not be as politically progressive as those committed to radical politics would like it to be.[18] It must be added that the empiricist formulation of universality is, in a sense, an idealist one too, even though it appears to open universality to the irreducible contingency of empirical, historical phenomena. For its aspiration for a universal encompassing all "actually existing" examples amounts to an idealism of inclusion—an idealism, which, being vulnerable to its own subversion by the contingency of experiences themselves, would fall prey to the poststructuralist trap of totally dispensing with the universal: "we can't have a universal unless we can have a *true* universal, which has been proved to be impossible in practice as well as in theory."

Toward an Alternative Universal

In seeking an alternative to these idealist, regulative approaches to the universal, both epistemologically and empirically, here I'd like to turn to Laclau's intervention on this issue. Refusing the rigid opposition of universalism versus particularism as well as the idealized notions of univer-

---

concepts or a universalism that can match capitalism's total reach and implications and systematicity—a universalism which they defend (Dirlik, 105; Lazarus et al., 75; Lazarus, 23–24, 61–62). Similarly, Ahmad postulates universality as a result of "the global operation of a single mode of operation" (*In Theory*, 103).

18 Take patriarchy, for example. Patriarchy could be empirically determined as a universal prior to the exceptions discovered (or until the exceptions could no longer be ignored). While it was, and still is, a preponderant tendency regulating most societies, locating universals in such tendencies and regularities would be theoretically fallible and politically hazardous.

sality/particularity that simultaneously drive a polarized debate and undergird its impasse, Laclau attempts to conceive the universal by situating the relation between the universal and the particular in the field of *political articulations*.[19] Universality/particularity, placed in this context, is constructed through such political processes, rather than emerging out of one term's indissoluble essence or some transcendental logic. The relationship between the two, therefore, is not one of mutual exclusion but mutual, irreducible contamination, which inexorably invalidates the positions of both ideal universality and pure particularism, thus undermining the binary oppositions of the universal/particular as well as true universalism/false universalism (cf. Torfing, 168; Zerilli, 10). But if, as we've mentioned, almost all parties involved in contemporary debates about universalism agree that the universal is little more than an "inflated particular"—an inflation which is certainly deemed of a political nature, then how is Laclau's position different from those sketched out earlier? Maintaining that the universal is an ineluctable category, both theoretically and politically, Laclau undoubtedly can't concur with the dismissal of universality by many poststructuralists and postcolonialists, as he is also rather critical of the penchant for pure particularism he sees in the latter (to which we will return later). On the other hand, Laclau's notion of the universal is distinct from that of the "new universalists" of the debate, as he swiftly rejects some sort of ideal universality—either a universality devoid of any trace of particularity or an idealist vision of universality as an all-inclusive receptacle of all particularities—expressed or clandestinely presupposed in the recent wave of the "return" of universalism, whose theoretical edifice, as we've seen, is inconsistent with its politically progressive agenda.

For Laclau, some ineradicable remainder of particularity always imbricates the universal (just as the universal is an irreducible dimension in the constitution of any particular identity); he even goes as far as to say that "the universal is no more than a particular that at some point has become dominant," sounding like a typical anti-universalist denouncing the legitimacy of the universal (*Emancipation(s)*, 26). However, taking this statement to interpret the universal, as Schor does, to be nothing but an

---

19   Zerilli observes that Laclau, like Hannah Arendt, attempts to "shift the discussion of universalism from the terrain of philosophy to that of politics." For Laclau, the question of the universal, therefore, is a "question of political community after metaphysics" (7).

inflated particular, hence a false universal, is missing Laclau's point (22). As Zerilli specifies, "a universalism could be false in the sense of never fully devoid of particularity and yet still stand for that which we call universal" (20). This "contaminated," partially particular universal can "stand for" all the particulars and thus functions as a universal only when we forego the idealist conception of the universal—which, as suggested above, is secretly shared by the anti-universalists and their universalist counterparts—because there is no such thing as ideal universality. It would also require that we conceive of the formation of universality not according to a representational logic (the universal fully, adequately representing the particulars) but through what Laclau and Mouffe call "articulation," which is defined as "any [discursive] practice establishing a relation among elements such that their identity is modified as a result of the articulatory practice" (105). For the notion of representation, rendered sufficiently problematic since the advent of poststructuralism, is likely to lead us to another impasse like the postulation of ideal universality. As Laclau perceives, the "modern idea of a 'universal class' and the various forms of Eurocentrism are nothing but the distant historical effects of the logic of incarnation," since they always posit a certain privileged agent whose particular body is "the expression of a universality transcending it."[20] But the constitutive inconsistency

---

20 Examining the historical forms of the conceptions of the binarism universality/particularity in ancient Greek philosophy, Christianity, and Enlightenment thought, Laclau seeks to demonstrate the emergence and limits of the logic of incarnation underlying the idea of representation. In classical philosophy (particularly that of Plato), the universal and the particular are absolutely incommensurable, with an "uncontaminated dividing line" separating the realm of reason (universality) and irrationality (particularity). The particular either "eliminates itself as particular and transforms itself in a transparent medium thorough which universality operates," writes Laclau, "or it negates the universal by asserting its particularism (but as the latter is purely irrational, it has no entity of its own and can only exist as corruption of being)" (*Emancipation(s)*, 22). This unbridgeable gap between the universal and the particular is overcome and these two incompatible orders are somehow brought together by Christianity in the logic of incarnation, by which the universal, as "mere event in an eschatological succession," is incarnated in a "finite and contingent succession" of worldly events—a revelation. Here God is the "only and absolute mediator," and since God's designs are inscrutable, the relationship between the two orders, between the universal and the particular, has to be opaque and incomprehensible to humans. Enlightenment thought sets out to demystify Christian eschatology and thus interrupt the logic of incarnation by replacing the arbitrary, unfathomable divine intervention with a universal, "rational grounding that has to be fully transparent to human reason" (ibid., 23). And then come the now familiar

of Enlightenment universality lies in its cancellation of this operative logic through its disavowal of such particularity embedded in the universal: "if everything has to be transparent to reason, the connection between the universal and the body incarnating it also has to be so; in that case, the incommensurability between the universal to be incarnated and the incarnating body has to be eliminated. We have to postulate a body which is, in and of itself, the universal" (23). Such a postulation would be to fall back on the illusion and pitfalls of pure, ideal universality.

To say that the universal is constructed through political articulations is to underline that the universal is not a preexistent entity to be discovered, nor an a priori principle to be followed or applied, but emerges via *a chain of equivalences* out of the various demands of particular groups. As Laclau points out, "the universal emerges out of the particular not as some principle underlying or explaining the particular" (28), but through a certain *contingent articulation* of the particular demands of particular groups into a relation of equivalence, which is established as a result of "all of them being antagonized by the dominant sectors" (54). "[This] 'something identical' shared by all the terms of the equivalential chain," emphasizes Laclau, "cannot be something positive (that is one more difference which could be defined in its particularity), but proceeds from the unifying effects that the external threat poses to an otherwise perfectly heterogeneous set of differences (particularities)" (57). One prime example is the colonial situation, as Laclau and Mouffe point out:

> In a colonized country, the presence of the dominant power is everyday made evident through a variety of contents: differences of dress, of language, of skin colour, of customs. Since each of these contents is equivalent to the others in terms of their common differentiation from the colonized people, it loses its condition of differential *moment* . . . . Thus, a relation of equivalence absorbing *all* the positive determinations of the colonizer in opposition to the colonized, does not create a system of positive differential positions between the two, simply because it dissolves all positivity: the colonizer is discursively constructed as the anti-colonized. In other words, the identity has come to be purely negative. (127–128; emphasis in original).

---

critiques of Enlightenment rationality, ushered in by Adorno and Horkheimer's "de-demystification" of an enlightenment repeating the very mythic gesture it seeks to do without and culminating in the postmodernist debunking of its universalist pretensions and inherent contradictions. Later in *Emancipation(s)*, Laclau proceeds to a similar historical re-examination of the concept of universal/particular, with emphasis on individual philosophers—Plato, Hobbes, Hegel, and Gramsci—who represent "four moments" in the thinking of ruling and universality (60–65).

Universality constructed or articulated through such equivalential relations is distinct from what we have explored so far. This universal—that "something identical" knotting together the equivalential chain—is not a common ground with positive, specified determinations, therefore it cannot represent any objective relations articulating the commonalities of the particular terms, or any communitarian essence; rather, it can only signify the "absent fullness of the community, which lacks . . . any direct form of *representation* and expresses itself through the equivalence of differential terms" (*Emancipation(s)* 57; emphasis mine). It is important to note that though universality is fundamentally incommensurable with particularity, as Laclau insists (see, for example, 34–35, 57), this universal can still only be expressed in the particular. Such universality thus highlights something which is inherently unrepresentable by means of any particularity— namely, the unreachable communitarian fullness—or foregrounds the limit of the logic of representation, because the universal is not based on any differentiable, positive characteristics, but on some radical negativity or exclusion.[21] The operation in which a certain particular emerges, through an equivalential relation and on an antagonistic ground, to assume this universal function and articulate such impossible universality is precisely what Laclau calls "hegemony."

One can sense that the universal, as Laclau conceives of it, has a radically *contingent* character and *transformative* function; as he argues: "the universal does not have a concrete content of its own (which would close it on itself), but is an always receding horizon resulting from the expansion of an indefinite chain of equivalent demands" (34). Whatever particularity there once was would be somehow "diluted" or hybridized in the process of equivalential aggregations resulting in eventual and inevitable universalization, which further complicates the interpenetration of the universal and the particular, since the differential identities of the particular terms

---

21 It comes as no surprise that this universal representing the absent fullness of community is often taken to be the "true" communitarian ground or "essence" of the community in reality; this fundamentally false universal thus assumes, in effect, the function of the "true" universal, however temporarily, tenuously, or erroneously. This once again resonates with Zerilli's comment on Schor that "a universalism could be false in the sense of never fully devoid of particularity and yet still stand for that which we call universal" (20).

of the chain wouldn't remain intact either. The universal is therefore subject to or has to open itself to contingency and transformation, since "it is essential that the chain of equivalences remains open: otherwise its closure could only be the result of one more difference specifiable in its particularity" (57). "The open character of the chain," continues Laclau, "means that what is expressed through it has to be universal and not particular" (ibid.). The place of the universal, which brings to the fore not the communitarian ground but precisely its impossibility or absence, is an "empty place" in which particular terms are necessarily engaged in *hegemonic struggles for and articulations of universality*, as Laclau argues: "the impossibility of a universal ground does not eliminate its need: it just transforms the ground into an empty place which can be partially filled in a variety of ways (the strategies of this filling is what politics is about)" (59).

This Universal Which Is Not One[22]

To work toward an understanding of universality/particularity that serves as the theoretical groundwork for the further inquiries of this book, I'd like to underscore a number of things in our exploration of the universal so far, place them under the aegis of the postcolonial problematic, and illuminate them with other discourses on the universal/particular as well as the central historical event to be examined in this book—Toussaint's Haitian Revolution.

First of all, antagonism is the precondition of universality: This universal is based on what Laclau and Mouffe define as "antagonism," a radical negativity or exclusion, which stems from the positing of some threatening otherness as its outside and which brings about the dissolution of all positive, differential determinations that characterizes the "emptiness" of universality. The universal consisting in such exclusion or negativity must divest itself of positivized or differentiable identities; otherwise, it would only be another particular and not a universal. One crucial point not to be mistaken is that antagonism, as Laclau conceives of it, is not reducible to antagonistic relations between *particular* sectors in a given social order; rather, antagonism is precisely the *internal limit* of the social itself (cf. Žižek, "Discourse," 253):

---

22   Here I am borrowing the title of Zerilli's essay, "This Universalism Which Is Not One."

> Antagonism as the negation of a given order is . . . the limit of that order, and not the moment of a broader totality in relation to which the two poles of the antagonism would constitute differential—i.e. objective—partial instances. . . . The limit of the social must be given *within* the social itself as something subverting it, destroying its ambition to constitute a full presence. Society never manages fully to be society, because *everything in it is penetrated by its limits*, which prevent it from constituting itself as an objective reality. (Laclau and Mouffe 126–127; emphasis mine)

"Society doesn't exist"—if we adopt Žižek's patently provocative phrasing when he comments on Laclau—because antagonism does ("Discourse," 249). It is important to note that in Laclau's political theory, antagonism is not only what prevents society from reaching a communitarian fullness—a utopian society with no strife, conflict, or unsatisfied demands—but is also what is *constitutive* of the social. That is, antagonism, which signals that there is something fundamentally antagonized and excluded, points to a radical absence of the fullness or impossibility of the community, yet this exclusion or impossibility is precisely the precondition of the social, much in the way that a certain primordial repression necessarily precedes the very constitution of the subject—exclusion as the price to be paid for access to the socio-symbolic order.[23] Universality predicated on antagonism therefore signals precisely the impossibility of pure universality (where the universal finds its ideal incarnating body), or the absence of any communitarian fullness, or universal ground.

This conception of universality has at least the following ramifications that are particularly relevant to our exploration and deserve more elaboration: This universal, first and foremost, is *divisive*, or a "contestatory universal" (MacCannell, "Stage Left," 41). It is divisive and contestatory not only because it is split between its universalist function and irreducible, ineradicable particularity, but also because this universal brings to the fore the inherent fissure or gap that constitutes the current hegemonic constellation, which strives to suture it. But how can a universal claim to be at once universalizing *and* dividing? Invoking Fanon, Hallward argues that "every emergence of a *new* figure of universality . . . must begin as no less divisive: there can be no new mobilisation of the universal interest that does not immediately threaten particular privileged beneficiaries of the old

---

23 Without such socially constitutive antagonism, we would have "the reconciled society," whose existence requires "the emergence of a social actor whose own particularity would express the pure essence of humanity" and therefore allows for "the full realization of a pure universality" (Laclau, *Reflections*, 78).

status quo" (xv, emphasis in original). Furthermore, the divide opened up by this new universal is *not* between particular sectors of society, but between *social and non-social*, between a given socio-political field and what is radically excluded so that the social order can be established. Citing Marx's *particular* example of the weavers' revolt in Germany, Juliet Flower MacCannell interprets this view of *antagonistic universal* as the result of the radical exclusion of "a class so fully devastated, so excluded, so dehumanized, and so dispossessed that it is not merely relegated to haunting the society that denies it all standing, but is forced to becoming *the* universal" ("Stage Left," 40; emphasis in original).[24] The universal character of this particular revolt, continues MacCannell, lies in the following message: "*no one* should suffer as we are suffering. This *no one* is a critical, negative universal. It conceals no petty self-interests. It has no particular content, even though its coming into existence depends entirely on the particular that has been squeezed down to become no more than a universal shout: '*No one should have to suffer this way*'" (40–41; emphasis in original).

This, too, was the message Toussaint saw in the precepts of the French Revolution, whose universalist vision and ramifications have been widely acknowledged, even though those who drafted the Declaration of the Rights of Man and the Citizen and those who championed its precepts hardly took into account the slaves, at least not in practice (we'll have more detailed discussion of how the question of colonial slavery was "forgotten" in Revolutionary France in Chapter 2). No other group in history was more

---

24 Here MacCannell is explicating Žižek's, or rather, a Lacanian, conception of the Universal in light of Marx. There are, of course, nuances between the Marxian formulation of the universal and the one we're advancing here. It goes without saying that Marx, in much of his writings, privileges the proletariat as the agency destined to incarnate the universal and carry out its universalizing function, whereas the discourses of universality we've enlisted do not exclusively attribute this radically excluded element to the proletariat. The difference, I think, lies mainly in who or what it is that is so systematically excluded and rendered *outside* the social or even the human, and whether such a non-social element is still considered a class, as part of society. Marx's ambivalence and inconsistency with regard to the status of the most victimized and oppressed strata of society—and hence their candidacy for the agency of universality—is revealed most explicitly in his notion of the lumpenproletariat, which he considers even more heterogeneous vis-à-vis the existing order than the proletariat, and which represents less the emergence of a new class than the unfixing of all class differentiation. See Peter Stallybrass's discussions of Marx's *The Eighteenth Brumaire*. I shall return to the question of the lumpenproletariat in Chapter 4.

dehumanized and farther removed from anything that might have consisted of a social fabric than the displaced African slaves. Since Toussaint, slave revolts and decolonization movements have gained a universalist dimension and been fought in the name of universal emancipation—which is why the revolt Toussaint led was not a mere revolt, like the numerous slave insurrections before it, but a Revolution (cf. Blackburn, Davis, and Genovese). The emancipatory message that resonated in the hearts of black slaves across the Western hemisphere in Toussaint's time, and later echoed on a global scale by the colonized peoples in the mid-twentieth century, however, amounted to little more than a resounding "No!" Stemming from the most drastic forms of oppression, it didn't need to have a specific, particular, positivized content to mobilize a constituency that was as diverse geographically as ethnically and linguistically.[25]

The struggle between Toussaint and post-Bastille France, therefore, was not a showdown between two particular forces within the same (existing) socio-political field; rather, it was an arena in which a given socio-symbolic order was confronted with what was foreclosed or precluded from it—an exclusion which was nevertheless constitutive of this order. For, as mentioned earlier and as will be further discussed in the next chapter, colonial slavery was what essentially funded the bourgeois Republic, yet had to be extricated from or disavowed by post-Bastille socio-political discourse so that the existence and functioning of the bourgeois order could be maintained and justified in the first place. It was a struggle, therefore, between an emerging universal defined by nothing more than a radical exclusion, a not-yet-specified antagonism, *and* an old universal that ossified into a particular, privileged sector within the status quo, which presupposed a radical exclusion of some element or antagonism that was constitutive of it.

Cast in Étienne Balibar's conception of the three moments, meanings, or modalities of universality—universality as reality, as fiction, and as ideal—the confrontation between these two universals here can be seen as that between ideal universality, which is premised on the notion of the "unconditional" (65) and sets in motion the destabilizing process of "in-

---

[25] It was common practice for owners to mix slaves of different tribal and regional origins so as to prevent mass communication and, hence, mass uprisings on their plantations.

surrection," in the name of *egaliberté*, against the status quo (64), *and* fictitious universality, by which most people, except those experiencing "internal exclusion" (55), reinforce their identification with their immediate social roles—hence solidifying universality as reality—by virtue of their imaginary identification with the ideological fiction of a higher order of belonging (such as State or Church). This new universal thus lays bare the universalist pretension of the existing socio-symbolic discourse and counters it precisely on the grounds of universality. In the case of Toussaint, the combative universal he appeals to follows that very same universalist logic put forth by the precepts of the French Revolution. As Hardt and Negri indicate, Toussaint simply "takes the Declaration of the Rights of Man to the letter and insists on its full translation into practice" (118). Toussaint's revolution is, I argue, a radical mimicry, as he turns the universalism of the French Revolution against it by pushing its lofty, universalist discourse till it reaches its internal limit, by being more Jacobin than the Jacobins.[26]

In other words, Toussaint's struggle exemplifies what Slavoj Žižek describes as a confrontation "between the social and its exteriority, the non-social" (*Contingency*, 92). The limit between these opposing camps, "the limit that separates society itself from non-society," again, has to be an *internal limit* instead of an external one (ibid.). If it's an external limit, it would only constitute another difference between *particular* elements within the same socio-symbolic edifice.[27] Such positioning of the internal limit, as at once radically outside and penetratingly internal, is precisely why this non-social element, this "constitutive exclusion," or what Žižek calls, *à la* Jacques Rancière, "the part of no part," can claim a *universal* status (*Ticklish*, 188). The radical exclusion of such a peculiar element, which entails the deprivation of its place *in* society and in the available representational system—hence, any specified, positive, particular content vis-à-vis the given socio-symbolic field, is crucial in its transformation into a universal, as MacCannell points out: "It is only in realizing their exclusion from the human that the universal is born, and that the human can be reconstructed" (40). The existing social order can thereby be restructured

---

26 More detailed elaborations of Toussaint's mimicry will follow in Chapter 2.
27 Or, rather, this non-social would be swiftly co-opted in an expanded yet structurally intact universe, and we would have another antagonistic fight between particularistic forces that pose themselves as "false universals," as postmodernists and many postcolonialists would have it.

because "such a universal," argues MacCannell, "offers what nothing 'in' society can: a standpoint to seize society as a '*whole*'" (41; emphasis in original). But, once again, this antagonistic universal opposes the existing social field not from without, but from within. For if this universal is born out of what we've called radical antagonism, which is foreclosed yet constitutive of the social, *everything* in society, we recall, would be penetrated by such antagonism as the internal limit of the social (Laclau and Mouffe, 127). The postulation of a radical "outside" does not result in the universal's differential relationship to the existing order, which is a relationship defined by the particularities of the terms; rather, the deprivation, degradation, and exclusion of the slaves, the plebs, the wretched (Fanon), or the subaltern (Spivak) is so total and profound that it divests itself of any particular, positivized content (of their antagonism) and cancels out any (previous and potential) differential relations with the "social." It is only in this sense that it becomes a universal, since, as Laclau reminds us, that "something identical" shared by the terms of the equivalential chain which stems from radical antagonism and which gives rise to a universality "cannot be something positive (that is one more difference which could be defined in its particularity)" (*Emancipation(s)*, 57). Now that I've deployed two terms—and names—frequently invoked in postcolonial discourse, let me dwell here on how our latest reflections on the (alternative) universal can shed light on some of the related issues in postcolonial criticism and theory.

Difference and Equivalence

In their attempts to valorize and thereby include the hitherto excluded, many postcolonial critics seem to be primarily driven by a glorification of and preoccupation with particularity, otherness, and most importantly, a logic of difference; the flip side of this penchant is, of course, "the postcolonial aversion to universals" or the "'universalizing' condemnations of the universal" of postcolonial theory, as Hallward puts it (176). Much has been said about the limits of particularism in radical politics—and that's the theoretical background of our earlier discussions of the recent reconsideration or even return to the universal in critical theory. Here, I'd like to first examine such postcolonial preoccupations in terms of the logics of difference and equivalence, which Laclau, following a structuralist/poststructuralist vein of thinking, employs in his critique of particularism. In the contemporary cultural milieu of celebrating difference, no one would seem to contest the idea that all identity is *differential*, that the identity of a group (ethnic, racial, religious, etc.) constitutes a difference. Yet this also means that no particular group leads a "monadic existence," but is always situated in a wider community or a larger context, since "part of the definition of its own identity is the construction of *a complex and elaborated system of relations with other groups*" (Laclau, *Emancipation(s)*, 48; emphasis mine). So far this view of differential identity appears to be similar to Said's conception of cultural identity, and by extension, hybridity, as always implicated in an elaborate web of interconnection, occupying a nodal or "contrapuntal" point at which different cultural elements intersect. Laclau's point, however, is that the logic of difference is necessarily entangled in the logic of equivalence. For, as Laclau argues, the very assertion of a given group's right to their difference already posits or appeals to some *universal* principle or equivalential relation, and "there is no particularism that does not make an appeal to such principles in the construction of its identity" (26). In the case of the political discourse of rights, "if it is asserted that all particular groups have the right to respect of their own particularity, this means that they are *equal* to each other in some way" (49; emphasis mine). Where the logic of difference is not contaminated by the logic of equivalence, where the pure logic of difference holds sway, we encounter the notion of "separate developments" lying "at the roots of apartheid"— in which case the mere assertion of particularity ends up "sanctioning the *status quo* in the [unequal] relation of power between the groups" (27, 49; emphasis in original).

It is noteworthy that the postulation of some universal principle is not merely the implementation of regulating norms and principles which transcend the particularism of any group—this, however, is what Said's inconsistent, mostly humanistic universalism appears to advance. If the universal emerges out of a radical antagonism that is nevertheless constitutive of the social, it is to be conceived as *the interruption or subversion* of differential identity, because, we recall, universality is expressed through an equivalential chain in which the dimension of equivalence is privileged "to the point that its differential nature is almost entirely obliterated" as a result of confrontation with radical exclusion or antagonism (ibid. 39). That is why Laclau writes, in a quite Lacanian way, that "the universal is part of my identity as far as I am penetrated by a constitutive lack, that is as far as my differential identity has failed in its process of constitution" (28).[28] Based on the conception of antagonism as the *internal limit* of the social, Laclau points out that "all political identity is internally split, because no particularity can be constituted except by maintaining an internal reference to universality as *that which is missing*" (31; emphasis mine).

Postcolonial theorists, who in general are wary, or even critical of the strong, sometimes essentialized identity claims in the broader postcolonial criticism and literatures[29] as well as in identity politics, adopt a different approach to undermine differential identities and their systematic certainties. Although this approach is also premised on a similar line of thinking regarding the insurmountable problematic of representation (Spivak) and the necessary incompletion of identity or subjectivation (Bhabha)—a poststructuralist contribution postcolonial theorists acknowledge—it is still largely bound by a logic of difference, not only because of the postcolonial theoretical resistance to universalization based on a logic of equivalence, but also due to own its tendency to generate more particularistic categories derived from the existing particularities whose fixed identities and epistemological certainties they seek to deconstruct or subvert. Take, for example, Bhabha's conception of the "third space," which is closely related to (or metonymic to) his well-known, yet ever elusive, terminologies of "in-between-ness" and "hybridity":

> If . . . the act of cultural translation (both as representation and as reproduction) denies the essentialism of a prior given original or originary culture, then we see that all forms of culture are continually in a process of hybridity. But for me the importance of hybridity is not to be able to trace two original moments from which the third emerges, rather hybridity to me is the 'third space' which enables other positions to emerge. This third space displaces the histories that constitute it, and sets up new structures of authority, new political initiatives, which are inadequately understood through received wisdom. . . . The process of cultural hybridity gives rise to something different, something new and unrecognisable, a new area of negotiation of meaning and representation. ("The Third Space," 211)

---

28 The universal *dimension* of individual social beings—since none of them can be a pure difference or fully incarnate the universal—therefore "depends on the very failure of the full constitution of a differential identity" (Laclau, *Emancipation(s)* 28).

29 Here I am referring to Moore-Gilbert's distinction between "postcolonial theory" and more broadly defined "postcolonial criticism," which is skeptical of its "theory" counterpart (1–33).

Under the rubric of our preceding discussions, I'd like first to query whether this "third space" is itself *another difference* accounted for in the current terrain of cultural embattlement (or "translation"), rather than the undermining or subversion of the differential identities of the "two original moments." For if those moments or existing identities constituting the "binary closure" are to be subverted in "the process of hybridity" beyond recognition, and everything leveled down to the same plane, then the designation "third space" has little meaning.[30] In much of his work, Bhabha undoes colonial discourse by demonstrating that mimicry can be deployed as a means of disrupting colonialist surveillance and authority by creating ambiguous identities that elude the gaze of the colonizer. However, the legitimacy of such mimicry as a strategy of resistance seems to hinge on a colonial control presumed to be airtight; its radicality appears to dissolve once it's removed from the reach of prohibition, since, as Bhabha himself points out, "the visibility of mimicry is always produced at the site of interdiction" (*Location*, 89).

A more sympathetic reading of Bhabha has to be proposed here, too, since Bhabha at times seems to border on positing, quite uncharacteristically and perhaps unwittingly, a new universal that redefines and restructures the given socio-symbolic field ("This third space . . . sets up new structures of authority, new political initiatives").[31] For, as mentioned earlier, both the initial particularity of the agent assuming the role of the universal and the differential identities of the terms entering the equivalential chain will somehow be "hybridized" in the process of universalization. This reading, however, appears to run counter to Bhabha's overall theoretical endeavor of anti-universalism. Furthermore, his conception of the "third space" as "a new area of negotiation" and his frequent references to the process of "reinscription and negotiation" (see, for instance, *Location*, 191) in the production of cultural identity never seem to make clear

---

30 It is widely acknowledged that the deconstruction of a dominant discourse or "originary culture" works within, and relies heavily on the logos or cultural logic of the dominant, and in this sense cannot avoid being complicit in reasserting the targeted discourse while deconstructing it.

31 Another example can be found in Bhabha's exploration of the "liminal" moment or element (*Location*, 185).

whether, in the actual arena of cultural embattlement,[32] the reference is to a space (or an agency?) in which mediating between (existent) *particularities* takes place, or where the existing social field confronts its radical outside: in other words, whether it is a (re)negotiation between the "particulars," or, more radically, between the social *and* the non-social, the "part of no part," the socially unrepresentable, which Bhabha's occasional invocation of "something new and unrecognizable" seems to suggest. If this process of hybridity or negotiatory space points to the former, then it is likely that the particular terms from which the third term derives would not be undermined—the hybrid can be accommodated and reduced to another difference, however fleetingly, juxtaposed with the originary particularities and constituting a merely differential relation. What we have, then, would be a proliferation of differences in an expanded socio-cultural field whose infrastructure remains relatively intact. One also has to be wary, as Laclau cautions us, that the model of negotiation—as ambiguous as this term has become—would lapse into an even worse scenario, in which "the agreement concerns only circumstantial matters, but the identity of the forces entering it remains uncontaminated by the process of negotiation" (*Emancipation(s)*, 32).

Articulation, Agency, and Misrecognition

Rather than indulging in the celebration of what appears to be an infinitely complex, indeterminable, yet ultimately conciliatory space of negotiation that absorbs antagonism, I'd like to propose "a contingent intervention taking place in an undecidable terrain," an intervention taken up by a *hegemonic agent who articulates radical antagonism* (ibid., 89). We understand, from our preceding analysis, that radical antagonism is irreducible to the antagonistic relations between the particulars within a given socio-political order; however, the gap or fissure opened up by constitutive antagonism (which is not merely another internal difference) can only be mapped, in a distorted way, onto a particular difference *within* the social (Žižek, *Contingency*, 92), since the universal emerges not simply out of struggles or "negotiations" between particulars, but points to something beyond the particulars that, nevertheless, can only be articulated through

---

32 Bhabha also conceives such a process of (incessant, indeterminate) negotiation as constitutive of the subject. We will elaborate on that in Chapter 2.

some particularity. The agency which assumes the universal function, therefore, is itself a particular, an intra-social difference onto which a fundamental difference (between the social and the non-social) is mapped and through which radical antagonism as well as a new universality are articulated. The equivalential chain that sustains this antagonistic universal, I argue, is not based on a logic of incarnation or representation (according to which the represented is coextensive with its agent), but on a profound misrecognition of the antagonism to be articulated; it is an *articulation* which does not necessarily reflect the positivity or objective differential relations of the social because antagonism, as constitutive and indissoluble, tends to dissolve objectivity into the social (but not totally). This universal therefore does not go beyond the well-documented problematic of representation; rather, it only foregrounds such a problematic, since the indispensable role of agency it presupposes represents, first and foremost, the impossibility of universal grounds.

Such impossibility of communitarian fullness, of *full* representation, is also famously figured in Spivak's *subaltern*, who is no less excluded and unrepresentable than the non-social elements we've enlisted so far. For Spivak pushes the logic of difference and the notion of representation to their limits, to the point where one has to postulate not only a constantly self-differentiating difference, but an absolute alterity, impenetrable to anyone who has the audacity to represent her—hence rendering suspect any form of agency seeking to "include" the subaltern. With her eye trained on the most excluded among the excluded, Spivak's insistence on relentlessly tracking or evoking the subaltern figure seems to suggest that radical antagonism be *either* left intact on the unfathomable fringe of any socio-political representation; *or* that it be fully, adequately represented, i.e., that antagonism coalesces on a coextensive content able finally to give the subaltern its due. For the latter, no representational system available, as the critic is well aware, can do the trick. Moreover, doesn't Spivak's theoretical probing of the subaltern itself demonstrate that subalternity can be somehow *articulated*, though certainly not without some degree of complicity with the socio-symbolic edifice that forecloses it? Spivak's ethical injunction on the subaltern question—which reads, from the subaltern perspective, "[since] we can be represented; [therefore] we must not represent ourselves"—is a "catachrestic rewriting" of Marx's formulation: "[they] cannot represent themselves; they must be represented" (Larsen, 207; cf.

Spivak, "Subaltern," 276–277).[33] Without the slightest intention of contesting the insurmountable problematic inherent in representation, I'd like to paraphrase Spivak and propose the following: The subaltern cannot speak; she cannot be represented, but she can be, and always has been, *articulated*, not only because her "constitutive exclusion" is the precondition of the socio-symbolic order vis-à-vis which she is subaltern, but also because she *can* be articulated in such a way that she (mis)recognizes her plight in the articulation and that may thus transform both her and the socio-symbolic order.[34]

Let me conclude this chapter—and introduce the next—by looking at, as an instance, the articulation of revolutionary ideals in the case of Toussaint and the Haitian Revolution. Toussaint and many other former slaves who devoted their lives to the liberation *of all* were profoundly impacted by the French Revolution, as they apparently identified with the proclaimed ideals of liberty and equality. Yet their identification, I argue, was based more or less on a *misrecognition*; or rather, the precepts of the metropolitan Revolution got articulated and transmuted in their part of the world in such a way that what united them was scarcely a unified message with a positivized, particular content: In the age of revolution (circa 1770–1823), writes David Brion Davis, revolutionary ideology took a myriad of forms, yet the "vague and often confused idea of revolution continued to spread." For example, in the Caribbean, British slaves "sometimes imagined that their masters were resisting and suppressing the king's efforts to free them; in 1790 this conviction sparked a revolt in Tortola" (76). Robin Blackburn also notes that, to the extent that "liberty and equality had become the religion of the formerly enslaved," the emancipatory message "might be conveyed in a variety of idioms—French, or *Kréyole* or some African language—and with a variety of political or religious inflexions—royalist, Republican, Catholic, voodoo—so long as slaveholder power was broken" (259). During his initial success against the French troops, Toussaint didn't have any specified goal other than overthrowing

---

33 The "they" Marx refers to, in his *Eighteenth Brumaire*, are the small peasant proprietors.
34 The discussion of Spivak in this passage is based mostly on her seminal essay, "Can the Subaltern Speak?" The admittance, or even valorization, of "constructive complicity" is highlighted in *Critique of Postcolonial Reason* (e.g. xii, 3–4, 9).

slavery in the colony of San Domingo.[35] After granting universal liberty to *all* the inhabitants of San Domingo (which was the first polity in the Americas to have done so), Toussaint went on to realize more specific goals of rebuilding war-torn San Domingo and meet the increasingly concrete demands of a diverse constituency, ranging from blacks to Mulattoes to the whites, which for some time Toussaint managed to satisfy (James, *Black Jacobins*, 251–256). In the later stage of his tenure, however, Toussaint was not able to raise any specific issue or slogan around which he could rally, as effectively as before, the black masses who had single-mindedly and willingly followed all of his commands, even though his authority and popularity were rarely challenged (cf. James, especially Ch. XII; Miller).[36]

As exemplified in Toussaint's case, it is precisely because the articulation of universality is based on misrecognition, and because what is to be expressed in the universal is an impossible object—the absence of communitarian fullness—that the place of the universal can only be filled temporarily and partially by the agency assuming the universal function. This "un-fulfilling" of the universal agent, paradoxically, is what gives it a universal character, since the filling of the place of universality—its coinciding with the agent's ineradicable particularity—can only mean it's a particular fully recognizable in its particularity. The place/placing of the universal is at once precarious and indispensable, both impossible and necessary, and it is for this reason that universality is always subject to contingent, contestatory articulations.

---

35 We will elaborate more on Toussaint's and the Black Jocobins' misrecognition and identification, from a more specifically psychoanalytic perspective, in Chapter 2.

36 One may argue, then, that the same Toussaint who was the emblem of liberation and the common ground for *all* across racial and class divides, who could mean so many things yet ultimately the same thing, later ceased to function as a universal mediator *precisely* because, when the race issue rent the colony asunder and the contradiction between the metropolis and the periphery on the question of colonialist interests escalated, Toussaint was not clear about what was to be on the top of his agenda, wavering between reconciling and collaborating with the French who continually threatened to restore slavery in the colony, and maintaining a political autonomy that would protect the hard-won fruits of liberty.

Chapter 2
Toussaint, Mimicry, and the Primal Scene of Postcoloniality

This chapter attempts to reconsider the conception and glorification of mimicry as subversion and the notion of postcoloniality premised on the pastness of colonialism by examining Toussaint L'Ouverture's Haitian Revolution, which has often been considered an imitation of its immediate historical precedent, the French Revolution, and was itself the model one and a half centuries later for Third World anticolonial movements. Being at once in strict adherence to and idiosyncratic variance from the precepts of the French Revolution and Western modernity, Toussaint's "mimicry," I argue, poses an uncanny specular relation in which the mimicker becomes the rem(a)inder of the impossibility of the projected ideal image for both itself and the mimicked simply by carrying out the other's revolutionary ideals to the letter. Mimicry in the "colonial mirror stage," however, hinges on identification with something besides the immediate, specular image, something the subject tends to disavow. The colonial state is such a mistaken image. Split between their willing identification with the French Revolution and unwitting mimicry of the colonial state, Toussaint and the Haitian Revolution become both a model for decolonization movements and an originary symptomatic representation of that traumatic impossibility of revolutionary ideals, mirroring and prefiguring not only the recurrent violence, corruption, and dependency of the postcolonial nation—which nevertheless exemplifies the inherent inconsistency/antagonism of the Western model nation-state—but also the ensuing and prevalent disillusion toward the—or any—nationalist or revolutionary project among postcolonial subjects. This chapter will advance and illuminate the abovementioned thesis by exploring C. L. R. James's, Eduard Glissant's, and Derek Walcott's symptomatic revisitings of Toussaint and the Haitian Revolution, conceived as "the primal scene of postcoloniality" in this book.

Mimicry: Strategy of Resistance and/or Means of Survival

Long before contemporary postcolonial and cultural critics' celebration of the seemingly inexhaustible subversiveness and complexities of mimicry, the commonplace view that the Haitian Revolution, taking place in the wake of the French Revolution, was an imitation of the latter, together with the perception of the slave leader Toussaint L'Ouverture as a mimic man who recited and copied the precepts of the French Republic in its richest colony, had already been problematized in the nineteenth century. In his *Mémoires d'Outre-Tombe*, the French Romantic writer Chateaubriand (François-Auguste-René) describes Toussaint as "the black Napoleon, imitated and killed by Napoleon, the white one" ('le Napoléon noir, imité et tué par le Napoléon blanc'; 326–327). The well-known title "black Napoleon," however, may confuse the copy with the original, since Toussaint broke into modern history before Napoleon attained his fame.[37] Reflecting the Eurocentric view of the commentators, this title—though a compliment to Toussaint's military feats and leadership—was certainly retroactively bestowed on a certain phenomenon unthinkable/unnamable for the French before Napoleon I gained prominence on the historical stage. Historians have pointed out the intertwining relationship between the French Revolution and its Haitian counterpart: While the Haitian Revolution may have been inspired by the uprisings in Paris, and was indeed inconceivable without its French precedent, the colonial question—a raging debate about whether freedom and the rights of citizenship should be extended to subjects in the colonies, regardless of color—in turn altered the course of the French Revolution.[38]

The case of Toussaint and the Haitian Revolution seems to be a classic example of mimicry as strategic resistance, since Toussaint in effect undermined the legitimacy and authenticity of French colonial rule in San

---

37 Much of this, of course, depends on whose history this is, how one defines "modern history," historiography, or even history itself. I am referring specifically to the point in time when either's military genius was recognized and exerted significant impact on the revolutions in France and its colonies. In this context, Toussaint had frustrated the French revolutionary troops in San Domingo even before he changed sides from fighting under the banner of royalist Spain (against colonialist France) to fighting for France as a Republican in May 1794. His conversion gave the Jacobins an edge to fend off the counter-revolutionary forces, including the pro-slavery colonials, and to promote their revolutionary programs and prestige in both France and San Domingo. Napoleon, on the other hand, helped secure the revolution by crushing a royalist rising in Paris in October 1795, and wasn't promoted to General-in-Chief of the Italian Army until March 1796. For a detailed timeline (up to the date) of Bonaparte's illustrious career, see Furet's 1992.

38 For James' views on how the Haitian Revolution was inconceivable without the French Revolution and how the two Revolutions were in "close parallel" see, for example, *Black Jacobins*, 385ff; see also Blackburn, 257–260.

Domingo simply by being more French than the French, more revolutionary than the Jacobins, by adhering to—by mimicking—the principles and language of the French Revolution. It is as if he were holding up a mirror to the French and saying, "Look! You don't even live up to your own image, as I do!"[39] Such a strategy of subversion, or mode of resistance, has also been echoed in Derrida's book, *Monoligualism of the Other*, where he, with rare reference to his personal experience in Algeria, problematizes the originality and authority of the master's discourse by perfecting his act of mimicking even unto hyperbole, by mastering the Other's language with incredible impeccability. This is what one might call "a logic of admiration,"[40] whereby the underdog's admiration for the dominant, such as Toussaint's for the French, weighs so much on the other that it eventually wears him down: "I shame you by admiring you."

The fact that slavery was still upheld in San Domingo in the first years following the Bastille should have been a slap in the face for the French who were still consumed by revolutionary fervor, if this glaring inconsistency of the new Republic had been brought to the fore. It eventually melted the initial reluctance of the ruling bourgeoisie to proclaim the abolition of slavery in the colony and helped the Jacobins consolidate their power by defeating the pro-slavery Girondists. The political significance and leverage of Toussaint's realization of revolutionary precepts in the colony, however, appear more like the product of chance than the result of a strategic move. First of all, one can make the case that Tousssaint never intended to dismantle the grand narratives of liberty, fraternity, and equality from within, nor did he show any ambition to "deconstruct," if you wish, French imperialism. On the contrary, he didn't conceal his single-minded admiration for French civilization, and constantly tried to instill the great ideas of the Revolution in his followers. Furthermore, if it was indeed a strategic move, the outcome, like the outcomes of all forms of

---

39   Although this point permeates Derrida's book, I came across this sentence—whether it's exactly the same phrasing I can no longer recall—in a remark by Shaun Irlam in his seminar titled "The Discontents of Postcolonialism," SUNY at Buffalo, Fall 2003.

40   In an earlier essay on Nelson Mandela, Derrida teases out, with a similar line of thought and a case as equally exemplary as that of Toussaint, the force as well as the source of "the admiration of Mandela," which lies not only in what Mandela inspires but also in what he feels—his admiration for Magna Carta, the Universal Declaration of the Rights of Man, and, ultimately, the Law. See Derrida's "The Laws of Reflection: Nelson Mandela, in Admiration," *For Nelson Mandela*, 11–42.

mimicry, was essentially incalculable. Such incalculability of the political efficacy of mimicry as resistance can be illuminated from both a theoretical perspective and a historical one.

The pendulum of history

Let me take up the narratives of historical events first, with perhaps a little bit of hindsight, drama, and the interventionist comments C. L. R. James offers in his purportedly historical account, *The Black Jacobins*:[41] Not only had there been twists and turns in the political struggles in Paris before the anti-slavery factions among the bourgeois revolutionaries finally gained the upper hand, but Toussaint had so much faith in France and its revolutionary ideals that he never dreamed of the possibility that Napoleon, the Son of the Revolution, would be so depraved as to be secretly plotting a restoration of slavery with a last French expedition to San Domingo.[42] James documents the exposure of Napoleon's intentions by referring to the solid evidence found in General Leclerc's correspondence with him and other officials close to the First Consul (341–346). Yet the illiterate ex-slaves, Toussaint's most loyal supporters, hardly needed such evidence to be convinced of the impending return of slavery, which had long been feared and suspected. Upon learning that the Convention in Paris, under the direction of Bonaparte, had voted to restore slavery in Martinique, Guadeloupe, and

---

41 Numerous scholars have pointed out this cross-genre characteristic of James's work. See, for example, Paul B. Miller's "Enlightened Hesitations"; Grant Farred's "A Thriving Postcolonialism" (235).

42 James reiterates this reading of Toussaint's mind in his book (cf., for example, 282, 290, 364). David Brion Davis echoes this judgment: "Toussaint . . . had also tried to reassure white settlers of his own good will and of his dependence on France, assuming that France made no attempt to reinstitute the old colonial regime. Toussaint's faith in compromise, unfortunately for him, helped to divide his followers and ultimately led to his capture" (151). This doesn't mean that Toussaint always trusted, or tended to trust, the French in his life-long dealing with them, whether militarily or politically. Abundant evidence points to the contrary. Yet it is sufficient to add that if the restoration of slavery had ever entered into his conception of post-Revolutionary France, Toussaint wouldn't have hesitated to set up resistance against a long-anticipated French expedition, or be reluctant to sever ties with the French, nor would he have sworn allegiance to France and reassured Napoleon that he would subordinate his power and authority as Governor of Saint-Domingue, along with its sovereignty, to the rule of Bonaparte on condition that the fruits of the Revolution be preserved in the colony.

other islands in the Caribbean (not including San Domingo), the black masses in San Domingo rose up in rampant insurrections.

On the other hand, Toussaint, the bearer of the torch of enlightenment for his race, couldn't see this light in his final days, confined in the frosty, damp, and dim cell Napoleon reserved for him in Fort Joux. After outmaneuvering Napoleon's troops on the battlefield and outwitting his rivals, French or black or Mulatto, in political intrigues, Toussaint wrote from jail to Bonaparte in a surprisingly subservient, naïve tone that might have cancelled what he had accomplished, did it not reflect less his degradation than what James calls his "fatal sincerity":

> I had the misfortune to incur your anger; but as to fidelity and probity, I am strong in your conscience, and I dare to say with truth that among all the servants of the State none is more honest than I. I was one of your soldiers and the first servant of the Republic in San Domingo. I am to-day wretched, ruined, dishonoured, a victim of my own services. Let your sensibility be touched at my position, you are too great in feeling and too just not to pronounce on my destiny. (quoted in James, 364)

This curious blindness could be seen as the *harmatia* of the historical tragedy of Toussaint,[43] and the silence with regard to the letter, whose receipt remained unacknowledged, irredeemably prevented Toussaint, who humbly requested a trial wherein the First Consul would do him justice, from a full-blooded disillusionment with Napoleon and the ideals of the Republic that he supposedly personified. Until his death Toussaint never put independence on his agenda, publicly or privately, as Bonaparte certainly thought he did, since he still saw himself as part of the Revolution and the French Republic, "one and indivisible," and believed his sacrifice would eventually "make the French see reason" (James, 364).

It is tempting, therefore, to argue that Toussaint's failed mimicry lies in his "fatal sincerity," which necessarily accompanies a too faithful, uncritical imitation, and which in turn results from the sudden elevation, amidst overwhelming ecstasy, from the lowest state of being (the slave) to that of a free, dignified man, much like the child in the mirror stage who revels in its projected, not yet fully differentiated image. What if the mimicker, after trial-and-error sessions in front of the mirror, masters the art of playing with his/her own image, that is, what if he/she learns how to simulate and dissimulate under the gaze of the other? Would mimicry as a

---

43 Critics have pointed out and elaborated the comparison of Toussaint's legend to Greek tragedy. See, for instance, Paul B. Miller's "Enlightened Hesitations."

conscious, strategic move, then, subvert the master's assumed position of domination and save us from repeating Toussaint's mistake? Let us indulge ourselves in the case of Toussaint a little longer and not forget that, first of all, Toussaint's identification with Revolutionary France, like all identification, belies a bilateral, strictly specular relationship (I will return to the theoretical underpinnings of this point later in the chapter). Moreover, Toussaint was scarcely a simple, one-dimensional, straightforward, and unwavering figure who single-mindedly carried out his championed ideals, despite the few dazzling misjudgments and inconsistencies that marked the enigmatic limits of his conception of the world around him and his fateful downfall. Quite to the contrary, Toussaint was, as James rightly remarks, "the embodiment of vacillation" between "two certainties," between two conflicting worlds (290): his hesitations before joining the already widespread slave revolt, which he later led; his precarious balancing act, during his brief tenure as Governor of San Domingo, between repeatedly assuring the white proprietors of his determination to safeguard their interests (in which he believed San Domingo's prosperity and progress toward civilization lay); *and* appeasing the growing discontent of the ex-slaves who still worked long hours under rigid regulations on the plantations and were bewildered, even angered, by the prerogatives of their former exploiters and the deference Toussaint displayed toward them. Most devastating were his demoralizing vacillations between fierce offensives and secret negotiations during the French expedition aimed at ousting Toussaint and his black generals—offensives that would prove to be too costly for Napoleon to regain his dominance in the New World, ensuring that the compromises proposed by Toussaint would be received by the exhausted French with joyous surprise. I argue that in each case, as in numerous similar situations, his vacillations were occasioned by the instability of a mimicry that wasn't laid bare except in moments of crisis: an uncanny resemblance with an irreducible incompatibility, for Toussaint was *at once more French than the French and foreclosed from being French.* When, where, and how does the pendulum come to a halt? As these cases exemplify, the outcomes of his vacillations can hardly be calculated.

And we cannot emphasize enough that *Toussaint was a man who calculated, and calculated well.* Many of his black and Mulatto followers looked up to him as someone wrapped in his own world of unfathomable and supreme intellect, while the French in San Domingo, after being stung and surprised by his superior maneuverings, revered and feared his cunning, prescient judgment, and remarkable leadership.[44] For most of his life, Toussaint was the type of the tactful politician who weighed the gains and losses of his every move, be it military, diplomatic, or political, and wound up outmaneuvering his adversaries. He might have unequivocally or unwittingly modeled his vision on that of Revolutionary France in his efforts to rebuild war-torn San Domingo, but he deployed this vision—of being a Frenchman as well as a black Jacobin—as a formidable weapon in what he did consciously and strategically for his struggles. Until the last of these, against his archrival Napoleon, the White Toussaint, when Toussaint's fatal miscalculations resulted in his arrest, imprisonment in France, the ruin of his lifework, and his eventual demise. Just when Toussaint and his loyalists had rendered Leclerc's troops helpless and demoralized, in spite of Toussaint's initial wavering between war and peace that led to a few black generals' surrender without a fight, Toussaint sought to come to terms with Leclerc, who happily accepted. Again, one may have to resort to James's insightful reading of Toussaint's mind to grasp this seemingly inexplicable move:

> Toussaint now wrote a reply to Bonaparte's letter and . . . assured Bonaparte of his devotion and submission to his orders, and *affected to believe* that Leclerc had acted in opposition to Bonaparte's instructions. If Bonaparte would send another general to take command of the colony all would be well. . . . By this offer he gave Bonaparte the opportunity to withdraw from a hopeless expedition with dignity and send someone else to negotiate with Toussaint for the new relation with France which Toussaint wanted. . . . *It was magnificent diplomacy but ruinous as a revolutionary policy.* (325, emphasis mine.)

It is not hard to see from the quote Toussaint's calculations, the desired result of which relied on his strategic mimicking of the stereotypical relation of a naively loyal black servant to his master, a relation Toussaint knew only too well, being a trusted coachman before joining the revolt. Yet Napoleon thought far better of him. In the end Toussaint was let down by his own strategic mimicry, entrapped in his own intricate scheme, whose scope and vision, unfortunately, never involved severing ties with France, let alone independence. And it wasn't the first time he outwitted himself.

---

44   For example, Vincent wrote of his heartfelt admiration for Toussaint in his letter to the Minister, after his advice against the expedition was rejected by Napoleon (James, 272).

Earlier in Leclerc's expedition, Toussaint's vacillation had already confused and dispirited some of his generals, including his own brother, Paul. Bracing for the impending French troops yet uncertain of what to do, Paul wrote to Toussaint to ask for orders. Pressed for a definite answer, Toussaint wrote back and demanded that Paul defend to the last and "even to the extent of capturing Kerverseau [the French officer leading the attack] and his troops," which, as James laments, was "a miserable and tell-tale indication of vacillation" (298). Interestingly, Toussaint somehow embodied or revealed his own wavering state of mind in the letters to Paul, since he, ever thinking ahead of others, forged by himself a second letter that contained the opposite message—asking his brother to conciliate—and instructed the three messengers, each carrying both letters, to present the false one to their captors in case of arrest. It was classic Toussaint, according to whose calculations the French would be caught off guard when he and other generals took on offensives, even if the worst scenario he expected—all three messengers were captured—happened. As it turned out, the messengers were killed, both letters were found on them, and Toussaint's scheme was turned against him when Kerserveau sent the false letter to Paul, who followed the order and opened the gates to let in the French. What else could Paul have done? If there hadn't been a faked letter, Paul would have had one of the toughest decisions to make, but now he probably was just relieved that he finally confirmed what everyone had been speculating, or wondered if it was part of his brother's inscrutable plot.

    Toussaint's failed mimicry two hundred years ago, whether regarded as strategic or unknowing, might throw light on later anti-colonial movements (this is exactly the message James attempts to deliver in his book) and contemporary postcolonial struggles and cultural politics. In certain situations, particularly in moments of crisis (such as a revolution), when the question of achieving the most significant political efficacy is at stake, wavering between positions, even in the case of Toussaint's astute maneuverings, can be deadly at worst, irrelevant or ineffectual at best. Besides the example of Toussaint, one has only to look at the fate of Rigaud, the Mulatto general who was second to none but Toussaint in San Domingo in terms of power and military feats, and who practically maintained a Mulatto state in the South. Faced with both the discrimination of the whites and the hostility of the blacks (this doesn't mean the Mulattoes didn't reproduce the whites' racism against the blacks—quite to the contrary), Mulatto vacillations at that time were less preordained by color than a necessary strategy of survival. Yet while Rigaud prevented black domination by collaborating with the French, who were uneasy with Toussaint's rapidly rising power, and curbed French power in south San Domingo by hinting at an alliance with the blacks or even cooperation with the British in trade, Mulattoes' strategic wavering couldn't always take advantage of their intermediate role. In the end, Bonaparte recognized the victor of the Black-Mulatto war, Toussaint, as de facto ruler of the colony—just to have a single target for later attacks—and poor Rigaud, after being used up, was then deported and imprisoned in France.[45] Upon hearing of Rigaud's deportation, Toussaint aptly summarized his rival's fate: "It was against me that they brought that general here. It is not for me that they are deporting him. I regret his fate" (James 322). Perhaps the most interesting—and least relevant politically—case of indeterminate vacillation is Beauvais, a Mulatto general who was beloved by everyone and on friendly terms with the blacks, especially with Toussaint. He was, as James dubbed, "a Mulatto of the Mulattoes," unable to take sides earlier in the struggle between Toussaint and Rigaud. What he eventually did—or did not do—can be described as a "suspended vacillation": Beauvais "threw up his command and sailed for France," being, as James puts it, "honest to the last" (231).

The often glamorized conception of postcolonial mimicry, therefore, seems to be focused exclusively on the colonized's or the minority's presumably transgressive mimicry of the colonizer (or the culturally dominant in the postcolonial era), without entertaining alternative forms of mimicry (the master unwittingly resembling the slave, for example) or the possibility of a failed strategy of mimicking, let alone elaborating on the common sight, in all resistance movements, of largely opportunistic collaboration/opposition or uncritical assimilation on the part of the native informant/informer that too often confuses means of survival with strategic mimicry as resistance, or even disguises its role as exploiter vis-à-vis the rest of the colonized.

---

45 After arriving in France, Rigaud sought an interview with Napoleon, who at the end told Rigaud, quite succinctly, "General, I blame you for only one thing, not to have been victorious" (James, 235).

Of mimicry and Lacan: a theoretical exploration

Now, theoretically speaking, why is mimicry, as a conscious, strategic move or mode of resistance, *not necessarily, inherently* subversive? I'd like to approach this theoretical question with reference to Homi Bhabha's idea of mimicry, which, of course, is based on his appropriation of Jacques Lacan. In his well-known essay on mimicry, "Of Mimicry and Man," Bhabha points out that "the visibility of mimicry is always produced at the site of interdiction" (89). Since his writings tend to lapse into a collage of instances of mimicry under authoritarian, stringent colonialist surveillance *and*, for example, mimicry by the figure of contemporary, postcolonial migrants on the margins of the metropoles, one may well wonder how the legitimacy and necessity of mimicry as a subversive gesture in the colonial era can still retain its political relevance and effectiveness in the postcolonial setting, where/when we are far removed from "the site of interdiction," the brutal control, the head-on confrontation between the colonizer and the colonized. Of course, Bhabha and many postcolonial theorists draw on a Foucauldian notion of power and the Law to conceptualize a much more refined, insidious, and ubiquitous system of domination in present-day postcolonial situations that call for new modes of resistance. While still clinging to, or persisting in creating a coexistence or symbiosis of colonizer/colonized, dominator/dominated, the law and its transgression, the law that fuels its own subversion, the postcolonial form of mimicry shifts from invoking alikeness, from a deceptive resemblance to valorizing elusiveness or indeterminacy of identities, establishing a fluidity of subject-positions, hybridity, or syncretism so as to keep its radicality current.

The combative, oppositionalist implications of mimicry in postcolonial theorizations are best exemplified, and perhaps gain their credibility and popularity in Bhabha's elaboration, in that same essay, of a quote from Lacan, which features a notion of mimicry as camouflage: "The effect of mimicry is camouflage in the strictly technical sense. It is not a question of harmonizing with the background, but against a mottled background, of becoming mottled—exactly like the technique of camouflage practiced in human warfare" (*Four Fundamental Concepts*, 99). Yet the model of negotiations between subject positions on the terrain of cultural warfare, which Bhabha advocates in his work, is hardly Lacanian. The wavering and negotiations between arrays of subject positions, even within the same subject, seem to befit the multicultural settings of the metropoles where migrants from the former colonies converge, yet they imply a flux of subject positions, somewhat free-floating, interchangeable, and ready to be assumed by the subject, thus remaining exclusively in the imaginary, or implying an imaginary instability untethered to the symbolic or the logic of the signifier. This would invoke, or presuppose, *multiple yet fully constituted* subject positions, rather than a barred, split subject. Thus mimicry in Lacan's sense, i.e. mimicry as camouflage, foregrounds an agonizing split in the subject, rather than facile oscillation or seemingly intricate negotiations between different (full) subject positions such as multiculturalism envisions. The subject that mimics, the subject that puts on a mask of camouflage, is a subject that "breaks up between its unconscious being and its conscious semblance" (Copjec, *Desire*, 37), just as Toussaint was split between the subject position he affected to assume, and the one he couldn't help always already, unwittingly, occupying, one that he couldn't really get rid of. It is in this light that we argue that the outcome of mimicry as resistance is incalculable because the subject is ultimately incalculable: a fundamentally split subject can hardly be manipulated at will in the game of negotiation (Cf. Copjec, *Desire*, 18, 208).

We've seen that Toussaint, in his faithful imitation of everything French, failed to anticipate Napoleon's betrayal of Revolutionary France's very own founding principles; nor did he foresee his own degradation into what the whites perceived as an untrustworthy, whimsical, and unreasonable savage, who is the very opposite of the civilized, honorable Frenchman. Although it's seldom acknowledged by the colonizer, colonial histories, especially those of Haiti, nevertheless testify to what Michael Taussig calls "the mimicry by the colonizer of the savagery imputed to the savage" (66). And here is another reason why the incalculability of the subject can lead to *a most unlikely target of identification, an image the subject tends to disavow*. To better elucidate such an ostensibly problematic identification, we may need to delve further into the formation and workings of identification, via Lacan's return to Freud.

Lacan reminds us that Freud's conception of identification, most notably in *Group Psychology and the Analysis of the Ego* (46–61) isn't limited to specular, immediate identification. Rather, as Lacan indicates, "the identification in question," is the *support* of such specular, immediate identification. For it "supports the perspective chosen by the subject in the field of the Other, from which specular identification may be seen in a satisfactory light" (*Four Fundamental Concepts*, 267–268). Herein lies the important distinction Lacan, following through on the threads initiated but not yet illuminated by Freud, makes between imaginary identification and symbolic identification. Our predominant, commonsensical understanding of identification certainly envisages a specular relation: We identify with someone, particularly a hero, pop star, celebrity, etc., because we want to be like him/her, because we identify with the likable image he/she projects. Yet such an idea of identification as a likable image we see in the other, as if in the mirror, doesn't take into account from whose perspective we appear likable to ourselves—"the perspective chosen by the subject in the field of the Other," as Lacan puts it—or it simply assumes, quite mistakenly, that one's judgment or spontaneous feeling about someone pleasant or agreeable is his/her "own," unique and free from others' influence. One crucial point that can't be missed in Lacan's distinction between imaginary and symbolic identifications is that they are not two types of identification, with some people falling under the former, and others the latter. While imaginary, specular identification is an ineluctable phenomenon in all identification, symbolic identification is what makes it possible, therefore it is constitutive of identification yet tends to elude one's awareness, since, as Slavoj Žižek points out, "the trait on the basis of which we identify with someone is usually hidden—it is by no means necessarily a glamour feature" (*Sublime*, 105).[46]

In terms of imitation or mimicry, imaginary identification is an imitation of the immediate, specular image, resorting to certain likeness with the image. Symbolic identification, on the other hand, no longer turns on the resemblance of the subject in question to the projected image. Rather, it is based on something unlike what the subject sees or likes in the image, something "outside the mirror," or, one can even say, something inimitable, as Žižek explains with his usual lucidity, accuracy, and richness of examples: "In imaginary identification we imitate the other at the level of resemblance—we identify ourselves with the image of the other inasmuch

---

[46] Žižek here is drawing on Jacques-Alain Miller's distinction between "constituted" and "constitutive" identifications, qtd. in his *Sublime* (105). Such a distinction is also parallel to that between the ideal ego *i(o)* and ego-ideal *I(O)*.

as we are 'like him', while in symbolic identification we identify ourselves with the other precisely at the point at which he is inimitable, at the point which eludes resemblance" (*Sublime*, 109). One of Žižek's numerous examples is "the Dickensian admiration of the 'good common people'" whose poor but simple, communal, and uncontaminated world is in sharp contrast with the high society that is characterized by its cruel struggles for power and money. But this imaginary identification with the "good common people" is made possible—that is, they appear likable—precisely by an unannounced symbolic identification with the perspective of "the corrupted world of power and money" (*Sublime*, 107).[47] Just as Lacan makes clear in his widely cited and appropriated theory of the mirror stage, the infant in the mirror stage, who is mimicking its own reflection in the mirror but who does not yet have the capacity to coordinate its movements, is actually positing something beyond the image it sees—some imagined unity (see, for example, *Ecrits*, 4–6; 18–19). Imaginary identification—identification with the immediate, specular image, therefore, is always accompanied by a ratification of the symbolic one, of something outside that specular or bilateral relation, even if the symbolic intervention sustains invariably a misrecognition, or involves an overturning of a previous perception, in phantasmatic bliss, of an ideal image.

What, then, do we make of Toussaint's identification with the French Revolution? I propose that Toussaint's project in San Domingo, including its undecided/undecidable relationship with France, results from his identification with something inimitable, and quite tragically so. Coincidentally, James, when calling our attention to Toussaint's excruciating vacillations between two irreconcilable worlds, comments that "Toussaint was attempting the impossible—the impossible that was for him the only reality that mattered" (291). The inimitable which Toussaint was mimicking was not only the inerasable differences in skin color, but also *the impossibility of revolutionary ideals*. The widespread, zealous identification with the lofty precepts of the Revolution, which certainly propelled both the revolutions in France and San Domingo, nevertheless appeared as a phantasmatic projection, an exemplary *méconnaissance*. Not only did the exist-

---

47   Is the hidden trait on which identification is based inimitable? In some examples Žižek himself gives, however, it seems possible to mimic that particular characteristic.

ence of colonialism and slavery present itself as a glaring, indelible reminder of the unfinished, or unfinishable, project of the Revolution—an irredeemable failure that leaders of the Revolution from Robespierre to Napoleon endeavored to cover up or simply ignored,[48] but the metropolitan revolution itself had to undergo a series of inglorious sequels—counter-revolution, excess in the Reign of Terror, and (bourgeois) restoration of monarchy by Bonaparte, who as the Son of the Revolution effectively killed the Revolution.[49] On the part of the black slaves in the colony, their misrecognition of the revolutionary precepts was conspicuous yet powerful in igniting the engine of the Revolution, since, as James notes, they "construed it in their own image: the white slaves in France had risen, and killed their masters and were now enjoying the fruits of the earth" (81).[50]

Generations of anti-colonial/postcolonial/minority literatures or discourses have sufficiently and rightly refuted the racial stereotypes constructed and imposed by the West's colonialist/racist regimes and their present-day successors in the advanced capitalist societies of Euro-America. If such misconceptions of the victims of colonialism or racism are void or at least far from characteristic of the colonized/dominated, the victims' perceptions of the colonizer/racist are just as often erroneous. This doesn't mean the colonizers were not racists and exploiters, but that the colonized's misrecognition is twofold: First, it tends unwittingly to internalize the colonizer's inscription of the colonized into the second terms of the oppositions white/colored, civilized/backward, good/evil, etc., hence rendering the colonizer mistakenly idealized; second, it masks the colonized's hidden identification with what it accuses the colonizer of doing, what it hates in the latter (I shall return to this second point shortly). Toussaint's error, therefore, did not lie in miscalculation, in failing to anticipate in the

---

48 After presenting Robespierre's arguments on slavery, James comments that "it was only the word slavery Robespierre was objecting to—not the thing" (77). As for Bonaparte, he didn't even bother to rationalize the restoration of slavery because he didn't have to.
49 Napoleon I once proclaimed, "The Revolution is over. I am the Revolution." Such a post-Revolutionary, Bonapartist monarchy was uncannily repeated by Napoleon III years later.
50 Similar observations can be found in David Brion Davis, who writes that the idea of "revolution" could mean "something very different" in different geographical and political contexts (76); in Robin Blackburn, who notes that slave resistance would manifest itself "with a variety of political or religious inflections" as long as slaveholder power was broken (259).

Other's potential moves—or in what might escape the Gaze, but in his total misrecognition of the Other's omnipotence—in the surprising truth that the Gaze doesn't see you, as Lacan reminds us.[51] Toussaint's mimicry as camouflage—and few had greater mastery of this art than he—had to presuppose a field of vision seen by the Other, the gaze of the Other, about which the subject can never get assurance or confirmation and without which the mimicker's enterprise would be nullified, thus locked in the dualities of master/slave, enlightenment/backwardness, dominator/dominated and likely reinforcing the existing hierarchy of this binary structure.

In light of the problematic of identification we sketched out earlier, what is the symbolic support of such a phantasmatic, imaginary identification with the Revolutionary ideals? The question we need to ask ourselves is: From whose point of view do the precepts of the Revolution appear noble, lofty, or even celestial, otherworldly? From whose if not that of the elite leaders who were involved daily in the sordid power struggles, bloody slaughter, and horrific savagery mercilessly inflicted on their opponents? The brutality and goriness of the revolutionary struggles are best epitomized in the dialogue between Toussaint and Calixte-Breda, for whom Toussaint used to serve as a trusted and devoted coachman, in Derek Walcott's play *Drums and Colours*, where Toussaint has a dramatic confrontation with his former master, now bound as a captive by the black rebels and lamenting that the revolt has turned San Domingo into a living hell. Upon hearing this Toussaint replies: "Where was God? All of a sudden from your nephew's body/You have grown a delicate orchid called a conscience./And blame the times. I have learnt to pick up a child/Limp on my sword's edge as you would lift an insect;/I have to learn this" (246). In *The Haitian Earth*, another play by Walcott where a similar exchange is curiously repeated, though with slightly altered phrasing, Calixte-Breda, in an emotional outburst, again asks the question, "What is happening to the world? To us?/When will there be peace?" to which Toussaint candidly responds: "Do you know what peace means to me, monsieur?/It is a rag soaked in blood I must squeeze dry/Before there can be peace" (366).

---

51   See Lacan's example in Petit-Jean's thought-provoking quipping (*Fundamental*, 95–96). Also see Copjec's penetrating illuminations of this point (*Desire*, 35–36).

This "underside" of the Revolution, so incongruous with the idealist visions it inspired, was an image that disgusted many involved in the revolutionary struggles yet was inadvertently adopted by them—a secret symbolic identification the subject tended to disavow. As we've pointed out earlier, identification belies a bilateral, immediately specular relationship and is always based on something beyond such specularity, so when the subject appears to imitate something, he/she ends up mimicking "something else," even something the subject hates in the other's image or an image that seems most unlikely for him/her to become. It is not hard to extrapolate that in identifying with the precepts of the French Revolution, the revolutionaries in San Domingo also unwittingly mimicked the violence and atrocity colonialist France, pre- or post-Revolutionary, had inflicted upon them. (Hence the reoccurrences of interior quasi-colonialist exploitation after they drove out the French.) For example, before the black revolt, the mostly free and rich Mulattoes in the colony had sought to demand their equal rights with the whites by appealing to the principle of equality, with which they undoubtedly identified. But at the same time they identified with and reproduced the whites' racism against the blacks, which, in effect, applied to all non-whites. Some Mulatto proprietors, for their own vested interests, even once spoke publicly in favor of slavery, and when Rigaud's Mulatto troops fought with Toussaint's, they fought, as James puts it, with "their pride . . . roused" (232). Dessalines is perhaps the most obvious yet extreme case in point. Robin Blackburn observes perceptively that when Dessalines declared himself Emperor in 1804 his "emulation of Napoleon was accompanied by a strongly anti-French orientation" (254). A prototypical, cruel killer and strong believer in "an eye for an eye," Dessalines never hid his intention to exterminate everything French: the people, the customs, the political system, the ideas, and "proper French" (*Trilogy*, 374). Turning on them the havoc the white colonialists wreaked on the blacks and sadistically enjoying doing it, Dessalines became in this way a white lyncher, and thus personifies, quite proportionally, a virulent racism which, though at the diametrically opposite end of the spectrum of skin color, is as essentialist as that of his white counterpart.

As for Toussaint, he was one of the few who always saw clearly—maybe too clearly—the gap between these different facets of identification yet still naively and tragically attempted the impossible task of bridging the gap. His identification with the Revolutionary ideals also hinged on a vision of their impediments or obverse, thus the structure of Revolution was no longer seamless to him. This was a gap someone like Dessalines, for instance, couldn't see, being an impetuous, one-dimensional military strongman who "saw what was under his nose so well because he saw no further" (James, 288). In his discussions of transference, Lacan highlights "the discovery of the analyst" as the climax, the end—purpose as well as termination—and perhaps the whole point of analysis. This discovery consists in a symbolic intervention into a previously constructed imaginary identification and necessarily involves a certain alienation, since it is "understandable only at the other level, the level at which we have situated the relation of alienation" (*Fundamental*, 268). Such alienation is important because it opens up a gap in which the subject, as fundamentally split, has to recognize itself:

> The operation and manipulation of the transference are to be regulated in a way that maintains a distance between the point at which the subject sees himself as lovable—and that other point where the subject sees himself as caused as a lack by *a*, and where *a* fills the gap constituted by the inaugural division of the subject. (*Fundamental*, 270)

This small *a* is precisely what Lacan has designated as the *objet a*, which certainly can never cross this gap nor cover up this point of lack that founds the subject. Toussaint's transference couldn't result in a perfect resemblance or a thoroughgoing immersion in French ideals, as Toussaint himself saw only too well. Yet what's extraordinary—and tragic too—about him was his futile but heroic efforts to bridge the gap, to grasp the *objet a*, while the rem(a)inder of the Revolutionary ideals is blinking at him.

Colonial Trauma and the Postcolonial Fantasy

Toussaint and the black Jacobins' identification with the French Revolution, I argue, turned on this underside of the Revolution and their imitation was not simply of the ideals but also an unwitting imitation of what hindered or failed the Revolution. And since the Revolutionary ideals are inevitably, irrevocably rendered impossible, the black General's revolutionary program in San Domingo, as mimicry par excellence, became a tragic impossibility *not only historically, but also structurally*. The hidden symbolic identification with the Revolutionary failures supports the imaginary identification with the ideals precisely at the point where they are impossible to attain, thus sustaining it traumatically. Such a structural impossibility is what constitutes the trauma of post-Revolutionary San Domingo and engenders—or invokes—what I call "the primal scene of postcoloniality."

Colonial slavery as Trauma

Before I go on to explore the ways in which Toussaint and the Haitian Revolution have been imagined and relived as post-revolutionary/postcolonial trauma (in Toussaint's as well as in our times) and how they can be construed or constructed as "the primal scene of postcoloniality," I'd like to look into the traumatic effects of the original Revolution, with a capital R, the one Toussaint and his black Jacobins were allegedly mimicking. In her study of post-Revolutionary French Romanticism, Deborah Jenson locates in almost all the major Romantic writers "a vacillation between ideological extremes of personal liberty and social likeness," wherein the fulfillment of the latter was typically at the expense of the former (13–14). In light of the first two terms of the Revolutionary precepts, post-Revolutionary mimesis or representation (an older sense of mimicry) of the two inevitably entails a certain traumatic impossibility, what Jenson calls "traumatic mimesis," which she conceives of as the following: "Traumatic mimesis occurs as a textually palpable sense of a utopian field of social mimesis—a politics of likeness—that has come to function instead as a social wound because of the failure of various aspects of the Revolutionary program" (14). We need not rehash all these quite visible—retrospectively, of course—failures, but I'd like to highlight one particular flaw—the *hamartia*, one could even say—of the idealist Revolutionary project: slavery.

We've mentioned that the colonial question didn't sit too well with the leadership of the Revolution, regardless of which faction or ideological camp they belonged to, since many of the shrewd bourgeois revolutionaries sensed that the colonies, especially Saint-Domingue, the richest of all, essentially funded the Revolution. It was the wealth accumulated in the highly profitable trade opportunities opened up by colonialist exploitation of cheap labor and fertile lands overseas that gave the bourgeoisie the economic means and political status to challenge the monarchical authorities and the monopoly of trade privileges of the *ancien régime*. Of all forms and relationships of exploitation, slavery was the most blatant, brutal, vicious, and weighed the heaviest on the human conscience, if it was ever awakened. Until the formal abolition of slavery proclaimed in 1794 (which was so precarious and provisional that it was soon followed by Bonaparte's restoration of slavery in 1802), the issue of slavery underwent what we might call an "institutionalized forgetting" in the post-Bastille bourgeois Republic, and emerged as a *constituent exception* of the new socio-political order. For it was at once what made the Revolution possible, economically at least, and what would render the Revolutionary ideals constitutively, irrevocably, and traumatically unreachable. In the early years after the Bastille, "everybody," as James puts it bluntly, "conspired to forget the slaves," except for some lukewarm attempts by the Friends of the Negro (70).[52]

Quite paradoxically, however, such a forgetting of the question of slavery, whether knowingly or unknowingly, coincided with a proliferation of the term slavery as *trope* in post-Revolutionary social and literary discourses. Jenson notes that "[a]ppropriation of the term *slavery* to describe other, less drastic, forms of oppression had been popularized during the Revolution," sometimes even to the extent of obliterating the original referent of the word and the troubling connotations it incurs (198). For example, in George Sand's novel *Indiana*, the theme of "marriage as a form of slavery by analogy" evolves into "a political mutation," whereby "the term *slavery* virtually sacrifices its meaning to the term *marriage*" (Jenson 197, emphasis in original). The suffering of the slaves themselves has been relegated to oblivion not only because it is merely a vehicle through which Indiana, the heroine as well as narrator, expresses her own sense of oppression and suffering *but also* because Indiana apparently forgets and in effect cloaks the fact that she still maintains a master/slave relationship with her own slaves even while bemoaning her fate in front of them. In the political

---

52 One conspicuous and close parallel of such a facile, convenient neglect and an often unnoticed failure to extend the Revolutionary precept of equality to slaves was the American Revolution. Of the states of this new-born nation that was premised on such ground-breaking pronouncements as "all men are created equal" in the Declaration of Independence, Vermont was the only one that outlawed slavery in its constitution (in 1777). However, as Robin Blackburn points out, it was "a break-away, not one of the original thirteen colonies, and it was not admitted to Congress until 1791" (112). His empirically-based analysis of the "exclusion implicit in revolutionary ideology" is also a helpful reminder of the limits and the historicity of the age of Revolution, however prophetic and influential it indeed was.

arena, many French deputies would take advantage of the strong emotional appeal of the word *esclaves* [slaves] to refer to the status of the French people they professed to represent, yet when issues of colonial slavery arose, the term, interestingly, "was sporadically replaced by the euphemism 'unfree persons'" (Jenson, 198).

Such a "forgetting" accompanied by recurring evocation of what's forgotten is characteristic of the experience of trauma. The traumatic event, however, can only return or be invoked in its variegated, symptomatic forms, displaced, transformed, disguised, and rendered unintelligible, expect for the palpable power it holds over the traumatized subject, since trauma cannot be subjected to conscious, voluntary recollection. Remembering trauma, therefore, can never be an act of retrieving or reconstructing the traumatic event because the traumatic event itself is marked by an inherent latency or unintelligibility, hence an irreducible impossibility with regard to the representation of trauma. Remembering trauma, rather, presupposes an inherent forgetting, as Cathy Caruth expounds with reference to Freud's ostensibly ahistorical account of the Moses legend, specifically of the murder of Moses by his people:

> The experience of trauma . . . would thus seem to consist, not in the forgetting of a reality that can hence never be fully known, but in an *inherent latency within the experience itself.* The historical power of trauma is not just that the experience is repeated after its forgetting, but that *it is only in and through its inherent forgetting that it is first experienced at all.* And it is this inherent latency of the event that paradoxically explains the peculiar, temporal structure, the belatedness, of the Jews' historical experience: since the murder is not experienced as it occurs, it is fully evident only in connection with another place, and in another time. (17, emphasis mine)

In the context of the dominant Revolutionary discourses, what is noteworthy is not only that its blindness toward colonial slavery wouldn't be revealed until after a certain temporal belatedness that involved the constitutive forgetting, but that the Revolutionary project was predicated precisely on the exclusion of the question of slavery, on rendering it unintelligible, incomprehensible, unrepresentable. Such an unintelligibility or foreclosure of the slave in the representations of post-Bastille France resulted in the recurring evocations of the slave as trope and testified to the traumatic nature of the Revolutionary event, since traumatic experience lies in the symptomatic recurrence of that which eludes the comprehension of memory yet has an impact on it. One can even argue that it was exactly the invocations of the figure of the slave that mobilized the metropolitan resistance against other, less drastic forms of oppression, even though that didn't immediately lead to the emancipation of all slaves. Revolutionary trauma, therefore, was not only registered diachronically, but also inscribed synchronically, in the very structure of the Revolutionary discourse.

If the Revolutionary trauma of French Romanticism, as Jenson contends, was "especially symptomatic of the trauma of *being belated*, of coming after the 'great' Revolution," and "of experiencing one's own era as a secondary text" (15, emphasis in original), wouldn't the San Domingo Revolution be doubly traumatic, since chronologically it came a little after the French Revolution and was allegedly a second-hand Revolution, an undeniable mimesis of (the impossibility of) the original, off the central stage of history? Drawing on Caruth's illumination, in the quote above, of the Freudian conception of trauma, I maintain that the San Domingo Revolution, far from being merely the shadow of its French counterpart, was precisely the manifestation of the traumatic kernel—the rem(a)inder of the impossibility of the projected ideals—of the purportedly original Revolution. For, as Caruth explains, the "inherent latency of the [traumatic] event" would become "fully evident only in connection with another place, and in another time." Whether the traumatic event itself can become fully evident may be questioned; however, what we can be certain of is its recurrent evocations and a series of attempts to come to grips with its haunting returns, to make sense of the inexplicably repeated scene of the traumatic event.

The constitutive unintelligibility of the memory of slavery, however, often results in convenient forgetting of slavery in "empirical memory," which, as Barnor Hesse contends, is entwined with "empirical forgetting" to effectively efface the history of slavery as trauma. Hesse points out that "the historical recurrence and impact of black anti-slavery movements, particularly symbolized by the Haitian Revolution, the only successful slave revolt in recorded history, is erased almost absolutely" in both Western abolitionist and colonialist representations (164), and is still relatively marginalized in certain Eurocentric postcolonial discourses. Utter obliteration or disavowal of the memory of slavery, however, is nothing but another form—albeit an extreme one—of testifying to the unrelenting effects of slavery as trauma. In fact, it is precisely such an "inherent latency" of "the originary event" of trauma—in our context, the indestructible yet inarticulable effects of slavery for the descendants of slaves, as well as the unspeakable question of slavery for France and other Western powers with a slave-holding history—that gave rise to its persistent returns, with temporal belatedness, in variegated forms, of course. Hence the uncanny repetitions of history on seemingly divergent historical paths in the aftermaths of the Revolutions.

The primal scene of postcoloniality

Although the two Revolutions were knotted together by the same traumatic impossibility of Revolutionary ideals and bear a certain resemblance in their post-Revolutionary developments (for example, the grotesque, ironically counter-revolutionary repetitions of monarchical restorations by Bonapartes I & III in France and the recurrences of despotic kings—or whatever titles they had—in Haiti), the originality and significance of the San Domingo Revolution cannot be overemphasized. As Blackburn points out, "Haiti was not the first independent American state but it was the first to guarantee civic liberty to all inhabitants" (260). Taking into account the slave revolts the Haitian Revolution inspired throughout the New World, and the impact it exerted on the policies and public opinions of slave-holding societies, one would be obliged to concur with Blackburn's conclusion that "the Haitian Revolution had involved more profound upheavals and mobilizations than even the French Revolution itself" (ibid.).[53] Yet it is in particular this extraordinary combination of the dazzling achievements as well as far-reaching influence of the Haitian Revolution *and* its ensuing disappointing mutations in the post-Revolutionary/post-independence era that reinforce and incarnate its traumatic nature.

While optimism, racial pride, and positive outlooks may have abounded in overseas slave insurrections stirred by the San Domingo Revolution, treacheries and betrayals in pursuit of personal power reached

---

53 For the effects of Toussaint's San Domingo Revolution on the slaves in the New World, specifically the American South, see Blackburn, Davis, and Genovese. One can also not forget the ways in which Toussaint and the projects he initiated, though they remained unfinished, changed profoundly the power structure of the West. Napoleon's withdrawal after the failed campaign against Haiti resulted in the Louisiana Purchase that ushered in the westward expansion of the US and ensured British dominance in the Caribbean.

their basest form at the original site of the events when Dessalines and Christophe conspired with Leclerc to mastermind an arrest of Toussaint that would procure the French promise of peace and secure his black generals' power on the island. After Toussaint had been deported to France and Napoleon subsequently sent more reinforcements to San Domingo to secure an unannounced yet expected restoration of slavery, most of the fence-sitting black and Mulatto generals, trying to figure out their gains and losses, still waited. Some of them—including Dessalines—even helped the French hunt down the insurgents for some time. Although Dessalines, according to James, only feigned to collaborate with the French, thanks partly to his consistent and intense hatred of the whites, and eventually cooperated with the Mulatto leader Pétion to spark a war for independence, it is plausible to contend that these generals were merely opportunistic warlords who, fearful of the return of slavery themselves, would die to defend—or bargain for—nothing more than the liberty of themselves and their families.[54] Long gone was the Toussaintian ideal of "emancipation for all" in the early years of the Revolution, and Dessalines's intimidating ferocity was demonstrated not only to the whites but also to those blacks and Mulattoes who didn't submit to his command.[55] Dessalines recruited and organized troops, as James describes it, by either winning over those who were suspicious of his position, which was only natural, given his track record, or else he ruthlessly "hunted them down and destroyed them" (358). All these scandalous subplots at the very beginning of a new, independent nation rendered the initial ideals of the Revolution even more irrevocably impossible and proved to be ominous foreboding of the ensuing

---

54 For instance, James notes that a black general who conciliated with the French once pointed to his children and questioned his white counterpart, "'Are these to go back to slavery?'" (347)

55 Robert Debs Heinl Jr. and Nancy Gordon Heinl comment on the difference between Toussaint and Dessalines by focusing on their distinct approaches to Spanish Santo Domingo, which was to become today's Dominican Republic: "The differences between Toussaint's campaign of 1801 [in Spanish Santo Domingo] and Dessalines's of 1805 illustrate the differences between the regimes and the men. Toussaint proclaimed liberty and unification, and revitalized commerce, administration, and even the road system of Santo Domingo. Where Toussaint came as liberator, Dessalines came as invader. So far as can be determined, the emperor [Dessalines] had no desire to stay and no motive save to extirpate the last trace of French influence and to break Dominicans to his fearful will. What he achieved was to lay the foundation of unending fear, hatred, suspicion, and recrimination between the two nations of Hispaniola" (134).

cycles, in the history of the island, of bloody *coups d'état* and the ruling elite's utter disregard for the populace after their ascendancy to power.

The traumatic effects of the legends of Toussaint and the Haitian Revolution (which also had to be elevated to the status of a legend to be traumatic), as in all traumatic experiences, didn't manifest themselves until after a certain "time lag"[56]—"in connection with another place, and in another time," when we witness the uncanny repetitions of this particular historical event. It is interesting to note the temporal lapse between this first successful slave uprising that, according to Eugene Genovese, was not merely another revolt but the first true revolution undertaken by slaves (94), this original anti-colonial revolution in the Third World which led to the first independent state in the Caribbean, *and* the burgeoning of Third-World nation-states born in a torrent of successful—in the strict sense that they ended direct colonial rules in the colonies—anti-colonial movements in the twentieth century that were either explicitly modeled after it, or inadvertently followed its historical trajectories.[57] The extent to which the two waves of revolution resemble each other in their anti-climactic, degenerating developments in the aftermath of revolution/independence, however, precipitate the second time around an unprecedented, quite disproportionately grand scale of disillusionment, tristesse, cynicism, bitterness, distrust, and a new kind of antagonism against the new socio-political order.

If, as Marx comments on Hegel's remark that "all facts and personages of great importance in world history occur, as it were, twice," these monumental historical events and personalities take place as tragedy the first time, but as farce the second time (15), then the repetition of (Haitian) anticolonial/independence revolution in the twentieth century probably

---

56 Such a time lag is similar to what Freud, in his explorations of the Moses legend as collective trauma of the Jews, formulated as the "latency period," during which "no trace is to be found of the monotheistic idea" that is supposed to be bequeathed by Moses (*Moses*, 84, 86).

57 The empirical studies of the complicated reasons and factors in play for this temporal lapse between anti-colonial movements of the nineteenth century that stopped short of overthrowing the colonial regimes and settled for the gradual abolition of slavery, and their twentieth-century successors would be beyond the scope and main fields of concentration of this book. Blackburn's, Davis's, and Genovese's books can no doubt throw some light on this broad issue, especially more on the earlier nineteenth-century struggles.

was an "unbearable lightness in life," if the comic element is ever as revealing as the original one. (And don't forget that the Haitian Revolution was itself modeled after the French one.) This post-independence sentiment of disillusionment—so prevalent among the post-colonial subjects, especially the intellectuals, since the end of the decolonizing revolutions—can be characterized as symptomatic of a more profound traumatic experience, which, as we've mentioned, consists in a "forgetting" accompanied by recurring evocations of what's forgotten. Apart from the apparently uncanny resemblance between twentieth-century anticolonial movements in the Third World and their historical predecessor, there has been a proliferation of literary, historical, social, and political discourses on this original revolution since the 1930s[58] that signals simultaneously—and paradoxically—recurrences to the now legendary scene of the Haitian Revolution, *and* counter-movements of forgetting, of disavowing the memories or significance of this event. It is precisely these repeated efforts to reinscribe and reedit the memories of the Haitian Revolution in the postcolonial era, to come to terms with its traumatic effects in another time, that render the event in question—as elusive as it is—the "primal scene of postcoloniality," since the "primal scene" is conceived in Freudian psychoanalysis to refer to "those actual traumatic events whose memory is sometimes elaborated and concealed by phantasies" (Laplanche, 331). Like the sexual connotations often associated with the term (most notably Freud's designation, in the case of Wolf Man, of the parental intercourse witnessed by the child as the primal scene), the "primal scene of postcoloniality" here also involves a mixture of a certain incomprehension, covert excitation, repudiation, and lasting mental hold. It is, as Derek Walcott succinctly puts it, "the sordid and degrading beginning of the West Indies" ("Caribbean," 57) that traumatizes the postcolonial subject by reenacting what gave birth to

---

58 To be sure, there had been numerous accounts of Toussaint and the Haitian Revolution since the outbreak of the event. On the one hand, there was indigenous folklore, legends, songs, and mainly historical documentation by Haitian or Caribbean historians and scholars. From Western perspectives, Romantic writers seem to have been fascinated by the figure of Toussaint and wrote repeatedly about him. Earlier, Eurocentric historical studies of Toussaint and Haiti certainly abound too. But it was not until James's book that a colonized's perspective of this historical figure and this particular event was resurrected, as it were, and gained its due recognition by reconnecting to a movement of planetary reach.

him/her; that embodies the inception of a first, though transient, post-colonial moment; that seizes and fires the postcolonial imagination. In the following pages, I'll explore how the Haitian Revolution has been repeatedly represented as the primal scene of postcoloniality by examining works by C. L. R. James, Derek Walcott, and Eduard Glissant that specifically deal with this historical event.

C. L. R. James and the original sin of the postcolonial

We've indicated that a certain inherent forgetting is characteristic of traumatic experience and necessarily precedes the returns of the memories of the traumatic event. Although such a forgetting concerns more the constitutive unintelligibility of the traumatic event itself due to its overwhelming impact on the subject than the temporal lapse that always seems to obliterate events in our memory, Toussaint's revolution, incidentally, had somehow been forgotten, that is, had been devoid of the luster and sway it once displayed by virtue of the sweeping reach of a revolution, before the "rediscovery" of this particular history by James's ground-breaking book *The Black Jacobins*. The importance of James's book on Toussaint and the Haitian Revolution lies in its anticipating and heralding the anti-colonial movements that would soon sweep across different parts of the world by excavating this long-forgotten or ignored story of decolonization one and a half centuries ago, as a model and inspiration. What makes *The Black Jacobins* stand out "as a profoundly 'original' political artifact," as Grant Farred points out, is not only the knowledge and scholarly endeavor to unearth this effaced chapter of history, but also James's prescience "to identify in Toussaint's slave rebellion of the late 1790s the antecedents of an anti-/postcolonialism" that could "inspire, shape, and inform the 'Third World' future, dialogically linking Toussaint with Nkrumah and Kenyatta" (235, 236).

James's prescience, however, like the patently prescient judgments and Enlightenment doctrines of Toussaint himself, has a "singular blindness" that prevents James from seeing what his narratives envisions and enables the reader to perceive (ibid., 237–238). In other words, in foregrounding the emancipatory prospect of the Haitian Revolution for contemporary struggles against abiding colonialism, James fails to see the underside of the Revolution—be it French or Haitian—we delineated earlier, thanks in part to his own engaging and almost exhaustive documentation of the succession of events. Apart from the inherent inconsistency and structural impossibility of the Revolutionary ideals, i.e. their failure even before independence, James seems to have forgotten, too, the deterioration of post-independence Haiti into recurrent violence and corruption in the state, and the perennial poverty of its people—a history with which James is definitely familiar. If such is indeed his abstemious conception of the San Domingo Revolution/Haitian Independence, then wouldn't his pushing for a revisiting of the "Haitian model" in his book be a move that is destined to elicit repetitions of the Haitian follies and brutalities? This is apparently the sentiment registered in Farred's critiques of James, though the blame is placed on the theoretical short circuit in James's writing, rather than the historical fact that there has been, unfortunately, a proliferation of the Haitian model—or more specifically, the "Dessalines model," as Farred terms it—among the anticolonial/independence revolutions since the mid-twentieth century (237).

What James should have foreseen but didn't, therefore, is the even more gloomy prospect of "the postcolonial future that was Dessalines." As Farred convincingly argues, "Dessalines's assuming power signals more than the replacement of Toussaint" because "in that succession the atrocities that Papa Doc and Baby Doc Duvalier would commit against the Haitian people were ideologically spawned" (237). It is as if the postcolonial is henceforth born with an original sin in that transition, an irredeemable Fall from the celestial vision of the Revolution. Dessalines here emerges as a disturbing metaphor which, according to Farred, invokes a long list of names that are synonymous with the "infinite repetition of the 'Haitian' as ongoing postcolonial tragedy," one that extends well beyond Haiti and into the Caribbean, Africa, Latin America, and Asia (ibid.): Papa Doc and Baby Doc Duvalier, Kwame Nkrumah, Eric Williams, Jawaharlal Nehru, Idi Amin, Edward Seaga, Basdeo Panday, etc. Farred's enumeration of the postcolonial failures or degradations is reminiscent of a pessimism that is an extension of the general rise of "Afro-pessimism," albeit of a leftist strand (the rightist views being that since Africa lacks the political will and capacity to cope with its predicament, it'd be better off being recolonized, or that Africa's problems are of its own making so there is nothing or very little one—read: the Western colonial powers—can do about it).[59] The arguments derived from such a pessimistic, though quite realistic picture of the post-independence Third World are of a nuanced variety.[60] However varied they seem, most of them either look at post-colonialism as what renders colonialism passé (and as something that, in turn, is rendered passé by globalization), or look for the roots of the repeated failures of the postcolonial state in their models—whether the Western model of the nation-state or the Haitian one.

Yet the so-called postcolonial failure results less from a direct copy of the Haitian model than from a clandestine identification with the colonial state. As we've illustrated above, in identifying with the idealism of the French Revolution, the black Jacobins in San Domingo were also secretly or unknowingly mimicking the colonialist state of Saint-Domingue. By the same token, when the postcolonial nation-states appear to model themselves after the metropoles or Haiti (as a successful revolution, not its infamous deterioration), they can be unwittingly mimicking the colonial state, which, though a copy of the mother country, primarily practices what Partha Chaterjee calls "a rule of colonial difference" (16) and whose demise is the precondition of the postcolonial state's existence in the first place. This third element in the bilateral, specular identification often goes unheeded in the colonial situation, even with its spatial propinquity. Benedict Anderson, for example, admitted in the preface to the revised edition of his widely cited *Imagined Communities* that one of the "serious theoretical flaws" in the first edition is that he failed to take into account "the question of the role of the local colonial state, rather than the metropole, in styling these nationalisms" (xiii). In linking the Haitian Revolution to

---

59 Though permeated by such pessimism about the postcolonial nation-state, Grant Farred's essay in the end strives to think a way out of this impasse by alluding to Gramsci's dictum, "pessimism of the intellect, optimism of the will." For cases of Afro-pessimism, particularly as "postcolony," see, for example, Achille Mbembe, Tejumola Olaniyan, and Adebayo Williams.
60 There is the postmodern/poststructuralist view that picks on the glaring wrongs of the postcolonial state to call for a thorough jettisoning of the institution of the nation-state and embrace seemingly unbridled mobility in a borderless world of globalization; there is also a postcolonial view that, while pronouncing the bankruptcy of the nation-state, argues for shifting terrains of resistance to international-based campaigns, such as those sponsored by NGOs, because the mode of exploitation has been reconfigured under such headings as "globalization," "neocolonialism," "cultural imperialism."

the French Revolution, James too seems to envision little beyond the immediate, specular image of the former in the latter.

If the postcolonial insight or its progressive gesture lies in its denunciation and distrust of any revolutionary/nationalist project, then we'll have to say James is presciently postcolonial on occasion. For instance, as Paul B. Miller points out, "James places the cause of Haiti's suffering over the next two centuries squarely on the massacre" of the whites ordered by Dessalines shortly after he declared himself Emperor of the island (1084). James soberly concludes as follows:

> The massacre of the whites was a tragedy; not for the whites.... Such purposeless massacres degrade and brutalise a population, especially one which was just beginning as a nation and had had so bitter a past.... As it was Haiti suffered terribly from the resulting isolation. Whites were banished from Haiti for generations, and the unfortunate country, ruined economically, its population lacking in social culture, had its inevitable difficulties doubled by this massacre. That the new nation survived at all is forever to its credit for if the Haitians thought that imperialism was finished with them, they were mistaken. (373–374)

As mentioned above, James ultimately falls short of following through on the threads of the insights his book brings to light. In most of his writings, he appears to be an unequivocal exponent of militant resistance against imperialism, with independence as a necessary step to take, if not the goal, thanks perhaps to the example of Toussaint's inability to choose between France and an independent San Domingo. James's error, however, lies in his willful determination to avoid, or even undo, the Toussaintian vacillation, in another historical conjuncture, and in this way he remains symptomatic of the unresolved preoccupation with that primal scene, of the traumatic kernel of the structural impossibility of revolutionary ideals, of the Toussaint figure he represents in the text. In other words, James's prescience should have allowed him to perceive, however fleetingly, the underside of the Revolution, but he strives to disavow the unannounced symbolic support—in the figure of Dessalines—for that phantasmatic vision of the Revolution. It comes as no surprise, then, that James writes in his bibliographical notes for the book, "In a revolution excesses are the normal" (385).[61]

---

61 Interestingly enough, in Walcott's plays, Dessalines, the emblem of excesses and destruction, twice drunkenly mocks Toussaint, "He hates excess" (242, 365).

His revolutionary fervor and determination notwithstanding, James's prescience almost certainly necessitates the undercurrents of conflicts or inconsistency in his work. Miller also echoes this point by identifying a similar "enlightened hesitation" in both Toussaint and James that features the inherent "contradictions of the Enlightenment"—here he highlights the unbridgeable gap between the popular masses and the enlightened few (1071, 1078–1079). "By elevating Toussaint to the level of extraordinary individual or historical protagonist," Miller contends, James, an ardent Marxist and believer in the power of the "the people," sometimes lapses into effacing the significance of the masses and thus reenacts in his narratives Toussaint's flaw of alienating the masses yet taking their support for granted, of over-privileging "the tenets, institutions and (broken) promises of the French (Revolution)" (1075). The story of the black Jacobins, as the plural in James's title suggests, therefore reads more like that of the black Jacobin Toussaint L'Ouverture. In spite of his attempts to *forcefully steer clear of repeating Toussaint's mistake*, James winds up reenacting Toussaint's vacillation, of *becoming a Toussaintian figure* himself. James in this sense is a transitional, anti-/postcolonial figure, flashing insights ahead of his time yet meanwhile remaining bound by his historicity. At the other end of the pendulum's swing, where the broken promises of the postcolonial state have precipitated the bankruptcy of the grand narratives of revolutionary/nationalist projects, James's postcolonial successors and/or critics seem to be more engaged in some sort of counter-movement of forgetting, of disavowing the memories or significance of the traumatic event—not necessarily the Haitian Revolution itself, but the experiences and effects of slavery and colonialism per se.

Derek Walcott and the disavowal of decolonization

Through both his creative and critical writings, Derek Walcott is known as one of the most illustrious postcolonial advocates and practitioners of the productivity, creativity, and validity of mimicry. Walcott's poetics of mimicry, quite paradoxically, is accompanied by his celebration of an "Adamic vision" and his identity as a "New World poet," as well as his provocative promoting of collective amnesia as "the true history of the New World" (*Twilight*, 39). In his seminal essay on mimicry, "The Caribbean: Culture or Mimicry?," for example, Walcott writes wryly: "In the

Caribbean history is irrelevant, not because it is not being created, or because it is sordid; but because it has never mattered. What has mattered is the loss of history, the amnesia of the races, what has become necessary is imagination, imagination as necessity, as invention" ("Caribbean," 53). Although his notion of mimicry is not a banal imitation of some model, or "the real thing," such an obliteration—in the temporal sense, at least—or denial of the materials or the mirror on the basis of which or against which the mimicker creates his/her art seems incompatible with any conception of mimicry. According to Walcott, "the children of slaves must *sear their memory as with a torch*" (*Twilight*, 5; emphasis mine). Despite his proposal of eradicating the bitter memory of slavery as a way of healing, Walcott, throughout his career, has visited and revisited a scene which would undoubtedly evoke the memory of slavery, or of the end of slavery: the Haitian Revolution.

The Haitian Trilogy, published in 2002 as a collection of new and old plays, comprises three "history plays" that, as Walcott himself points out, center on the Haitian Revolution: *Henri Christophe*, *Drums and Colours*, and *The Haytian Earth*. The structure of the trilogy strikes us as that of repetition. Not only does the putatively central event, the Haitian Revolution, return throughout the plays as the backdrop against which the actions take place, but certain scenes, dialogues, and the "minor" fictional characters—as opposed to the recurring colossal historical figures such as Toussaint, Dessalines, and Christophe—repeat themselves, especially in the last two plays: the above-quoted scene of Toussaint confronting his former master Calixte-Breda, now as a captive after the revolt; the seduction of Anton, Calixte-Breda's illegitimate mulatto son, by white women; the characters with the names of Pompey and Yette, etc. But it is not exactly such recurrence of events and personages that testifies to or exemplifies the uncanny repetitions of this particular history, just as what returns in a history as trauma is not precisely the exact recurring minutiae (I'll return to this point about repetition in history later). Recall that the experience of trauma is characterized by an inherent forgetting that goes along with recurrent evocations of what is forgotten. Walcott's call for amnesia as history, therefore, can be considered a conscious, willful, and intensified act of forgetting which, nevertheless, happens to attest to the overwhelming force of a traumatic event that could result in involuntary amnesia. If one views the postcolonial failures as the seemingly endless repetitions of the

Haitian model, then amnesia would seem to be a solution that would cure the traumatized subject once and for all. What, then, does Walcott incinerate in his ostensibly paradoxical counter-movement of retrieving remnants of memory, again and again? In what ways and/or to what extent does Walcott "treat" this particular history as trauma?

Henri Christophe, first published in 1948, was Walcott's very first play. It begins, as Paul Breslin points out, where James's *The Black Jacobins* left off, when the news of Toussaint's death in his cell in France has just reached Haiti and ushers in the new era of Dessaline's repressive monarchy, soon followed by that of Christophe (76). In other words, we are thrown into the *aftermath* of the Haitian Revolution right from the very beginning of the play. The Revolution, together with its Toussaintian idealism, is officially over, coinciding with the death of its spokesman Toussaint, as well as with Dessalines's proclamation of himself as Emperor and his severing of Haiti's French connection by subsequent massacres of the remaining whites. We're already too late from the very beginning; the beginning is already the end. The inception of this first black independent state can therefore be presented as at once burial and birth, bound in "its swaddling cerements," to borrow the unsettling imagery of Walcott's poem "Laventille" (*Collected Poems*, 88). Indeed, the play is preoccupied with its post-Revolutionary tristesse and disillusionment, in contrast with James's revolutionary enthusiasm. The early signs of the withering of a revolutionary era can be discerned in the impatience and indifference with which Dessalines, with his generals looking on, receives the news of Toussaint's death. Before the messenger announces what everyone has long expected, Dessalines tells him: "Be eloquent without elaboration;/Talk quickly . . ." (9). After his elaborate story has been forcibly shortened by Dessalines, the messenger says, "I expected to move iron men to tears;/You look as if I had discussed the weather" (11). Dessalines is planning to seize on the occasion and rally around Toussaint's demise to assert his status as the heir apparent of Toussaint, however incongruous that seems. He then moves on impetuously to gain control of Haiti before the news reaches Christophe, who is repeatedly portrayed as a pal of Dessalines not only in this play, but also in the other plays of the *Trilogy*. Treacheries and betrayals of all kinds—of revolutionary precepts, comrades, leaders, followers—are nothing but commonplace in the Haitian Revolution and its sequels.

When Christophe finally learns of Toussaint's death, he laments to his soldiers, "the man is dead, history has betrayed us . . ." One of his soldiers reminds him, however: "You talk of duplicity; you yourself betrayed him./I think we mock-turtle him with tears" (24). Upon this Christophe, who is more sophisticated than Dessalines and embodies complicated inclinations like "a two-sided mirror" (29), replies with eloquence and a startling truth:

> These sharp tears that prick my heart are genuine,
> And as for betrayal, who has not betrayed?
> Mainvielle the archbishop, Ogé, Dessalines, Telemaque,
> And I, time, I.
> Toussaint . . .
> I cannot list his braveries, I can only tell
> Things that the memory shudders to remember,
> Hurt by its love. . . . (25)

As Walcott reflects retrospectively on this early work, *Henri Christophe* is about "the corruption of slaves into tyrants" (*Twilight*, 12). What Walcott wants to foreground in memory are premonitory failures of "those slave-kings, Dessalines and Christophe, men who had structured their own despair. Their tragic bulk is massive as a citadel at twilight. They were our only noble ruins" (*Twilight*, 11). As someone who keeps a skeptical distance from the political activism of fellow Caribbeans Aimé Césaire and Frantz Fanon, what Walcott seeks to sear in the gaping wounds of history, with the torch of historical hindsight, are the dizzying heights of revolutionary ideals and expectations that precipitate the unbearable plunge into cycles of corruption, violence, and the abiding economic dependence and exploitation which recur on the heels of the optimistic prospect of independence in Walcott's time. Such a disavowal of the emancipatory significance of decolonization, whether in the eighteenth or twentieth century, however, belies his wish to treat colonialism as passé or even nonexistent in his call for amnesia as history, for it also has to recognize the persistence of varied forms of colonization and exploitation, within or beyond national borders.

Breslin notes that Walcott leaves out some events that are "perhaps as significant as those he emphasizes" (77). One such event defines "Christophe's finest moment as king," when in 1814 he foiled France's secret plan, with the acquiescence of the British who were bound by the Treaty of Paris, to not only repossess Haiti but also to restore slavery (ibid.). Perhaps the most conspicuous and interesting omission in Walcott's "treatment" of this traumatic history is, as felicitously instantiated in the quote above, "Toussaint . . ." The dots signal more than the erasure of Toussaint; they somehow represent his grotesque, haunting presence, "things that the memory shudders to remember." For Toussaint emerges and reemerges as *the absent center* of the play, even though the character Toussaint isn't actually acted out in *Henri Christophe*. It is the death of Papa Toussaint that allows Dessalines to rally around the Name-of-the-Father in establishing his rule; it is also Toussaint's death that sets in motion a series of struggles for power by lesser historical figures who apparently are not worthy of the name of Toussaint. The sordid betrayal of Toussaint by his two trusted generals, Dessalines and Christrophe, is later repeated and turned against Dessalines himself, while Christophe is duped by his own self-deception which disavows his eventual resemblance to Dessalines (for example, he chastises Vastey, his secretary, "Do not mention Dessalines/And I in the same breath"; 82). The overarching significance and ubiquitous presence of Toussaint in relation to the purportedly central event—the Haitian Revolution—are somehow diluted in the rest of the *Trilogy*. In *The Haytian Earth* Dessalines is clearly the protagonist who, emblematic of excess and lust for power, contrasts not only with Toussaint, who is known for his decorum and love of order, but also with Pompey and Yette, the "nobody" couple who till the Haitian earth and "endure so many kings on their heads."[62] In *Drums and Colours*, whose ambitious, epic framework encompasses hundreds of years of history of the Caribbean since Columbus's landing, Toussaint is juxtapositioned with other monumental historical figures—Christopher Columbus, Sir Walter Raleigh, and George William Gordon—and appears as no more than one of the four greats.[63]

By highlighting the horrific deteriorations of the Haitian Revolution/Independence, "the corruption of slaves into tyrants," Walcott inad-

---

62 I borrow this from a line by Toussaint in Glissant's play, *Monsieur Toussaint* (36).
63 The play is structured as if the Carnival band, which consists of masqueraders Emmanuel Mano, Pompey, Yette, Ram, and General Yu, was reenacting bits of histories of these heroes. From scene 16 to the end of the play, these fictional, comical characters are even engaged in farcical mimicking of a petty guerilla band which seems to parody the recurrence of gangs of warlords in the history of the island, and thus also borders on taking away the aura of the historical figures it enacts earlier.

vertently (or knowingly) downplays Toussaint's presence as a source of inspiration for generations of the oppressed and the idealist, emancipatory implications he stands for, while in effect effacing the subtle yet profound contradictions in Toussaint (for instance, being at once an exponent of the modern republican state and a paternalist despot).[64] It is precisely Walcott's disavowal of certain aspects of the memories of the Haitian Revolution, which stems from his disillusioned perception of his own post-revolutionary conjuncture, that renders his recurring representations of the historical event a primal scene of postcoloniality, a traumatic scene vested with convoluted fantasies. In exterminating the whites, Dessalines, one can argue, sought to exterminate every trace of slavery as well as the memory of subjugation and indignity, to "wipe the slate clean," to support a fantasized amnesia. Walcott's advocacy of collective amnesia is contradicted by his own textual practices, since he does foreground some of the most painful memories of the Haitian people. His violent, willful forgetting of bitter memory, therefore, is *selective amnesia* at best, and the idea of a *willed amnesia* wouldn't sustain itself theoretically, either.

First of all, if a traumatic event, including the historical kind, is predetermined by its inherent unintelligibility, then one can't really forget what's always already forgotten, since there is nothing to be forgotten, given the unintelligibility or unrepresentability of the event that prevents itself from being registered in memory and expunged later. Moreover, though such a traumatic event is not subject to conscious recollection, paradoxically it can never be successfully forgotten either, thanks to the haunting nature of trauma, of the unrepresentable event as an indelible remainder in memory. There can never be a clean slate to begin with; there is always a certain remainder of history that threatens to return and disturb the consistency of a historical narrative. But what survives Walcott's willful amnesia is not coincident with what he leaves out in his dramatization of

---

64 In addition to the contradictions touched on elsewhere in the chapter, Juris Silenieks lists the following: "there are deep contradictions and contrasting inconsistencies of a man who was both a freedom fighter and a despot, as well as a devout Catholic suffused with the ideas of the Enlightenment, a royalist with the passion for the French Revolution, and a revolutionary with an administrator's zeal for law, order, and prosperity" (6). Grant Farred, on the other hand, attributes Toussaint's inability to establish democracy in San Domingo to a certain deeper structural failure, rather than the flaws in his personality, as James argues.

this particular history. What, then, do we make of such a remainder of traumatic history? What exactly returns, if the traumatic event is said to be constitutively unintelligible? What are the significance and implications of the structure of repetition in both the history of the colonized world and the representations of the particular history of Haiti? I'd like to address these questions, starting with the last one, by means of a reading of Édouard Glissant's play *Monsieur Toussaint*.

Glissant, the (Post)Colonial, and the Remainder of History

In addition to being a model and inspiration for some, as well as a reminder of disillusionment and ongoing predicament for others (and a combination of both for still many more), the Haitian Revolution, as a historical event, also strikes us as a thought-provoking case to reexamine the burning question posed by many contemporary scholars engaged in the field of postcolonial studies: "When was the postcolonial?"[65] For if the "post" in "postcolonial" denotes the formal cessation of colonialism, then post-revolution/independence Haiti, as the first successful decolonization movement, would appear to be "proto-postcolonial." This "original" but often forgotten postcolonial moment would thus call into question the temporality and antagonistic position the postcolonial assumes against not only Western colonialist oppression/discourses, but also the mode of resistance/thinking (read: binary opposition) of its historical antecedent, the mid-twentieth-century Third-World anticolonial movements. This proto-postcolonial before the anticolonial, however, seems to be precarious and exemplary of the now scandalized binary opposition, as the new nation splintered into two (black and mulatto states) shortly after its creation. On the other hand, the abiding interior and exterior relationships of economic exploitation, as well as the long-standing autocracy and corruption of its ruling class make Haiti an uneasy reminder of an "undead coloniality" in a current intellectual milieu where many First World or cosmopolitan intellectuals celebrate the superseded colonial era (and a new age of global

---

65 The question was first, and most famously, brought up by Elaine Shohat. The special issue of *Social Text* in 1992 initiated the most visible, and perhaps the first large-scale debate about the postcolonial—a watershed that generated a series of responses to the issue.

postcoloniality). It is precisely this complicated juncture of the coloniality/postcoloniality of Haiti that precipitates the contestatory nature, the interventionist gesture, the convoluted temporality and the vested historicity of the authors who often characterize contemporary representations of the Haitian Revolution. Édouard Glissant's *Monsieur Toussaint* stands out as the most fitting of these characterizations.

The most striking feature of Glissant's play is its non-linear plot line, with different time frames traversing each other and collapsing the distinction between the past and the present, between different locales concomitant with the events. *Monsieur Toussaint* consists of four parts—the Gods, the Dead, the People, the Heroes—while the scenes are divided between the insular space of San Domingo and the prison in Fort Joux, France, where Toussaint appears to be experiencing flashbacks of past events in his mind and communicating easily with the dead as well as the living who are apparently not present in the cramped cell. The play opens with Toussaint already confined in the prison, which, as Glissant points out in the preface to the first edition, "marks the end of [Toussaint's] story" and functions as a "single act" around which various scenes revolve and present themselves according to "the logic of his life" (*Toussaint*, 18). The beginning, which is also the end, and to which all scenes of the past return, thus constitutes a structure of repetition in the play. What returns, what emerges throughout Toussaint's repeated evocations of things in the past, is not his stalling at the dead end of his career—his imprisonment—nor a final crystallization of a certain pivotal moment in time that defines his tragedy, but the convergence of the past, the present, and the future in a convoluted temporality.

According to Glissant, "the equivalence of past and present is essential in light of what [Toussaint] has or has not accomplished and of what he expects—or no longer expects" (17–18). Exemplifying such a convergence of different temporalities (and spatialities), the play is thereby "linked to what [Glissant] would call, paradoxically, a *prophetic vision of the past*" (17; emphasis in original). This is "a poetic endeavor" which does not rest content with uncovering or reconstructing historical facts, but seeks to "renew acquaintance with one's history" (ibid.). It involves "not only correction of factual inaccuracies and white bias, but also re-creation of the past concurrent with the vision of the future" (Silenieks, 11). Glissant's postulation of a prophetic vision of the past, of course, can be considered part of the general cause of the colonized or the newly decolonized to reclaim their right to write their own history, to interpret their history from their perspective, which has long been excluded. Yet *Monsieur Toussaint* is more than a literary work committed to bending or editing memories of past events to fit neatly into the agenda of the present struggle. Although Dessalines is listed as "Toussaint's lieutenant and liberator of Haiti" on the "Cast of Characters" page (21)—which means Glissant has a more sympathetic view of Desssalines than Walcott—his treason is nevertheless highlighted in his dialogue with Granville, Toussaint's secretary, when Dessalines defiantly taunts Granville, "And yet I betrayed Toussaint; I'll say it for you since you do not dare say it" (91). While the play records Toussaint's heroics at length, it is centered on the prison scene where Toussaint is presented as an aging, dishonored, humiliated, and backward-looking general who, in the eyes of the jailer and the officers in charge of Fort Joux, appears to be hallucinating about his past, "sitting there in his armchair, reviewing his troops" (23).

I argue that Glissant is preoccupied in this play with recreating, in the present, a particular history in its *totality and opacity* in order to place it under a scouring, pains-taking scrutiny. For Glissant, totality is necessarily bound up with certain opacity.[66] *Monsieur Toussaint* is permeated with a certain opacity primarily because of the convoluted temporality and the blurred boundaries between different spaces, between the living and the dead; even as it seeks to conjure up a totality, or its semblance, by enumerating a plethora of historical details—the large number of characters that are evidently far more than necessary, as well as place names and events that, as Juris Silenieks points out, "have no significance in the story line" (13). The convoluted temporality seems to be exemplified in, and can be rationalized by, Toussaint's reminiscences of past events, in which he converses freely with the dead as well as the living who are supposed to be in San Domingo instead of Fort Joux. The dead, especially Mama Dio, a Voodoo priestess, Macaïa, an early leader of the slave revolt, and Mackandal, a leader of runaway slaves who died before Toussaint's time, emerge as spectators and commentators of the reenacted events, rather than as participants. In fact, Toussaint calls them "my shadows" (*Toussaint*, 58) who constantly haunt him,

---

66   This is one of the central notions in Glissant's critical writings as a whole.

consoling and advising him sometimes, but more often contesting, bickering with, or sneering at him about his every move. They thus embody the perpetual conflicts inside the protagonist and the polyvalence of Toussaint's significance in the play as in history.

While Toussaint keeps revisiting, with his shadows, scenes from the past, he doesn't just seek to explain or justify what he or others did. His conversations with his supernatural companions are filled with prescient comments and predictions (for example, Toussaint announces to Macaïa his "destiny" of being betrayed and arrested before these events are reenacted in the ensuing pages [59]), but they are not merely historical hindsights or second-guesses. Toussaint appears to be willing to confront the most excruciating memories by reliving the events in all their minutiae; the meanings of the events, however, are subject to the unsettled debates between Toussaint and his shadows. Without attempting to undo what went wrong when he revisits earlier scenes (in fact, he never identifies specifically what went wrong or what could have changed the course of the events), Toussaint shows a tranquil resolve to accept whatever has taken place, though certainly not with quiet resignation, as his continual arguments with the dead attest. The converged temporality Glissant envisions in the play, therefore, is not that of superimposed temporalities—the present on the past, as in the case of denials of certain historical facts for the sake of present needs and a present agenda, or the past on the present, like the familiar neurotic obsession with, and compulsive repetitions of, past failures. One event that many historians single out as one of the gravest mistakes Toussaint made, and as the pivotal event that led to his eventual alienation from his people, was the execution of Moyse, Toussaint's nephew and heir apparent. I'd like to elaborate in some detail on Glissant's treatment of this event, not to prove it to be pivotal to the history of Toussaint and his project in San Domingo, but because it instantiates Glissant's "prophetic vision of the past."

Moyse was executed, on Toussaint's orders, because he refused to obey Toussaint's command to repress the ex-slave laborers who rebelled against the white planters and what they perceived to be a pro-white government led by Toussaint. Though he never led the insurrection, Moyse had been reluctant to implement Toussaint's policy to rigorously protect the white proprietors' properties. Moyse's execution is bewildering to many and Toussaint's motives can only be speculated. Whether to reassert his authority, which Toussaint perhaps thought he was losing, and prove yet again he was a man of his word, or under pressure from the former colonials as well as from jealous generals like Dessalines and Christophe, who wanted to rid themselves of a major rival, Toussaint in the end made no exception for his own nephew and the general most loved by the masses.[67] In Glissant's play, Moyse returns from death and reels off an eloquent speech which he didn't really make before his execution and which reflects more of Toussaint's sober thoughts, style, and his projection into the future through this specular reflection:

> **Moyse:** I seek the people. You say the people, I say the wretched.... There they are, awaiting only a sign, a signal, and I join them in my turn. The Republic made us governor or general. Why? Why? A blinding mirror turned about in the officer's epaulet; we were dazzled by it. But the gold braid is tarnished, my eyes are open now on the dusty death. They are there, General Toussaint, behind the wall. Those whom you call the people and who shouted: "Long live Moyse." *I was your successor; today I precede you in joining their band.* For you who commanded them to be killed, you will be their commander in eternity.
> **Toussaint:** You held back then for this speech... Go to your eternity. Go! You carry with you at least this bit of Toussaint which belonged to Moyse, since I had Moyse executed! Very well, I do not miss you. (65–66; emphasis mine).

Moyse, of course, did not join the insurgents. What consigned him to his death sentence was that simple sentence, that fatal salute: "Long live Moyse!" But when Toussaint imagines Moyse saying "I join them in my turn," it may be that "bit of Toussaint which belong[s] to Moyse" that, preceded by Moyse, wants to join them, if not today, then in the future.

No matter what kind of future one envisages, what (new) relevance one intends to invest in a certain history, Caribbean history, and in a broader sense, the history of those parts of the world with a common past of colonial slavery, cannot escape a sense of trauma that is deeply rooted in the experience of "the Middle Passage," the abrupt dislocation of African slaves, without preparation and comprehension on their part, from their native lands, into the slave ships, to unknown lands and their unknown fate.[68] Particularly in the case of Toussaint and the Haitian Revolution, owing to the juxtaposition of what he "has or has not accomplished,"

---

67 James says that Toussaint "recognized his error" and showed "the remorse which moved him" and made him seem "so agitated" (278).
68 Toni Morrison offers a comparable description of such an experience of abrupt dislocation in the Middle Passage when she talks about her *Beloved*: "snatched, yanked, thrown into an environment completely foreign... Snatched just like the slaves were

of the rapid uplift from slavery to freedom with the ensuing broken promises of that change of status. Glissant thus says of this history of an acute sense of dislocation: "Our historical consciousness could not be deposited gradually and continuously like sediment . . . but came together in the context of shock, contradiction, painful negation, and explosive forces. This dislocation of the continuum, and the inability of the collective consciousness to absorb it all, characterize what I call a nonhistory" (*Caribbean*, 61–62). The elements of shock, discontinuity, and belated absorption of such disruptive experiences into consciousness are also characteristic of trauma. The sudden, overwhelming infusion of otherwise discrete sediments of history into memory, therefore, seems to be felicitously represented in *Monsieur Toussaint* by the surplus of signifiers, of superfluous historical facts, coming together in a lacuna of history opened up by the "dislocation of the continuum" which is registered in neither the present nor the past, but in the convoluted temporality that is the *internal* limit of history. For what Glissant calls "nonhistory" is nonetheless historically produced, helpless before others' establishment of the slave trade (Breslin, 5). It is, as it were, *an empty place in history* that, produced by a violent discontinuity, a traumatic dislocation, *foregrounds the limit of the representation of the historical narrative as continuum*. Precipitately discontinued, it keeps returning to and encircling the same (empty) place in history, as if attempting to fill the gap.

Such a convergence of temporality is nowhere to be found in reality, except in liminal and/or traumatic experiences of entangled temporalities. "For the Caribbean," as Juris Silenieks points out, "the trauma of the past is ever present" (10), and "the simultaneity of the two time frames in the play" happens to signify "the Caribbean's ever present trauma of the past which now must be transformed into a lucid apprehension of history's rich heritage" (13). Whether such historical heritage can be lucidly "apprehended" or not, there is nevertheless some remainder of history that cannot be wiped out even after that violent disruption of the continuum and persists in returning in its variegated forms (from the past which is no longer the past per se). Although the formal device of the non-linear plot line, the large number of characters, the abrupt shifts of fictional locales—

---

from one place to another, from any place to another, without preparation and without defense" ("Unspeakable," 32).

even within the same scene, and the idiosyncratic language (revolutionary rhetoric mixed with vernacular idioms, Creole and aristocratic French) may perplex the reader or the audience, they are not an attempt at "technical sophistication," as Glissant puts it in his preface (17), typical of (Western) modernist/experimentalist art. Rather, these devices to some extent reflect, as Silenieks argues, "the structures and the modes of perception of the Afro-Caribbean mind. Time is not perceived as an irreversible and evanescing flow but rather as *a cyclic return* that assures a permanence partaken by the living and the dead as well as by those not yet born—a feature of many African beliefs" (13; emphasis mine). This recourse to the African conception of time, of course, is not a simple atavistic move to African origin, either. Mama Dio, symbol of this kind of supernatural communion, appears as no more than one of the shadows of Toussaint who never totally possess him. Toussaint's tragedy, like the tragedy of those victimized by colonial slavery, is a modern one, which is based on the irrevocable loss of that premodern origin, despite the latter's haunting power.

In the context of our analysis, the continual resurgences or evocations of the Haitian Revolution in the writings of certain postcolonial writers are symptomatic of that traumatic event, or signs of its unabating effects, but the ostensible repetitions of similar or identical scenes, characters, plots in the recollection or remembering of the event do not amount to reconstructing or reproducing the event in question. To better illustrate the traumatic repetition and the return of the remainder of traumatic history, I'd like to briefly return to Freudian/Lacanian psychoanalytic theory. Given that the repetition compulsions common in traumatic neurosis doesn't really help the patient reconstruct and comprehend the traumatic event, repetition in Freudian theory, as Lacan asserts, is not reproduction (*Fundamental*, 50). The difficulty of reproducing in dream the traumatic scene, however, doesn't seem to bother the traumatized person as long as he/she is awake. "What, then," asks Lacan, "is this function of traumatic repetition if nothing . . . seems to justify it from the point of view of the pleasure principle?" (51). In his ensuing arguments, Lacan teases out something that lies behind the symptomatic repetitions and might serve as the impetus of repetition—the real, as Lacan contends: "The real is beyond the *automaton*, the return, the coming-back, the insistence of signs, by which we see ourselves governed by the pleasure principle" (53–54). The real, which is irreducible to reality in Lacanian theory, is closely linked to

CHAPTER II: TOUSSAINT, MIMICRY, AND POSTCOLONIALITY   89

liminal experiences such as those of trauma. While the real is inassimilable to, and cannot be reconstructed in, the analytic experience, it can present itself "in the form of the trauma."[69] In fact, Lacan goes further to say that the real *can* be encountered in liminal, traumatic experiences—in the tuché, which he defines as the encounter with the real (53). One can argue, therefore, that the real is the kernel of the traumatic experience which remains inaccessible, inarticulable except in the rare, unexpected moments of the tuché.

The relation between the real and the phenomenon of repetition in traumatic experiences, however, appears problematic and has to be examined more carefully. On the one hand, the real is characterized by its tendency to return, by the movement of repetition, but repetition doesn't make the real, ever elusive, any easier to grasp. As Lacan writes, "the real is that which always comes back to the same place—to the place where the subject in so far as he thinks, where the *res cogitans*, does not meet it" (49). On the other hand, repetition that happens to bring along the encounter with the real cannot be confused with "either the return of the signs, or reproduction, or the modulation by *the act of a sort of acted-out remembering*" (54; emphasis mine). This last point is important because the traumatic kernel of memory cannot be willed or acted out, much as the encounter with the real can hardly be orchestrated or calculated. As Lacan says of such an encounter in traumatic repetition, "what is repeated, in fact, is always something that occurs ... *as if by chance*" (54; emphasis in original). What returns in the structure of traumatic repetition, in the repeated visitations to the purportedly historical event, therefore, is not *a historical reality* made up of its constitutive details, but *the real of history itself.*

The real manifests itself in history—as its internal limit, since it's parasitical of history—when something veers from its projected or calculated historical trajectory and turns out to be a *déjà vu*. One prime example from the texts we have analyzed is Christophe's relationship to Dessalines. As the latter's trusted pal, Christophe is the only person who can afford to

---

69 Referring to Freud's interpretation of a father's dream of the burning of his child, who was actually being burned while the father was having this dream, Lacan remarks as follows: "Is it not remarkable that, at the origin of the analytic experience, the real should have presented itself in the form of that which is *unassimilable* in it—in the form of the trauma, determining all that follows, and imposing on it an apparently accidental origin?" (55; emphasis in original).

advise against Dessalines's wrongs without seriously risking his own life, and, as Walcott shows us, he does that a number of times throughout *The Haitian Trilogy*. In *The Haytian Earth*, for instance, Christophe looks a drunken Dessalines in the eye while he engages the latter in a long, rather philosophical talk. When Dessalines asks Christophe what he is staring at, Christophe answers that it's an animal Dessalines can't see, because "you would have to be where I am to see him" (421). Later in the conversation Christophe gives the warmongering king a piece of insightful advice which also proves to be useful to Christophe himself at a much later time:

> If you find that peace has less purpose than war,
> Then make a war inside yourself, fight with yourself,
> And then I'd crown you myself, but all your actions
> Endanger the republic, or what was once
> A republic, before you made yourself a king.
> . . . .
> You should give back the crown
> To the republic, dissolve the monarchy,
> Dissolve yourself, and then you'll know yourself.
> And I am saying what everyone around you feels
> But is too scared to tell you. (424)

Although Christophe rationalizes his masterminding the assassination of Dessalines by highlighting the latter's tyranny and betrayal of their revolutionary, republican ideals, he himself, ironically, creates a monarchy shortly after he seizes power and is known for his despotism too. In other words, Christophe warns Dessalines of the latter's degradation into "a peevish king with terrible whims" (*Christophe*, 49) and even into an animal, and despite Christophe's aversion to being compared to Dessalines, of being mentioned with Dessalines even "in the same breath" (83), he ends up becoming a Dessalines himself, initiating the cycle of autocratic rule composed of the long list of despots in the history of Haiti, and, as mentioned earlier, of the postcolonial world.

We call the recurrence or resemblance of historical events uncanny repetition when some initially discrete historical event veers from its supposed historical trajectory—or brings to the fore the limit of its historical logic—and turns out to be a *déjà vu*. Coming back to Marx's comment on Hegel, the second time a historical phenomenon emerges it appears as farce because, in aiming to imitate the precedent or the original, it pales beside the model, and is thus forever condemned to an inherent lack of authenticity, just like Naipaul's mimic men. On the other hand, a tragedy is uncannily repeated, and its traumatic effects triggered, when one strives to steer away from a historical precedent, but, under the sway of something beyond one's control, something inarticulable, winds up retreading that historical path. The real of history, again, is the impetus of the repetition running beneath the resemblance of appearances, of historical details. It is what remains in excess of the repetition, as an irreducible remainder of history. Let me briefly illustrate such a remainder of history in light of Glissant and Walcott.

In contrast with Walcott's erasure of certain aspects of memory as "a sort of acted-out remembering" and his proposal of collective amnesia as "the true history" of the New World, Glissant tends to give us an overflow of the details of a memory that encompasses different spaces and times—*an abundance of historical contents infused into an arrested moment in time that is neither past nor present*. It is, as Silenieks points out, an attempt to "raise the past to a higher level of conscious apprehension" (10). While not glossing over or deliberately searing the historical wounds, Glissant's representation of the traumatic history seems to undertake a desperate attempt to render the inherently unintelligible event of trauma as though it were intelligible, *intense scrutiny of the representation resulting in the appearance of a surplus of signifiers*. Yet accompanying the totality of such a postulated representation is the indelible opacity persisting throughout the play, despite the repeated effort of summoning past and present into the convoluted temporality on which the protagonist reflects. The unarticulated/inarticulable remainder of history, therefore, is what remains opaque and resistant to scrutiny after Glissant proffers time and time again a plethora of historical minutiae that aspire to approximate historical totality. It is also what would survive Walcott's willful, sweeping liquidation of his memory bank—which, however, ends up being a selective, hence unsuccessful, amnesia, as we explained earlier.

Such a remainder of history, as the instantiation of the real of history, is by no means outside history, just as the real is the internal limit of the socio-symbolic order, rather than its outside or beyond. Drawing on Freud's interpretation of Jewish history, as elaborated in *Moses and Monotheism*, Joan Copjec thus writes of a Freudian/Lacanian notion of history: "There is no history without an internal limit within history itself, without an irreducible element, a negation that forbids the emergence of an outside of history.... [T]his negation is able to be designated by its Lacanian name:

the real" (*Imagine*, 96). Having no existence in historical time, the real can nevertheless show its effects in history by marking the limit of a historical trajectory—and the ensuing unexpected change of course—or by foregrounding the inherent impossibility of a historical representation, of a traumatic event, for example. The real manifests itself in history when it "produces temporal anamorphoses within historical time that take the form of uncanny repetitions or anachronisms" (ibid.). Glissant succeeds in invoking such a convoluted temporality which recreates, as faithfully as possible, the liminal experience of historical trauma. The real can be encountered; however, it cannot always be "apprehended" when we place bits of memory under our conscious scrutiny, in all its totality and opacity. It catches one by surprise only in "one of those" moments, when, for instance, Toussaint comes to realize that his intended successor Moyse turns out to be his predecessor in (re)joining the people, and the execution of Moyse also signals the death of the Toussaint of old, as the leader of the people. It is also such an irreducible remainder of history that, as *real*, repeatedly brings about that complicated temporality of the representations of the Haitian Revolution—of the primal scene of postcoloniality that is simultaneously the harbinger of the postcolonial and of an enduring, undead coloniality.

Chapter 3
In the Name of the Father: Representing Postcolonial Nationalisms

One of the constitutive contradictions of the modern nation is its ambivalent temporality which, as Homi Bhabha points out, turns on its recurrent evocations of antiquity in the face of the contemporaneity of the national present ("DissemiNation," 295). In this chapter, I will take as a point of departure this "archaic ambivalence that informs modernity" and Ernest Renan's postulation of a forgotten traumatic event at the very inception of the nation and examine their instantiations in anticolonial/postcolonial nationalisms, especially in the case of the Haitian Revolution, in light of the Freudian scene of the murder of the primal father and his subsequent returns in variegated forms. This, of course, will involve some theoretical questions about nationalism and the nation-state in general. I will take into consideration Frantz Fanon's and Benedict Anderson's conceptions of nationalism in order to highlight the question of spontaneity in nationalist feelings, which are approached in terms of the psychoanalytic notion of *jouissance* closely linked to the positing of the killing of the primal father. After and exploration of the problematics of the temporality of the postcolonial in the previous chapter, I will then bring in the spatial dimension into our inquiry of the workings of postcolonial nationalisms and the formations of national literatures, not merely those limited to the Caribbean.

The Traumatic Antiquity of the Modern Nation-State

In an argument bearing striking a resemblance to Freud's notion of group formation and touching on the psychoanalytic conception of trauma, Renan writes as follows in his seminal essay on the modern nation, "What is a Nation?": "Forgetting, I would even go as far as to say historical error, is a crucial factor in the creation of a nation" (11). What needs to be forgotten, according to Renan, are the traumatic events of violence at the very origin of the nation, which occur as the precondition of the nation, yet have to be obliterated or excluded from its system of representation in order for the current, *modern regime* to function. For the emergence of the modern nation signals a severance with antiquity, or at least, certain aspects of the past: "The essence of a nation is that all individuals have many things in common, and also that they have forgotten many things. No French citizen knows whether he is a Burgundian, an Alan, a Taifale, or a Visigoth, yet every French citizen has to have forgotten the massacre of Saint Bartholomew" (ibid.). Nations, in the sense Renan conceives them, "are something fairly new in history" (9). In fact, Renan sets out to propose a notion of the *modern nation* and to debunk, in the spirit of the Enlightenment,[70] some "dangerous misunderstandings" of the nation, as he makes clear toward the beginning of the essay: "Nowadays ... race is confused with nation and a sovereignty analogous to that of really existing peoples is attributed to ethnographic or, rather linguistic groups" (8). Later in the essay Renan proceeds to refute the bearing of other "natural categories," such as race and geography, on the "principles" of the formation of a nation.

However, such a "constructivist" view of the nation—so ahead of its time—doesn't seem to stop Renan from conferring a transcendental, theological character on the nation later in the essay, where he claims that "a nation is a soul, a spiritual principle" (19). It is as if the nation gained an eternal life after the institutionalized forgetting, after the burial of its originary trauma, the symbolic death of its founding violence. Having said earlier that "antiquity was unfamiliar with [modern nations]," Renan surprisingly concludes with an atavistic move: "The nation, like the individual, is the culmination of a long past of endeavours, sacrifice, and devotion. Of all cults, that of the ancestors is the most legitimate, for the ancestors have made us what we are" (19). The modern nation, therefore, consists of a dual temporality, since the "soul" or "spiritual principle" which is the nation is constituted by two things—one, as Renan argues, "lies in the past, one in the present" (ibid.). Such a dual temporality is what Bhabha calls "the 'double and split' time of national representation" ("DissemiNation," 295). In a curiously oblique way, the modern nation's persistent recourse to a certain antiquity testifies to the abiding power of the founding traumatic events of the nation that one conveniently forgets, just as Renan's inadvertent enumeration of events of a traumatic nature does in his own writing. "It is good

---

70 Renan indeed deploys an avowedly scientific, objectivist gesture which borders on so-called "epistemic violence," as he declares: "It is a delicate thing that I propose to do here, somewhat akin to *vivisection*; I am going to treat the living much as one ordinarily treats the dead. I shall adopt an absolutely cool and impartial attitude" (8; emphasis mine).

for everyone to know how to forget" (16), says Renan, advising against "too searching a scrutiny," against historical enquiry that might "bring to light deeds of violence . . . whose consequences have been altogether beneficial" and thus undermine national unity (11). What Renan forgets, though, is that sometimes people "forget to forget." Not because they want to, or can, remember the inherently forgotten, unintelligible trauma, but because the modern nation doesn't initiate history with a clean slate. Those wiped out from memory can manifest themselves in that strange antiquity in the present. To gain some perspective on the return of the foreclosed traumatic event, on the "distracting presence of another temporality that disturbs the contemporaneity of the national present" (Bhabha 295), I'd like to turn to the Freudian scene of the murder of the primal father.

It is well known that in *Totem and Taboo*, Freud pronounces us guilty of killing our father in time immemorial, a crime we can all now easily shrug off. The point of positing a primal father, however, is not to verify a certain mythological figure's existence at some point in history, since Freud insists that the primordial patricide is a prehistoric *fact* that "really had to happen" to allow for the passage from the animal state to the realm of Culture (cf. Žižek, *Ticklish*, 315). Rather, such a postulation is to account for the traumatic event necessarily *constituting and foreclosed by* human communities: The father with unconditional power has to be murdered so that the symbolic Law can be established in the Name-of-the-Father, which returns in place of the reigning father, yet the unspeakable nature of the horrific act that makes possible the new regime of brothers has to be maintained to ensure the efficacy of the symbolic authority. The surprising and even troubling discovery by Freud, which marks the shift from Oedipus to *Totem and Taboo*, is that with the death of the despotic father, we don't consequently obtain the enjoyments previously monopolized by him. Quite to the contrary, it is the very realization of the Oedipal wish (the killing of the father) that results in the symbolic prohibition of the Law. Totem and taboo hence are two sides of the same coin, coming into being at the same time, just as the father-function consists in being both the Ego-Ideal and the ferocious superego.[71]

---

71 Slavoj Žižek reminds us that Lacan points out in his early work that in modern bourgeois nuclear family, these two father-functions, which were previously separated, are now "united in one and the same person" (*Ticklish* 313).

What follows the murder of the primordial father is the "regime of the Brother," which, according to Juliet Flower MacCannell, also characterizes modernity and is no less repressive than the old regime. For the leader of this new regime, the Brother, assumes in "the 'name' of the father another and sadistic Other—unconscious, superego" (12–13). It is simultaneously modern and archaic because it is premised on equality and fraternity—precepts of Enlightenment modernity—yet imposes interdictions of excess enjoyment, i.e. more than what is rationally distributed, precisely in the image of the tyrannical father who forbids others' enjoyment since he monopolizes all *jouissance*. Modernity's persistent recourse to an archaic temporality, which I brought up earlier, here appears in its attempt to "raise the merely spectral symbol of a dead ancestor to privilege one contemporary figure (who steps in to represent the law in modernized form)" (18). Hence the reign of terror of the primal father returns in its modern form. Joan Copjec also points out that in the wake of the demise of the primal father, who embodies *jouissance* or excess enjoyment, "the signifier of his absence will be the son who promises to protect society from the trauma of *jouissance*'s return" (*Read My Desire*, 154; emphasis in original). This too marks the inception of the modern regime of equals, of which democracy is one prime example. Yet this new, democratic group can easily give way to the return of the totalitarian regime of the primal father. First of all, this fraternal regime is predicated on the interdiction of excessive enjoyment, which is itself an indication of the haunting power of the murdered father and a constantly threatening possibility of his return. Furthermore, the renouncement of enjoyment, which is characteristic of this new regime, only reinforces the reign of the superego incarnated by the ideal father who now succeeds the deceased primal father, since the superego, as Freud reminds us in *Civilization and Its Discontents*, becomes even more ferociously demanding once one submits to its demand to renounce enjoyment. Such an increasingly repressive regime is likely to implode due to its constitutive interdictions—required to curb the conflicts between the brothers. Hence "the law of the ideal father is repealed, and the despotic primal father returns. A totalitarian regime takes over" (Copjec, *Desire*, 157).[72] Before I elaborate further on the

---

72 Copec makes clear that "psychoanalysis does not . . . argue that all groups are basically totalitarian in nature," nor does it claim that totalitarianism necessarily follow from democracy (158). Although there is certain nuance between their lines of arguments (about the modern leader as an Ideal Ego or Ego-Ideal), neither does MacCannell think

"regime change" in group formations, I'd like to go back to the case of Toussaint and the Haitian Revolution to illustrate and perhaps also "test" the theoretical points outlined above.

The Postcolonial Fathers

We know that Toussaint was betrayed and sold to the French by his trusted generals, most notably Christophe and Dessalines, the latter becoming later the leader in the struggle for independence and hence the symbol of Haitian independence. In retrospect, i.e., with the confirmed supposition that Bonaparte was determined to restore slavery in San Domingo, the removal of Toussaint would seem a necessary step toward liberation from colonial slavery, since Toussaint, as James points out, could not think in terms of independence, seeing himself, until his final years, as part of the French Republic, "one and indivisible" (364). The simplistic Dessalines, on the other hand, couldn't think in terms other than independence, whether out of personal ambition or for the good of the Haitian people. Long before the temporary truce that led to Toussaint's arrest, Dessalines had pronounced a vision of independence in a fiery speech to boost the morale of his troops: "I shall make you *independent*. There will be no more whites among us" (qtd. in James 315; emphasis in original). "Independence. It was the first time a leader had put it before his men," James reports (315). Shortly before Toussaint's arrest, James continues, "Dessalines, who had formerly worshipped Toussaint, determined to get him out of the way, as well as Christophe, for their pro-French leanings. . . . Faithful and loyal assistant to Toussaint, he knew his chief well enough to doubt his capacity to take the steps Dessalines saw would be necessary" (333).

Seen in this light, Toussaint's demise would be an exemplary case of the necessary murder of the primal father (though Toussaint did not actually die at the hands of his generals, but of cold and malnutrition in prison) so that a new regime of brothers, in this case an independent state with warring generals, could be established—in the *name* of Toussaint, literally. Dessalines knew only too well the importance of Toussaint as Name-of-the-Father, not his physical presence, which had to removed, to that far-

---

the modern regime, structured around the principles of liberty, equality, and fraternity, is innately repressive or is bound to turn totalitarian. It could have, but did not, fulfill its promises (12).

off cell on a French mountain. In Glissant's *Monsieur Toussaint*, Dessalines, after his willing complicity in Toussaint's arrest, rallies his troops precisely around the death of Papa Toussaint:

> **Dessalines**: *Our commander* has fallen into their hands, he is already dead, he has passed into the shadows of the earth! . . . To arms! The time has come to sweep the land clean! . . . Remember! Those who fall will go to Africa. Commander Toussaint is in Africa, preparing an army for the deliverance of our brothers! Those who fall will meet Toussaint and fight under his orders.
> **Christophe**: Why all this empty talk? Freedom is enough to arouse them!
> **Dessalines**: Be quiet. I command, you fight. But *it's Toussaint who leads us*. (85–86; emphasis mine)

Dessalines's successful campaigns against the French and for his own ascension to power, as the number-one son, the Brother, prove Christophe wrong. As Walcott's play *Henri Christophe* shows us, immediately after the news of Toussaint's death in France reaches Haiti, Dessalines seizes the occasion to further consolidate his status as the heir of Toussaint, making a preemptive move against Christophe, the archrival who presumably has the capability to contest Dessalines's rule but hasn't received the news (10–19). The historical accounts have it that Toussaint died on April 7, 1803 in Fort Joux, France; on May 18 of the same year, black and Mulatto generals swore allegiance to Dessalines; seven months after Toussaint's death. In late November 1803, Dessalines's troops won a decisive battle after which the French forces decided to evacuate the island;[73] on January 1, 1804, San Domingo moved swiftly to declare independence and renamed itself Haiti.

Indeed, isn't "Papa Toussaint," as the nickname suggests, an avatar of the omnipotent, and even omniscient, Father, given his reputed prescience? In the heyday of his absolute authority, Toussaint had only to give orders, and the masses would follow blindly and willingly. This was especially true because, as James describes it, "nobody ever knew what he was doing" (287), not even his generals, perhaps imagining, along with the least

---

73 The French commander Rochambeau tried to come to terms with both Dessalines and the British, the latter being at war with France and blockading the seaways. Dessalines refused ruthlessly, threatening more fierce attacks if the French didn't pull out immediately. The British didn't budge either, and Rochambeau had no choice but to surrender to the British, as Dessalines warned that they would definitely be much more miserable if they ended up in his hands. As it turned out, "of the 60,000 soldiers and sailors who had sailed for France nearly all had perished, and the few who remained were to rot and waste for years in English prisons" (James, 369).

enlightened slaves, Toussaint as a superhuman being masterminding schemes beyond human comprehension. (His tendency to think things out by himself and to not explain himself, of course, turned out to be one critical weakness after he, for a constellation of reasons, gradually lost favor with the people.) "Toussaint's word by 1796 was law," writes James, as he was the only person whom the slaves could be depended on to obey (154). Even Dessalines, a man known for his ferocity and intractability, is no exception to submitting himself to such a Father and his unconditional power, though he nonetheless senses the necessity of patricide, as he confesses to Granville: "If Toussaint had cried, 'Dessalines, you must die,' Dessalines would be dead. And yet I see that one day I had to betray him, and let him be arrested, and yes, be carried off across the ocean on the last voyage" (Glissant, *Monsieur Toussaint*, 92).

The felt need to remove Toussaint, however, was not exactly out of a certain Oedipal complex, since other fellow generals, watching each other's moves, had to take part in this treachery for the conspiracy to be successful. More precisely, it exemplified the necessary step to take toward the establishment of a rule no longer of direct, natural, or plainly brute force, but of symbolic Law/Prohibition, which is embodied by the dead father who returns as his Name. Herein lies the structural necessity of patricide: Law is grounded in a constitutive exemption, a traumatic act of violence, and the Father is elevated to the status of a hollow symbol of Law *only after* his betrayal and murder.[74] The symbolic death of the primal father, therefore, characterizes the modern forms of power, the modern nation-state, for example. The birth of the nation requires the sacrifice of its founding figures. Note that every nationalist discourse is centered on the allusion to, or at least the rhetoric of, sacrifice, which attests to the inherently forgotten, yet constitutive traumatic events of violence at the very beginning of every nation. What better suits such sacrifice than the (symbolic) death of a colossal father-figure like Toussaint? Precisely because power in the modern nation doesn't have a theological ground, that is, power is no longer immanent to or coincident with the leader (as in the

---

74   Žižek points out this shift from Oedipus to *Totem and Taboo* in Freud's oeuvre. While in the former patricide and incestuous relation with the mother emerge as unconscious wish, with Oedipus being the only exception, in the latter we no longer dream about patricide—"we all do it" in order for the regime of brothers to take place. I owe a great deal to this reading of Freud's *Totem and Taboo*. See *Ticklish*, 313–316.

case of the Prince in absolute monarchies) who now occupies the place of power, the nation-state needs to be built on such a sacrificed, hence venerated, Name-of-the-Father—an invocation of a death which thus stretches the national present to eternal antiquity. Toussaint, testifying to his prescience yet again, seems to be aware that his sacrifice is necessary, as he wistfully utters the following Christ-like statement to his secretary Granville, who warns him of Dessalines's treachery and agenda for independence:

> What Dessalines wants is far beyond my life. What Dessalines wants I could not want. *However, he needs me.* It's essential for me to identify his treason, for his treason to become fidelity. It's necessary for me to accept his ingratitude, for his ingratitude to become my recompense. It is necessary for me to fall again, and for him to forget me again, so that my defeat may light up his victory. (Glissant, *Monsieur Toussaint*, 78; emphasis mine)

Up until now, we've treated Toussaint as the primal father to be removed and elevated to the status of the Name-of-the-Father, the Law on which a new regime, the independent state of Haiti, was founded. Dessalines, on the other hand, would appear to be the Brother/ideal father who, in the name of Toussaint the ultra-Father, represents the repressive superego and interdicts excess enjoyment, since he issued a series of severe measures restricting ex-slave laborers' movements and penalizing indolence. However, we should be quick to point out that Dessalines is more of an emblem of excess than its curtailment: excess in his hatred of whites; his merciless ferocity against enemies, whether white or colored; his cruelty toward the masses (he whipped slack laborers—something Toussaint specifically forbade); his unbridled debauchery after seizing power; and his unabashedly vulgar manners even after his coronation (Walcott describes in *The Haytian Earth* a drunken Dessalines peeing in a courtyard and hollering to Christophe, "Pee with me, Minister. That is a command"; 419). Dessalines, in this sense, seems to more befit a primal father—at least in his brief term as Emperor—who monopolizes all the obscene enjoyment and rules by sheer, brutal force.

Moreover, it is not hard to notice that Toussaint appears to be an ideal father who guards against excess enjoyment: his role as a devout Catholic and revered general who preaches discipline, decorum, and virtues; as a tireless administrator who demonstrates his zeal for law and order; as a tactful arbiter who, according to James, has a knack of satisfying everyone's needs in settling disputes. In *Drums and Colours*, Walcott offers a scene that best illustrates the stark contrast between Toussaint and Dessalines in terms of excess: A weary Toussaint returns to camp after a long, exhausting, and bloody expedition, deplores the brutality of the slaughter they must deal with, and says to his generals while "washing his hands" (a telling sign of his aversion): "I hate excess." A drunken Dessalines then roars with laughter, mocking his chief: "Ho, ha! He kills ten thousand or more defenceless citizens . . . . And shrugs his shoulders and says he hates excess. Oh, oh/I love, I kiss this hypocrite!" (*The Haitian Trilogy*, 242; a similar scene is repeated in *The Haytian Earth*, 364–365). What do we make of such role reversals of Toussaint and Dessalines? Or rather, the ostensible error in our interpretations of the fathers of the first postcolonial nation-state? To better elucidate this issue, I'd like to briefly return to Freud's explorations of the father-figure(s) of group formations in the final stage of his career.

In *Moses and Monotheism*, we recall, there are two Moseses—one Egyptian, the other Semitic—who represent two distinct father-figures. What signals the crucial turn from the earlier postulation of a primal father is that in the Moses legend the father who is betrayed and killed is not the pre-symbolic father of *jouissance* who monopolizes all obscene enjoyment, but the very rational father who embodies the symbolic authority, the Egyptian Moses who gives the Jews the monotheistic religion based on the doctrine of a universe ruled by a universalist, rational order, since it's the Egyptian origin of this monotheism introduced by the Egyptian Moses that the Jews must disavow and obliterate. Such an inherently forgotten murder, of course, has its lingering traumatic effects. For the Semitic Moses, the personification of the ferocious, fearsome, and volatile Jehovah, is now perceived to exhibit implacable rage and lay down unpredictable punishment as a result of his betrayal by his followers/sons. What returns after the patricide—this time of the rational father who is the bearer of the symbolic function—is the "irrational" father, whimsical, unfathomable, and as ferocious as the "unforgiving superego figure of God full of murderous rage." This Mosaic God/Father certainly is different from the primordial Father-*Joussissance*, as Žižek points out: "in contrast to the primordial father endowed with a *knowledge* of *jouissance*, the fundamental feature of this uncompromising God [the Semitic Moses] is that He says 'No!' to *jouissance*" (*Ticklish*, 318]; emphasis in original). What returns, therefore, in the wake of the destruction of the symbolic authority of the regime of brothers, whose establishment still hinges on the Name-of-the-Father as Law bequeathed by the murdered primal father, is the prohibitive, capricious, and tyrannical father who cannot be satisfied and forbids satisfaction. Though bearing a certain resemblance to the primordial father, this father is not equivalent to the primal father and can only be considered the return of the primal father in his modern form, in the constitutive gap between the prohibitive superego and the Ego-Ideal. It is important to note that the two fathers are represented in the same, Janus-faced persona of Moses, which indicates that the rationalist paternal function is always already implicated or grounded in arbitrary acts of willing—a mythical operation Enlightenment rationality seeks to do without. Hence the vulnerability of democracy to the rise of totalitarianism: a regime of equals, which is defined by its structural uncertainties, is likely—though not inevitably—to give way to the temptation of certainty proffered by the ideal father who in turn can easily become the obverse of certainty, as the ferocious, irrational father, by his unbounded, unpredictable willing, in addition to this superego figure's increasingly repressive demand for our relinquishment of excess enjoyment.

Seen in this light, Toussaint too would appear to embody the multiplicity of the father-figure, and the Haitian Revolution seems an exemplification of the susceptibility of the modern democratic state to the subsequent degenerative mutations witnessed in history. Toussaint's revolutionary program in San Domingo was to establish a modern regime of brothers, based on the precepts of liberty, equality, and fraternity—one that was also a brother regime of the French Republic.[75] Such a regime of equals, however, was made possible by the larger-than-life character of Toussaint, who emerged as an enlightened leader and ideal father whose relationships with the rest of the new regime were far from equal. He

---

75 It is tempting to say that this regime of brothers Toussaint founded was wrested from a regime of the primal father par excellence—the colonial state which monopolized all enjoyment and enslaved the rest of the group, yet the common experience of dislocation of the slaves belies this characterization of originating from the same group, even if the slaves did somehow regard their master as the absolutist father. I maintain, though, as argued elsewhere in the book, that the new regime the ex-colonized establish is founded on their misrecognition of the mother country and their unwitting, disavowed mimicry of the colonial state.

quickly turned into the unfathomable and unpredictable father who willfully defied Reason itself, as he left his actions unaccounted for even when others were bewildered by them. Nevertheless, Toussaint the Mosaic father has to be postulated as a primal father (just like the primordial father has to be posited, though the postulation is not to verify his actual existence in history) vis-à-vis the new nation-state.

Despite his anti-modern penchants, Dessalines symbolizes more than the return of the pre-symbolic, pre-modern father of obscene enjoyment. He is at once the incarnation of the Brother/ideal father and that capricious, ferocious, difficult father full of murderous rage. In addition to betraying and (symbolically) murdering Toussaint the primal father, Dessalines the Emperor also in effect killed Dessalines the Brother who enforces the Law instituted at the cost of Toussaint's death. It is important, though, to point out again that the rapid deterioration of the postcolonial nation-state into virulent autocracy or the blatant betrayal of its revolutionary ideals, epitomized in the case of Dessalines ("the Dessalines model"!), does not exactly signal the persistent return of the absolutist regime of the primal father. Whether out of egoistic ambition or not, Dessalines's plan of independence was a fundamentally modern gesture. During the final, decisive campaign at Fort Verdières, the bravery of Dessalines's men moved the French to send an officer over to compliment, in the manner of the chevaliers, their gallantry, which he claimed was worthy of the name of France the fatherland, but Dessalines snapped and shouted, "Words! Words! *My fatherland is San Domingo, nowhere else*! I take back my original dignity. We will be independent!" (Glissant, *Monsieur Toussaint* 88; emphasis mine). What returns, in the wake of the dismantling of the symbolic authority, is *not some earlier forms of despotism, but a modern(ized) one*.[76] For *jouissance* is irrevocable once the primordial father is murdered, once we are thrown into irreversible modernity. In the following section, I'd like to elaborate on such *jouissance* as impossible in terms of its invocation and instantiation in postcolonial nationalisms.

---

76 This is why nationalism is a predominantly *modern* phenomenon, even with its atavistic tendency.

Postcolonial Nationalism and Its Enjoyment

Another significance of the murder of the primordial father is that it opens up an empty place of power, an absence of originary communitarian fullness. The place around which the primal horde—or any community—is structured is empty not only because we are left with an emptying of power[77] in the wake of the death of the primal father, but also because the Father-Thing or Father-*jouissance* is irrevocably severed from our sociosymbolic existence the moment the symbolic order is instituted with the emergence of the-Name-of-the-Father. It is therefore the empty place of the Thing, empty apropos of the symbolic system, since it is without content or predicate, unrepresentable or unsymbolizable (yet it is exactly this impossibility that makes possible the system of representation). Taboo then arises, working against anyone who tries to take over the role of the murdered father, thereby rendering father-figures or political leaders seeking to fill in the empty place "impotent" or incongruous in the position once occupied by the primal father. Civilization therefore lies in the establishment of the constitutive gap initiated by the demise of the primordial father, between the prohibitive superego and the Ego-Ideal. We now witness in modern democracies the opening up of another gap, the one between the Leader in the immediacy of his personality, and the empty symbolic place he now occupies or fills, a gap through which he may be perceived as ridiculous or impotent (cf. Žižek, *Ticklish*, 313, 316).[78]

It is interesting to note that the "empty place," so essential to Lacan's notion of desire as a primordial lack, also appears to be a key term in Claude Lefort's conception of democracy.[79] For example, Lefort writes,

---

77 In accordance with Lefort's notion of power and the Freudian postulation of group formation, this book maintains that the emptying of power here is to be considered a drastic weakening, or a certain degree of decentralization of power, with radical change in its structure; it is, however, never a vacuum of power, as is too often posited by certain strains of the poststructuralist conception of the immanent disintegration of all power as an ideal politics—in which case there would be no politics at all.

78 Besides, as we've mentioned, the regime of brothers, notably democracy, is structurally impotent, "paralyzed by the interdictions that are required to stave off the conflict between the brothers" (Copjec, *Read My Desire*, 157).

79 Jacob Torfing contends that Lefort writes about power in democratic society "in a language that is not foreign to Lacanian psychoanalysis" (192). I owe this association of Lacan with Lefort to the psychoanalytic accounts of democracy in Copjec (158–161), Yannis Stavrakakis, and Žižek (*Ticklish*, 192).

"the *locus* of power is an empty place, it cannot be occupied—it is such that no individual or no group can be cosubstantial with it—and it cannot be represented" (17). This empty place of power, historically, is produced by the elimination of the sovereign God, or the prince under the guarantee of God—that is, unconditional power on eschatological or transcendental ground. Democracy hence seeks to come to terms with this recognized empty place and the inherent lack of communitarian ground in democratic society by institutionalizing political antagonism, as Lefort argues: "The erection of a political stage on which competition can take place shows that division is, in a general way, constitutive of the very unity of society" (18).

The parallel positing of an empty place on the ontological level (by Lacan) and in the political proper (by Lefort) would seem less like a coincidence if one were to go back to Freud's elaborations on Moses's personification of God in *Moses and Monotheism*, and follow Lacan's return to Freud in his conception of Father-Thing as both the unrepresentable apropos of the symbolic order *and* the latter's precondition. In a move similar to the psychoanalytic insight that the demise of the prohibitive father with absolute power doesn't lead to a situation of "everything goes" for the rest of us, Lefort conceives of democratic society as one that "undermines the representation of an organic unity" and is characterized by "the dissolution of the ultimate markers of certainty" (27). But he is quick to add that it doesn't follow that there is no unity or definite identity in democracy. As he goes on to contend, "on the contrary, the disappearance of natural determination, which was once linked to the person of the prince, or the existence of a nobility, leads to the emergence of a purely social society in which the people, the nation, and the state take on the status of universal entities" (18). We argue that in its attempts to come to terms with the recognized empty place, democracy in a way foregrounds the lack of a communitarian ground for the democratic state, yet it still has to presuppose a "*point de capiton*," a leader or an idea assuming the status of a Lacanian Master-Signifier, totalizing the socio-symbolic field. "Nation," whatever its connotations might be, more often than not emerges as such a signifier, as sometimes does "the people," or as the precepts of "liberty, equality, fraternity" did in Toussaint's time. It is as if the deceased primal father returned, in variegated forms, to the empty place he vacated, as the return of the Real, always, to the same place, temporarily filling the lack until the phantasmatic fullness can no longer be sustained.

Although the state doesn't have to assume the nation-form of democracy, democracy has an inextricable affiliation with the notion of the nation-state, as an open society nonetheless marked by necessary boundaries (which in fact function as the precondition of its very existence). Indeed, aren't the traumatic memories of Toussaint and the Haitian Revolution those of the premature death or abortion of a modern democracy and the ensuing deterioration of the nation-state cloaked in an expedient nationalism, which in turn is presented as a (retroactively discovered) premonition of the failures of the postcolonial nation of our time?[80] And isn't postcolonial Haiti, and by extension the postcolonial nation-state in general, envisioned and founded—initially at least—on a sense of liberation, an allegedly egalitarian principle, and fraternity (we'll all henceforth be free, equal, and fraternal under the roof of the new nation)? I propose that the postcolonial nation-state, as a modern regime of brothers, is structured around, and to some extent foregrounds, *an empty place* bequeathed by the murdered primordial father, which cannot be cosubstantial with or filled by any particular individual or political force, except for the evocation of an elusive Nation-Thing. For the *jouissance* appropriated by the primal father is irretrievable once we enter into the modern regime of power; it thereafter can only be approximated in the recurring evocations of the Nation-Thing, instantiated in the articulations of nationalism.

In the case of post-independence Haiti, the inadequacy of the subsequent leaders of the state who occupied the place vacated by Toussaint is conspicuous, as they pale in comparison with Toussaint, now as the deceased primal father elevated to the status of backbone of the new nation. The constitutive gap of the emerging symbolic order, as Dessalines and the successive leaders soon realized, can only, or most effectively, be bridged (however temporarily) by the evocation of the Nation-Thing organized around expressions of nationalism. Even Toussaint himself, before his death, was not isomorphic with this empty place. Like many leaders of decolonizing revolutions in the twentieth century whose charisma and aura

---

80 Critics of the postcolonial state mostly focus on its failure to be and/or become a democracy, following the Western model. Such a critique is not just limited to liberals, but is also echoed by leftist critics such as James and Grant Farred. The latter, however, rightly underscores that Toussaint's "inability to produce a democratic Haitian society" is "representative of larger structural failure," rather than "the consequence of [Toussaint's] personal shortcomings," as James's work suggests (237).

couldn't sustain the shift from the decolonial to the postcolonial,[81] Toussaint underwent a kind of "symbolic death" in which Toussaint the governor, in the latter stage of his brief tenure, in effect killed Toussaint the revolutionary leader. What is tragic about Toussaint is that he didn't have nationalism at his disposal, or never thought of resorting to nationalism, to deflect growing internal discontent, since he never had independence on his agenda; he became an incarnation of nationalist ideals only by an ironic role reversal—by being removed, for impeding the nationalist project, by the "real" nationalist leader who betrayed the national icon to the enemy for a purportedly nationalist cause. In other words, it is only after Toussaint became a Thing (Name-of-the-Father for the new nation) that he gained full identity with the empty place.

Such a Nation-Thing, like what Lacan calls the Thing (*Das Ding*), has no predicate or content; it is irreducible to the things that happen to be used to designate it (a collection of the "traits" and special "way of life" of a people, for instance), for there always seems to be "something more" in it than those designations. Though having no physical existence of its own, "the national Thing," writes Žižek, "exists as long as members of the community believe in it; it is literally an effect of this belief in itself" (*Tarrying*, 202). The Nation-Thing is, therefore, primarily an imaginary construct, yet this doesn't mean that its instantiation in the discourse of nationalism is tantamount to purely discursive effects, for it has its "substance" in *enjoyment*, just as Žižek argues:

> A nation *exists* only as long as its specific *enjoyment* continues to be materialized in a set of social practices and transmitted through national myths that structure these practices. To emphasize ... that Nation is not a biological or transhistorical fact but a contingent discursive construction, an overdetermined result of textual practices, is thus misleading: such an emphasis overlooks the remainder of some *real*, nondiscursive kernel of enjoyment which must be present for the Nation qua discursive entity-effect to achieve its ontological consistency. (ibid.; emphasis in original)

How, then, does one enjoy one's nation? Paradoxically, or tautologically, we can only enjoy our nation by discursively articulating our enjoyment of the nation, by organizing our enjoyment around a certain nondiscursive kernel, an unnamed or unnamable "Thing" which is reminiscent of the

---

81 Think, for example, Kwame Nkrumah, Eric Williams, Jomo Kenyatta, etc., among others on a long list.

traumatic event, as Renan indicates, at the very beginning of the modern nation. Nationalism can only assert its presence or have its effects on the national subject through its representations. The problem with nationalism as enjoyment is that it tends to become "an imperative to enjoy," when it evokes the *jouissance* of the Nation-Thing. This inherent problematic of *jouissance*, an extreme form of enjoyment, or excess enjoyment, is best illustrated by Lacan's explication, with his characteristic play on words: "Nothing forces anyone to enjoy (*jouir*) except the superego. The superego is the imperative of *jouissance*—Enjoy! (*jouissance-Jouis!*)" (*Encore*, 3; the original French phrase in the second parenthesis added by me).[82] The evocation of *jouissance* thus is, paradoxically, prone to prevent one from accessing the excess enjoyment of *jouissance*. The Nation-Thing promises *jouissance* to the nationals, but *jouissance* is by definition, in this context, impossible—which happens to suit the appetite of the insatiable, ferocious, superegoic father incarnated in the new leader of the modern nation, who now keeps intensifying his demand for our enjoyment (in the form of sacrifice for the nation, for example). For it is precisely *jouissance* that the modern nation-state, as a regime of brothers, wants to thwart, since it is premised, as we've pointed out, on the interdiction of excess enjoyment.

It follows that one is either eventually disenchanted by the unfulfilled or unreachable promise of the Nation-Thing (this doesn't mean that it cannot regain its appeal at a later time—the recent history of the ex-colonized world points to the contrary), or is willfully involved in a sort of perverse staging of enjoyment (I will enjoy it, I will keep enjoying it all I want, regardless of the betrayed founding ideals of the nation, or the continued

---

82   This is not to say, however, that all *jouissance* is linked to the superego. Spurred by his explorations of feminine sexuality in the final stage of his career, Lacan postulates, along with an uncharacteristically "non-skeptical" attitude toward love, a more sophisticated distinction between different "types" of *jouissance* in his *Encore* Seminar (Seminar XX), where "*jouissance* of the Other" is distinguished from "phallic *jouissance*," the most pervasive idea about *jouissance* (see for example, 7–9, 23–24, 82–83). Lacan is clearly trying to envision here a conception of *jouissance* that is not governed or driven solely by the superego's imperative "Enjoy!" (see especially 3, 7). This parallels, and testifies to, his move to positing "love beyond law" in the *Encore* Seminar. Drawing on Lacan's later formulation of *jouissance*, Copjec, in a much less cryptic way, further designates this *jouissance* of the Other as "feminine *jouissance*"—as distinct from phallic *jouissance*—in the final chapter in her book *Read My Desire* (224). For the purpose and scope of this chapter, I will focus on a conception of *jouissance* specifically in relation to the superego.

economic exploitation both inside and outside the national borders). The problem with many postcolonial nationalisms is not only the rapid disillusionment, from the decolonial to the postcolonial, felt by scores of postcolonial subjects, but also the sadistic "subreption" of the ruling class—their "suppression of truth to obtain indulgence" in their nationalist discourses.[83] In a theoretical move similar to that of Lacan's "Kant avec Sade," Copjec argues that "thorough subreption, a supersensible idea, that is, one that can never be experienced, is falsely represented as if it were a possible object of experience" (*Imagine*, 149).[84] The postcolonial nation-state, as Farred describes it, "is overburdened with the specter of subreption" (239). In his phantasmatic misrecognition of the Nation-Thing, the ferocious Mosaic father of the postcolonial nation, the "subreptive" leader who is so alienated from the people, "loses" himself in his fantasized relation to the supersensible Thing, imagining himself to be equivalent to the nation, to be cosubstantial with the constitutive empty place at the inception of the nation, thus duped by the nationalist sentiment he certainly helped articulate and even tried to manipulate.

In *The Haytian Earth*, Walcott proffers a scene that perhaps best epitomizes the subreption of Dessalines (and Dessalines*es*). When Dessalines once again asks Christophe, then Minister of Agriculture, to flog a plantation worker who refuses to work, Christophe declines, sensing the growing discontent:

> **Christophe**: Not me, Jacko.
> *(Silence.)*
> **Dessalines**: All right, then me. Is I who do everything anyway.
> I who begin, and I who end. You come in, you join
> When everything was going good. I am the beginning,
> And I am the end. Haiti is me. *Ous tender?* This!
> *(He stamps his foot.)*
> Is. Me. I will send you his two ears.
> *(He exits.)* (426; emphasis in original)

---

83 Farred brings in this term by quoting Gayatri Spivak, who in turns quotes the OED definition (as quoted here) but is discussing it in the context of Kant's use of the term. See Farred ("Thriving," 238), and Spivak (*Critique*, 149).

84 In *Philosophy in the Bedroom*, Sade exemplifies again and again subreption par excellence, wherein *jouissance* is obtained by deliberately arranged rituals and the victims repeatedly survive, with his/her beauty and body unblemished, the most horrific tortures imaginable.

In the context of the play, the Haitian earth is what the "ordinary people," Pompey and Yette, hold on to. Though they've got nothing to lose, all that the ex-slaves can claim to is the earth under their bare feet. Dessalines's equating himself with the Haitian earth would thus be sacrilegious to the peasants who no longer buy into his discourse of nationalism. Christophe, who is a sobering voice here, doesn't fare much better. In *Henri Christophe*, he twice attempts to manipulate mass support to endorse his self-conceived coronation in public rallies. The first one fails miserably, bringing embarrassment and humiliation in the public eye. After the second attempt barely succeeds thanks largely to a paid instigator they had installed in the crowd, a soldier who also hushes dissent, Christophe's secretary says, "That soldier did it; we must fatten him/He never gives up" (72). Christophe, on the other hand, can no longer hide his self-deceit, as he replies, "Their love goes further than the corporal./So, I am king" (ibid.). One may wonder, then, that since the Nation-Thing is by nature elusive, wouldn't there be substantially different "misrecognitions" of the Thing that result in distinct nationalisms in the masses and the ruling class? I shall take up this issue in the next section.

Love and Death in the Story of the Nation-State

Let me continue our theoretical inquiry into nationalism and its representations by taking a closer look at the works of two preeminent theorists on anti-colonialism and nationalism who also exemplify at once specific knowledge or engagement in particular cases of struggle and a universalizing move in advancing their theories of nationalism: Frantz Fanon and Benedict Anderson.[85] Although Fanon cautions us against "the pitfalls of national consciousness" in his book *The Wretched of the Earth*, he is nevertheless celebrating a sort of spontaneous, grassroots nationalism in revolutionary decolonizations in Africa, as he writes: "The many peasant risings which have their roots in country districts bear witness wherever they occur to the ubiquitous and usually solidly massed presence of the new

---

85 Here I am thinking about Anderson's less known identity as a Southeast Asia specialist, compared with his identity as an expert in nationalism, with his widely cited, and appropriated, notion of the nation. The "poststructuralist Fanon" recuperated or reconstructed by Bhabha would appear incongruous with his activist role in the nationalist movements in Algeria.

nation. Every native who takes up arms is part of the nation which from henceforward will spring to life" (*Wretched*, 131). Fanon's conception of nation here chimes with his justification of the use of violence by the oppressed as an action that could lead to both mental catharsis and meaningful political change. If the state-representing-the-nation is the only institution that can legally use armed force, what Fanon is advocating is the notion of the nation-people that seeks to *do without the representation of the state and become one with the nation*. Obviously, the familiar opposition between state and nation is present here. And if we go on to read his comparison of the post-independence nation-states of the Third World to "hollow shell[s] of nationality" (159), we'll understand how essential this idea of the spontaneous organic dynamism of the nation-people is in his conception of the nation and nationalism. Accompanying this idea of the spontaneous organic dynamism of the nation-people is his critique of the official, statist, "artificial" version of nationalism commonly seen in the post-independence era.

According to Fanon, the institution of the postcolonial state is built on an empty form of national consciousness, on an almost unchanged political and economic system inherited from the colonialist state, taken over by the national bourgeoisie who end up exploiting the nation-people in place of their ex-colonizers. Since "nationalization quite simply means the transfer into the native hands of those unfair advantages which are a legacy of the colonial period," the national middle-class is also the national elite in charge of the apparatus of the state (152). The national bourgeoisie of an underdeveloped country is a self-interested class that, however, lacks the entrepreneurial spirit and accumulated capital of the Western bourgeoisie.[86] For, as Fanon points out, it "is not engaged in production, nor building, nor labor; it is completely canalized into activities of *the intermediary type*" (149–150; emphasis mine). The postcolonial bourgeoisie therefore is not only an intermediary class with intellectual and technical capital that profits from mediating between the local and the metropolitan; it also plays an intermediary role between the nation-people and the nation-state,

---

86 In denouncing—quite rightly—the uncreative, self-interested, and destructive role the postcolonial bourgeoisie plays in post-independence nation-building projects, Fanon nevertheless idealizes the Western bourgeoisie, yet its profit-driven enterprises across national borders, as, for example, James's work demonstrates, were the driving force of colonial slavery and the most adamant resistance to its abolition.

a role which nevertheless prevents the former from coinciding with the latter. Monopolized by the national elite and alienated from the rest of the population, the political organization of the postcolonial state thus fails to represent the national-popular will, despite the elite's efforts to instill in the people an official version of nationalism through national institutions.[87] However, such a top-down indoctrination of nationalism, in Fanon's eyes, results in no more than an empty symbol of the nation, just as the flag and the palace where the government sits cease to mean anything to the people. Fanon insists that "it is only when men and women are included on a vast scale in enlightened and fruitful work that form and body are given to [national] consciousness." An authentic nation-state, therefore, should rid itself of the static, lifeless, exclusionary, and manipulative apparatus, desert the "brightly lit, empty shells and [take] shelter in the country, where it is given life and dynamic power" (204).

In Fanon's conception of nationalism, one can see a radical change in the formation and articulation of political identity from the pre-independence to the postcolonial era. In the colonial period or during revolutionary decolonization, nationalism emerges as a legitimate expression—and probably the only means available—of political identity. Here the people and the nation become one; nationalism is isomorphic with the political identity of the resisting people. The spontaneous invocation of nationalism in the people, the national-popular will, doesn't have to be represented by any agency because the political identity of the nation-people can be fully constituted by their own actions. After the cessation of colonial rule, the postcolonial nation-state, however, takes over the task of representing the national-popular will and assumes the role of the agency of political identity. It is at this point that the nation-people realize that they are alienated from the nation-state. The once fully constituted political identity can no longer sustain itself. The nation-people begin to question their shaken and increasingly ambiguous political identity because they can no longer identify with their bourgeois leaders and the postcolonial nation-

---

87 It is also instructive to note that this alienation of the ruling bourgeoisie and the state apparatus they control from the people is reinforced by the fact that the "national languages"—even if they are the same as the colonial language—in most postcolonial nations in Africa are used almost exclusively by the national bourgeoisie who make up only a tiny portion of the population.

state that is supposed to be the materialization of their spontaneous nationalism and realize the nation-popular will.

The kind of distinction Fanon draws between a populist nationalism and an official one, between a vitalist conception of nation and a notion of the nation-state as an artificial-technical construct also underlies Benedict Anderson's explorations of the origin and spread of nationalism.[88] Like Fanon, Anderson valorizes the people's spontaneous attachment to their imagined nation as the popular, progressive (in the sense of superseding the older, monarchical conception of communities), good model of nationalism, and denounces the official version as the statist, artificial, undesirable model of nationalism. Although Anderson's delineation of nationalism is far from being a simplistic binary opposition, as he explains postcolonial nationalism in terms of Janus-like modulations between the two models of nationalism,[89] he nevertheless links grassroots patriotism to something natural or organic, an association that can be evidenced in the common use, in many languages, of terms such as "fatherland," "motherland" or "home country" to refer to one's nation. Thus, Anderson conceives of this spontaneous "political love" as one of the categories that *universally, irreversibly divide people into particular groups*:

> ... in everything 'natural' there is always something unchosen. In this way, nationness is assimilated to skin-colour, gender, parentage, and birth-era—all those things one can not help. And in these 'natural ties' one senses what one might call 'the beauty of *gemeinschaft*'. To put it another way, precisely because such ties are not chosen, they have about them a halo of disinterestedness. (*Imagined Communities*, 143)

The characterization of populist nationalism as a natural, given, and universal category, of course, has to be qualified by Anderson's well-known association of the rise of nationalism (in Europe, at least) with the breakthrough in the technology of reproduction made possible by the emergence of "print capitalism." This materialist interpretation, however, cannot escape a sense of the "unchosen" fatality mentioned in the quote above,

---

[88] I am indebted to Pheng Cheah's observation of the similarity of the distinction made by the two authors in question. See his essay "Spectral Nationality."

[89] Detailed discussions of this feature of decolonizing/postcolonial nationalisms are presented in the Chapters "The Last Wave" (113–140) and "The Angel of History" (155–162) in the revised edition of *Imagined Communities* (1991). This Janus-faced character of nationalism is highlighted in Anderson's analyses of the origins and developments of the European "models."

as Anderson emphasizes again: "What, in a positive sense, made the new communities [of modern nations] imaginable was a half-fortuitous, but explosive, interaction between a system of production and productive relations (capitalism), a technology of communication (print), and *the fatality of human linguistic diversity*" (42–43; emphasis mine). The element of fatality is essential, as Anderson underlines, because the unavoidable diversity of languages would enable vernaculars to maintain to a certain degree their particularities in the face of print capitalism's potent capacity to stabilize the printed forms of vernaculars or unify different local languages. This in turn would allow for particular, yet unified fields of exchange and communication on which imaginings of individual national communities are based while at the same time testifying to the universalizing reach and imitability of the nation as an imagined community. At any rate, nationalism in this conception is something "one can not help," since "the fixings of print-languages and the differentiation of status between them were largely unselfconscious processes" resulting from forces beyond one's control, or even comprehension—"the explosive interaction between capitalism, technology and human linguistic diversity" (45).[90]

Such a (relatively) spontaneous and taken-for-granted mode of nationalism is, without exception, considered side by side with the other term of the duality—official nationalism. In his examination of the official nationalism deployed by European dynastic states, Anderson calls this nationalism a "willed merger of nation and dynastic empire," a strategy developed by the ruling class to "naturalize" themselves "*after*, and *in reaction to* the popular national movements proliferating in Europe since the 1820s" (86; emphasis in original). In other words, official nationalism is a statism "made natural" in order to accommodate and take advantage of the prevalence of spontaneous nationalism; its reactionary, secondary nature is also clearly exemplified in this case. A prime example Anderson gives is the early twentieth-century Anglicized Thai monarch Wachirawut. Wachirawut quite successfully promoted anti-Chinese nationalism in a preemptive move to frustrate the dissemination of an increasingly popular republicanism after the overthrow of the last Chinese dynasty by an assortment of revolutionaries, supported and financed by numerous overseas

---

90   Recall Marx's description of the experience of capitalist modernity as "all that is solid melts into air."

Chinese residing in Southeast Asia, including those merchants and laborers who had long ago immigrated to Thailand.[91] As for the "proto-postcolonial" nationalisms surging along with the wave of anticolonial revolutions around the mid-twentieth century, Anderson observes among them "that 'state' Machiavellism which is so striking a feature of post-revolutionary regimes in contrast to revolutionary nationalist movements" (160). Like Fanon, Anderson further singles out a profound disjunction in the manifestation and significance of nationalism between the revolutionary and post-revolutionary moments, when he writes: "the model of official nationalism assumes its relevance above all at the moment when revolutionaries successfully take control of the state, and are for the first time in a position to use the power of the state in pursuit of their visions" (159).

In both Fanon and Anderson, it appears that the emergence of the state, in a sense, signals the death of the nation as an emblem of spontaneity. Yet such a problematic relationship between birth and death apropos of "the nation-state" (this designation therefore seeming to invoke both life and death) is by no means simply a matter of gaining one at the cost of the annulment of the other. Indeed, Anderson also reminds us that the birth of a nation seems to always presuppose the death of anonymous national martyrs, commemorated with cenotaphs or tombs of the Unknown Soldier of the kind seen in almost every modern nation (*Imagined Communities*, 9–11; *Spectre of Comparisons*, 363–364). State monuments such as national cenotaphs are the indispensable, retroactive expression and reinforcement of a national consciousness born before the nation-state came into being. Such a strong affinity or willingness to sacrifice oneself for the nation cannot be easily explained away by dismissing it as a backward practice or a kind of "false consciousness" of the merely artificial construct of the "imagined community" we call the nation.[92] By insisting on the line drawn between the two modes of nationalism, both Fanon and Anderson

---

91 What was ironic about this instance was that Wachirawut himself, whether he knew it or not, actually had more Chinese than Thai blood due to interracial marriages in much earlier times (Anderson, *Imagined Communities*, 101).

92 Anderson's notion of "the nation as an imagined community" has been hailed by many postcolonialist/poststructuralist critics as a testimony to the bankruptcy of the modern concept of the nation. However, few people take note of his insistence on the spontaneity of nationalism once the imagined community of the nation is formed (however contingent its grounds) and his difference from the diasporic, rootless position of the transnationalists and postnationalists.

attempt to alert us to the pitfalls of nationalism while affirming its emancipatory potentialities and acknowledging its power over the members of the national communities.

The Question of Representation and the National Community

Now it is clear that both Fanon and Anderson privilege a primordial, spontaneous, natural attachment to the nation, an authentic affection that cannot be represented by the establishment of the nation-state, and will certainly be contaminated by such an empty, artificial construct. Since Fanon does not suggest an alternative political institution that can represent this spontaneous nationalism without contamination, he seems to imply that in the decolonizing process, the resisting people speak for themselves through revolutionary actions, without any discursive means of representing the primordial nationalism. However, in the postcolonial nation, it is the national bourgeoisie who fail to represent the national-popular will, exclude the people from the organic body of the nation, and turn the nation-state into the "empty shell" of a governing apparatus, a hollow emblem of a coercive, stagnant, and statist nationalism. Here one can discern a certain problematic of representation arising once the ruling class takes over the task of representing the spontaneous nationalism and popular will in the postcolonial era. But how does this kind of spontaneous, emancipatory popular national consciousness get represented or articulated in any way other than the "official" or "statist" one after the political independence of ex-colonies? Fanon does not elaborate on an alternative, except that Gramscian "organic intellectuals" or progressive party members can go about educating the people and spreading the idea that the nation doesn't belong in the hands of the leader(s) once synonymous with the liberation movement but no longer representing their interests.

Anderson, on the other hand, locates the representation of the national-popular will in the emergence of the technology of the mechanical reproduction of information and knowledge. According to Anderson, the rise of the nation is situated in a constellation of historical forces in the late eighteenth and early nineteenth centuries, the two most prominent of which are the rise of print-capitalism and a new apprehension of time. Print-languages created unified fields of exchange and communication among communities within national borders that either are physically far apart or speak mutually unintelligible vernaculars. The advent of the newspaper and the novel marked the accessibility of mechanically reproducible products to the masses and enabled people to think of time in a way we have long taken for granted. Unlike medieval Europeans, we now all imagine, and are sure that we are engaged in our own activities, in the same clock, calendrical time as our fellow countrymen are, but we may be largely unaware of one another. This imagining, this awareness, is what makes possible the concept of the nation as an imagined community beyond our immediate physical existence. Thus, Anderson defines the nation in terms of a new apprehension of time: "The idea of a sociological organism moving calendrically through homogeneous, empty time is a precise analogue of the idea of the nation, which also is conceived as a solid community moving steadily down (or up) history" (26). And it is through such imaginings and mediations of print-capitalism that the formation of nationalism—in fact, of any political identity—can come into being, appeal to its readers, and gain political impact.

We have to be aware that in Anderson's conception, the primordial attachment to the nation still needs print-capitalism and a new conception of time to be articulated and circulate. It may have been true that, at that particular historical juncture, a genuinely populist nationalism was successfully articulated through newspapers, books, and pamphlets—already a mediation—without being contaminated by the statist ideology; however, the same means of representation may not work—actually, did not work—in the contexts of decolonizing and postcolonial Asia and Africa. In post-independence Africa, there was still a large illiterate population, so print-capitalism was unlikely to achieve in Africa the effect Anderson describes occurring in the European context before a state-sponsored educational system could be established. In many African countries, the only written language was the colonial language, which could also be the only common spoken language that different ethnic or tribal groups in the new nation shared. This could render the representation of national consciousness more problematic because the medium of representation bore the legacy of the colonial rule that nationalism sought to overcome and could thus undermine the authenticity of a new national identity. Since the nation-people as a bounded community was arbitrarily generated from colonial state frontiers, popular national consciousness was initially weak and needed to be actively fostered through the artifice of political organization, which could always be monitored by the state. An authentic, unmediated affection for the imagined community that is the nation can therefore exist, or is conceivable, only before the birth of a nation-state.

One question we can perhaps ask about Fanon's valorization of popular struggle for a native nation that coincides with the nation-people is: If the uprisings in the rural areas are confined to the natives' own or neighboring villages, their immediate, and most intimate communities, how is this spontaneous revolt against the colonizer different from the primordial territorial defense in tribalism? How is it expanded into nationalistic emotions that involve a larger sense of community? How is the spontaneous, populist nationalism, or the national-popular will, represented, articulated, and circulated within national borders? Given the fact that the villagers' spontaneous attachment to the nation has to go beyond their immediate communities to become an imagining of a national community, a certain means of representing, mediating, and circulating such nationalism is necessary. But as long as there is representation or mediation, the communal space of the unmediated nation, the oneness of the nation and the people, which spontaneous nationalism envisages, is destined to disintegrate once the imagining of the nation materializes in the establishment of the state. Or rather, if one is to view it the other way around, the people have to be indoctrinated by the official nationalism to become fully identified with the state, to maintain a fully constituted political identity in nationalism.

The same query should also be directed to our other theorist: How is the spontaneous, populist nationalism, or the national-popular will, represented, articulated, and circulated in the European context from which Anderson's model derives? As mentioned earlier, Anderson's answer is that print-capitalism and a new apprehension of time played crucial roles in the rise of European nation-states. However, it is hard to determine if Europeans would have readily accepted people who spoke the same language as members of their imagined national communities had the ruling dynasties not privileged and elevated a certain language to the status of the official language (which usually wasn't the language the ruling families spoke). It is also unlikely that they could imagine the location of their fellow countrymen and how far their extended communities could go, if there had not been long established national borders. Moreover, why didn't the newspaper and the novel bring about a sense of simultaneity, and therefore, a sense of belonging to the same imagined community, among people in neighboring countries in Europe, which might have populations that spoke the same language on both sides of the frontier? In other words, a populist, spontaneous nationalism may have existed, but the imagining of a national community can hardly be represented, mediated, and reinforced without the intervention, or "contamination" of the official version of nationalism.

Spatial Images/Imaginings of the Postcolonial Nation

Perhaps the more important question is not whether we can call the spontaneous antagonism against the oppressor nationalism, but whether it's possible to imagine a nation without projecting the image of the colonial state. The postcolonial nation took over a host of things from the colonial state, ranging from the colonial language, the borders, the infrastructure, the bureaucratic system, the military organization, and, as Fanon observed that the secret services were not disbanded after independence (117), even part of the native personnel of the colonialist regime. In the revised version of *Imagined Communities*, Anderson modifies his earlier assumption and argues that the postcolonial nation-states of Asia and Africa, instead of being modeled directly upon the former mother countries of the metropole, are based on "the imaginings of the colonial state." Along with the new technology of mechanical reproduction, such nationalist imaginings were made possible by three state-sponsored institutions that "profoundly shaped the way in which the colonial state imagined its dominion"—the census, the map, and the museum (163–164). The common practices involving these institutions in every modern nation are prime examples that the spatial dimension of the formation of popular national consciousness is evidenced and given salience in state-related establishments.

Obviously, the map is the primary means by which a nation defines its sovereignty and demarcates its physical boundaries, and any dispute about territory can be a righteous cause to wage war against other nations. Anderson points out that in colonial situations, the modern technology of mapping emerged as a way of regulating and keeping track of people within the national borders, of putting "space under the surveillance which the census-makers were trying to impose on persons" (173). The census can be seen as the compilation of "identity categories" (164), a way of classifying or cataloging the people the colonial state rules. Since, as Anderson observes, the colonized people were often made up of complicated ethnicities (166), census-taking was the means by which the colonial administrator made sense of the multiple, blurred identities of the constituency by (re)ordering them into charts and thus giving them a "fixed" spatiality on paper. Museums are structured around the ordering and distributing of space, whether they be the deliberately reconstructed and maintained monuments of precolonial civilizations, or the well-planned exhibitions of cultural artifacts in modern buildings. They can be described as some sort of "time-space compression" because the (re)ordering of spatiality somehow captures and epitomizes the authority of the temporality demonstrated in atavism, to which nationalism invariably resorts. Although museums are apparently artificial, static collections of the lived experiences of the indigenous cultures in the past, it is this artificial character and deliberately maintained distance that bestow a kind of "secular sanctity" in the secularizing or secularized world of the colonial and postcolonial nations. Such spatial inscriptions of the imaginings of the nation on state-sanctioned maps, museums, and cenotaphs are paramount in the deepening and dissemination of "national consciousness" and nationalist discourses in the post-independence era, especially among the educated groups. Though the seemingly spontaneous nationalist feelings of the pre-independence period are somehow channeled into regulated venues and expressions, such a "symbolic death" of spontaneity curiously gives rise to a strengthened structure of feelings in which the nation seems to be endowed with an everlasting life *beyond* the simultaneity shared by the finite lives of individual nationals now able to imagine themselves as part of the infinity of the nation.

I argue that *the living on of the nation, nevertheless, presupposes death*—hence the universal practice of sanctifying the founding father(s) and tombs of unknown soldiers, despite the modern nation's disavowal of the previous sacred, eschatological basis of power. This again testifies to the necessary presupposition of the symbolic death so central to our conception of group formation. The techno-bureaucratic establishments of the state will also have to somehow "sap" the "life" of the nation—the originary vitalism Fanon and Anderson have in mind—in order for the socio-symbolic field of the nation-state to be instituted. The inevitability of the institution of the nation-state, and its subsequent stifling of any organic, natural attachment to the nation is rendered especially salient in the postcolonial nation, which exemplifies the absence of a communitarian ground of the national community, since most colonies did not have a unified political organization and homogeneous ethnic composition prior to colonization. In fact, the new nation inherited from its former oppressor the whole idea of the nation, which was a typically Western concept and had never been part of native traditions. Radhakrishnan points out that before the British colonialist invasion, there had been "all kinds of battles, skirmishes, conquests for territories, negotiations among the Moghul emperors, Hindu and Rajput kings and chieftains" within the borders of today's India, but "there was no real attempt at unification for purposes of effective administration." In other words, if there had not been an Indian Empire unified by the British, there wouldn't have been a unified contemporary India. In their efforts at empire building, the British administrators also undertook "a task of nation-building on behalf of the native people" (755). Postcolonial India wasn't founded on any bond between the people of the nation-state other than their common identity as subjects of the British-ruled Indian Empire, which was privileged over their different identities in ethnicity, religion, and caste. The same is true for many newly founded nation-states in Africa, the Americas, and Asia that broke loose from their colonizers after World War II, yet seemed to resemble the colonial states in many ways.

The Spatial Configurations of Postcolonial Nationalism

The spatial proximity between the colonized and the colonizer highlighted in the preceding discussion appears to undergird the character of the postcolonial nation-state (which unwittingly mimics the colonial state it denounces) and the ways in which political identities of the colonized are constituted (negatively vis-à-vis the colonizer). Furthermore, spatiality is crucial in reinforcing postcolonial nationalisms when the spatial elements of nationalist discourse—maps, museums, cenotaphs, etc.—are grafted onto the temporal dimension, thereby immobilizing and immortalizing post-independence nationalisms. Postcolonial nationalism, therefore, seems always to be grounded in the (native) land once occupied by the colonizer. This appears to be especially true in the Caribbean, where land is scarce and the descendants of slaves have nothing to hold on to but the tiny, sparse lands dotted around the Caribbean Sea. In the earlier stage of his career, Édouard Glissant, for example, claims that "every way of speaking is a land" (*The Ripening*, 105), and such articulation would precipitate the coming into consciousness of the colonized, via the critical agent of the nation.[93]

What is peculiar about postcolonial nationalisms in the Caribbean, however, is that the traumatic experience of the colonial encounter is compounded by a profound sense of dislocation or displacement that further exacerbates the most ruthless, basest form of colonization—slavery. The slaves and their descendants are neither the natives (the aboriginal Indian tribes had been virtually exterminated—which was why the colonials brought African slaves for cheap labor) nor the intruders into the native land. The spatial element hence still plays a pivotal role here, but anticolonial and postcolonial nationalisms in the Caribbean are overshadowed by a certain sense of uprooted-ness which results in nationalist feelings of nuanced twinges, pending on the different responses to that oroginary experience of dislocation. I will focus in this chapter on a strain of nationalisms that stems from such responses to the traumatic, constitutive dislocation yet nowadays often goes by names other than nationalism—such as the black diaspora, the black Atlantic, postcolonialism, or the Africentric movement, etc.[94] I attempt to show in the following pages how they may be more aptly categorized as a sort of "long-distance nationalism" which, however internationalist and transnational in vision and practice, don't really twist free of the logic of the nation-state or go beyond a nationalist thinking, even though, in certain cases, they strive to replace the category of the nation with others (for example, 'culture' or 'blackness').

---

93 This is a period when Glissant still placed anticolonial movements and an imagined nation on the top of his agenda, which is organized around the pursuit of a national specificity, to be distinguished from the particular vécu of "peuple" or folklore.
94 Such transnational projects certainly include the black nationalisms that have emerged in the United States, which are not conventionally (or even loosely) considered part of the postcolonial proper. For the latter term, see Molefi Kete Asante, *Afrocentricity*.

National Pastime, International Obsession

Based on the wide circulation and palpable influence of the legend of Toussaint and the Haitian Revolution in both the popular imagination and literary representations beyond Haiti, and even the Caribbean, one is tempted to postulate a certain manifestation of postcolonial nationalism in the Caribbean and beyond—a kind of transnational nationalist literature or cultural production—which, interestingly, hinges on the representation or imagining of a certain history beyond one's own national borders, as evidenced in the works of Aimé Césaire, Glissant, James, and Derek Walcott, etc. on this topic.[95] Césaire, Glissant, and James were apparently writing with the revolutionary fervor of mid-twentieth century decolonizing/independence movements in mind, striving to render the Haitian Revolution a communitarian ground, a constitutive traumatic event, on which the emerging national communities in the Caribbean could be built, as well as an inspirational story for anticolonial struggles far beyond their countries of birth, across the Atlantic Ocean to Africa. Apart from his affirmation of the race's blackness in his celebration of negritude, which is distinct from Fanon's agonizing ambivalence between "black skin and white masks," Césaire, like Fanon, was personally involved in decolonizations in Africa, where his nationalist vision was put into practice. Glissant delved into the collective memory of Toussaint and the Haitian Revolution to gain a "prophetic vision of the past" that, as Michael Dash argues, points to a sustained critique of the Martinican's "psychic dispossession" or dependence on the mother country, which was prefigured by Toussaint's "disastrous fascination with France and his dismaying lack of faith in his own community" (xvii). As a world-roving radical intellectual, James established ties with Marxist/Communist groups on both sides of the Atlantic and produced a body of work that serves as a theoretical arsenal at the disposal of anti-imperial nationalisms.

All these important figures from the Caribbean, in addition to Marcus Garvey and George Padmore, were involved in intellectual, political, or cultural activities that were nationalist in nature and international in

---

95   Other works not yet mentioned include Césaire's critical work *Toussaint Louverture: La révolution française et le problème colonial* and the play *The Tragedy of King Christophe*. For folklore about Toussaint and its influence on slaves in the American South, see Blackburn, Davis, and Genovese.

scope: they took part in resistance movements that centered on individual nationalist projects in order to counter their respective colonial states, while also targeting a universal colonialism that was characteristically global in its reach and sustained its particular materializations in individual colonies. Although Fanon wasn't engaged in any patently nationalist discourse or nation-building project in the Caribbean,[96] he, incredibly, devoted the last years of his life (1956–1961) to the radical anticolonial movement of the *Front de Libération Nationale* (FLN) in Algeria. It was a nationalist cause that had little to do with his own race or ethnicity (a narrower, pre-modern sense of "nation"), as distinct from the cases of other cosmopolitan activists who participated in African national liberation movements, except that Fanon was fighting with the Arabs in Algeria against their common colonialist mother country—France.

Fanon's nationalist project therefore can be considered the universalization of nationalism par excellence—an "abstract nationalism," devoid of particular nationalist content and hovering in international space, seeking to be given embodiment in particular nationalist struggles. Neil Lazarus describes Fanon's commitment to anti-colonial nationalist struggles as "nationalist internationalism," a "would-be hegemonic form of national consciousness" (79) which has to be distinguished categorically from the kind of bourgeois nationalism that, as indicated in Chapter 3, Fanon castigates. This new, burgeoning form of national consciousness, according to Fanon, is not equivalent to nationalism per se, but is the only thing that will give nationalist movements "an international dimension" (247). For Fanon, nation-building projects, which emerged as a route of *decolonization without alternative* in that historical juncture, were never an isolated or isolatable phenomenon, but necessarily "accompanied by the discovery and encouragement of universalizing values." As he argues: "Far from keeping aloof from other nations, therefore, it is national liberation which leads the nation to play its part on the stage of history. It is at the heart of national consciousness that international consciousness lives and grows" (247–248). As a militant Marxist (not that he didn't recognize

---

96 Fanon's *Black Skin, White Masks* is the only work of his that deals extensively with the problems arising from the colonial situations in his native Antilles. His writings on anti-colonial nationalisms are drawn mostly from his experiences in Africa.

the Eurocentrism of Marx), Fanon was ever attentive to the internationalist vision and struggles of socialism. However, unlike the (European) Marxists of a different generation who bemoaned the defenselessness of international workers' movements when confronted with populist nationalism, Fanon saw clearly not only the emancipatory implications of anticolonial nationalisms, but "the indispensability (and relative privilege) of the national liberation struggle to the wider struggle for socialism" (Lazarus, 242).

Commenting on "national culture" in the context of decolonizing/postcolonial Africa, Fanon maintains that "the birth of national consciousness in Africa has a strictly contemporaneous connection with the African consciousness. The responsibility of the African as regards national culture is also a responsibility with regard to African Negro culture" (247). Here Fanon is obviously echoing the Pan-Africanism advocated by monumental figures like Kwame Nkrumah, though with an accent on "cultural" rather than political unity. Such a Pan-Africanist, black cultural nationalism has had a strong hold on black populaces—especially the educated classes—outside of Africa, perhaps even more than on those residing in Africa. For if nationalism cannot be free from, and is actually premised on, an international dimension—the presupposition of other nations whose differences from us help define our nation, cultural nationalism is characteristically marked and reinforced by its long-distance, border-crossing movements. It is an imagined community that can now be infinitely idealized as it is not to be materialized in or cosubstantial with a real, existing, bounded nation-state which would inevitably appear as an inadequate representation of such an idealization. It is either posited as the imagined extension of territories of an existing powerful state, as in imperialist ideology, or the projection of a longing for a would-be powerful nation-state which results from the non-existence or marginalized status of that state, as in Zionism or Pan-Africanism. In recent years, the latter has assumed the aspect of the supersession of the national by the cultural, and glorifies its transnational movements as a new, progressive actor in the context of globalization or as an alternative means of political empowerment and legitimization. We'll focus on such cultural and political mobilizations in the black diaspora, in the New World of the descendants of the slaves defined by their traumatic dislocation and severance from Africa, which set in motion the process of a globalizing economy based on colonial slavery.

As Michael Dash points out, "too often the Caribbean intellectuals had led other people's revolutions—Fanon in Algeria, Padmore in Ghana, Garvey in the United States, and Césaire's role in African decolonization—but had had little or no impact at home" (xvi).[97] Whether indigenous or vernacular anticolonial nationalisms in the Caribbean were indeed relatively weak is open to debate and deserves further inquiry, but it is undeniable that the kind of long-distance, cultural nationalism(s) we've just described have prevailed in the New World, especially among the North American and West Indian black intelligentsia. This certainly had a great deal to do with the collective memory of slavery, which enabled them to think of their existence in the New World as fundamentally *in exile*, cut off from some irretrievable origin, as well as with the highly educated class's relatively privileged status, cultural capital, and economic ability to move between different countries, continents, and cultures. Paul Gilroy's seminal book, *The Black Atlantic*, is an ambitious recent attempt to theorize and delineate the trajectories of the cultural productions and political movements across the Atlantic Ocean that are inextricably linked to the experience of colonial slavery, and which form a counterculture to (Western) modernity which he calls "the black Atlantic." Gilroy offers detailed analyses of the contributions of generations of black intellectuals (mostly African-Americans—Martin Delany, Fredrick Douglass, W. E. B. Du Bois, Richard Wright, etc.) to the formation of this counterculture. At its own historical juncture, Gilroy's project was prompted and somehow motivated by his desire to argue against the rise of identity politics in cultural studies and "repudiate the dangerous obsession with [black] 'racial' purity" (xi), since, as he observes, "[r]egardless of their affiliation to the right, left, or centre, groups have fallen back on the idea of cultural nationalism" (2). With its renunciation of essentialism of any sort and emphasis on the mobility of cultural practices and political identities, one of the main targets

---

97 Césaire had been actively involved in local politics in Martinique; however, it was obvious that he couldn't bring about the kind of radical change of colonial or protectorate system in his native land. Late in his career, James also played a role in Eric Williams's government of Trinidad and Tobago. Glissant was a notable exception in the earlier stage of his career in concentrating on cultural life at home, though he became a typical cosmopolitan, traveling postcolonial intellectual in his later years.

of Gilroy's project of the black Atlantic, as one can expect, is the nation-state and all the sorts of borders that may be associated with it: "The specificity of the modern political and cultural formation I want to call the black Atlantic can be defined . . . through this desire to transcend both the structures of the nation state and the constraints of ethnicity and national particularity" (19).

The Routes of Cultural Nationalism

It is noteworthy that Gilroy omits from the bulk of his examples and analyses the international, even hemispheric movement of anticolonial nationalisms that mobilized countless black masses and their distinguished leaders on both sides of the Atlantic.[98] This glaring omission is probably a reflection of his hostility to or distrust of the category of the nation, something all too common in today's intellectual scene that often attributes, soberly or unthinkingly, all kinds of essentialist vices to it and scorns the artificiality and constructedness of boundaries and identities it imposes. I do not wish to argue with Gilroy's warning against identitarian essentialisms and his stress on the ineluctable, or even constitutive, "double consciousness" (à la Du Bois, one of the major figures he analyses at length) and hybridity of these important players of the black Atlantic, who, however, should be qualified as "blacks of the West" (2). I only want to question the disproportionate glamorization of the border-crossing movements, the spatial mobility so crucial to the cultural productions and political legacies of the black Atlantic, which, Gilroy insists, is not an actually existing political entity like a nation but a transnational "counterculture" positioned between at least "two great cultural assemblages" (1). Drawing on the pivotal image of "ships in motion," which invokes the slaves ships of the Middle Passage, Gilroy charts the "chronotopes" of the black Atlantic in order to conceive of identity on *routes rather than roots*, playing cleverly on the homonyms (17, 19).

---

98 In the preface, Gilroy does acknowledge the fact that he leaves out of his book Fanon and James, "the two best-known black Atlantic thinkers," citing the enormous body of work that has been devoted to the study of their lives and thought. Later on he also alludes to "Garvey and Garveyism, pan-Africanism, and Black Power as hemispheric if not global phenomena" (17).

As Gilroy says of these significant black intellectuals, the common "experience of exile," whether enforced, chosen, temporary or permanent, characterizes "these figures who begin as African-Americans or Caribbean people and are then changed," through their transcontinental, intercultural movements, "into something else which evades those specific labels and with them all fixed notions of nationality and national identity" (19). But doesn't this characterization, one that claims to elude all characterizations, paradoxically fit neatly into the mold of the transnational nationalist revolutionaries such as Fanon, Césaire, and many others who, as pointed out above, adamantly support a certain internationalist nationalism or cultural nationalism, whose name, if not substance, Gilroy wishes to repudiate? How does one define Fanon's or Césaire's nationality? Fanon deserves to be regarded as one of the founding figures of postcolonial Algeria; however, his native land of Martinique, as of this writing, is not (yet) an independent nation-state but a French "department." Moreover, exiles, as Benedict Anderson observes in the history of nationalism, have proved to be the breeding ground of nationalisms or, at least, as border-crossing leaders, they sow the seeds of nationalisms. For it is true that the first nationalist movements took place in the form of Creole nationalisms in North America and later in the Catholic, Iberian colonies to the south, prior to the flowering of nationalist movements in Europe (*Spectre*, 61-62). The experience of exile was not simply a strictly spatial matter, but also extended to exile in different languages and cultures as a necessary accompaniment of spatial displacements. This abstract sense of exile, then, accounts for the phenomenon that, as Anderson points out, "the nationalist movements which transformed the map of Europe by 1919 were so often led by young bilinguals, a pattern to be followed after 1919 in Asia and Africa" (65). Long-distance nationalism, as "routed" as it is, therefore, often serves as the precondition or catalyst that fosters and mobilizes the vernacular nationalism rooted firmly in the land of the emerging nation.

As further illustration of my point that spatial mobility across national borders and the boundaries of ethnicities and cultures doesn't guarantee that such movement is not governed by a logic of nationalism, or is free from the constraints of a system of nation-states, I'd like to turn to the only example Gilroy offers of black Atlantic cultural production not centered on a certain phenomenal black intellectual: vernacular black music culture. Gilroy notes that hip hop culture, "the powerful expressive medium of America's urban black poor," consists in a hybrid music form originating from the "Jamaican sound system culture" that was transplanted, along with Jamaican immigrants, in the 1970s and put down new roots in the South Bronx. The result was that "this routed and re-rooted Caribbean culture set in train a process that was to transform black America's sense of itself and a large portion of the popular music industry as well" (33). What troubles Gilroy, though, is the later appropriation of the routed, hybrid form in the name of black essentialism. His concern is expressed in a very incisive question: "how [does] a form which flaunts and glories in its own malleability as well as its transnational character [become] interpreted as an expression of some authentic African-American essence?" (33–34).

The answer, it seems to me, lies in the vagueness of the term "black nationalism" and the looseness of its usage. It is not even clear if it alludes to ethnic or racial essentialism. Such slippages in a transnational space like the black Atlantic, by a sleight of hand and in the name of a "global culture," often allow a particular "national" or local culture to be privileged as "ethnic" according to the cultural logic of a dominant nation-state disguised as transnational, and which in this case remains recognizably American. Although in the US context, black nationalism is frequently pitted against a mainstream white culture perceived as imbued with racism, it is US global economic dominance and technological advantage that allows hip hop culture, a means of expression of African-American discontent, to create what Gilroy calls "a global youth movement of considerable significance" (33). It would be no surprise if this hip hop culture, after a certain period of time, gets re-routed to Jamaica, obliterating the earlier routes. As Gilroy himself points out, what is called "Africentricity" by some contemporary African-American writers "might be more properly termed 'Americocentricity,'" even though these writers claim "a special status for their particular version of African culture" (191). Such complicity with the ideology they forcefully critique is often unwitting but is not limited to those black nationalists born or residing in the US. For example, Walcott, a well-known proponent of cultural hybridity and now a typical border-crossing cosmopolitan intellectual, writes as follows: "We live in the shadow of an America that is economically benign yet politically malevolent. That malevolence, because of its size, threatens an eclipse of identity." Yet this concern is eventually assuaged by his conclusion that "that shadow is less malevolent than it appears, and we can absorb it because we know that America is black . . . that what is most original in it has come out of its ghettos, its river-cultures, its plantations" ("Caribbean," 51). This initially ambivalent, yet ultimately affirmative identification with American blacks contributes to a sort of black nationalism, one which claims to transcend the artificial structures and boundaries of the nation-state, but which cannot be said to be free of the sway of the economic benevolence and political might of the nation-state that dominates such transnational, or even "global," cultural production.

Even though Walcott is an outspoken critic of postcolonial nation-states, especially those in the Caribbean, and an avowed New World poet who denounces the nostalgia for Africa prevalent among many of his peers, his cultural nationalism, as revealed above, is most explicitly demonstrated in his enthusiasm for the West Indies Federation. Walcott's *Drums and Colours* was commissioned to celebrate the creation of the Federation and the play offers a multicultural, multiracial background, with scenes taking place in major parts of the West Indies and covering a history that encompasses the experiences of both the colonized and the colonizer over the last four centuries. The reasons for the collapse of the short-lived West Indies Federation (1958–1962) are overdetermined and beyond the scope of the current project; its failure, however, epitomizes structural and theoretical difficulties and limitations underlying postcolonial attempts to go *beyond* colonial legacies.

Chapter 4
Toussaint, Globalization, and the Postcolonial Spectacle

Writing in the 1930s, C. L. R. James provided an ominous, disturbingly prescient depiction of what was to become the postcolonial future of much of the colonized world under the aegis of a ruthlessly expanding capitalist world order:

> On October 1804 [Dessalines] had himself crowned Emperor. Private merchants of Philadelphia presented him with the crown, brought on the American boat the *Connecticut*, his coronation robes reached Haiti from Jamaica on an English frigate from London. He made a solemn entry into Le Cap in a six-horse carriage brought for him by the English agent, Ogden, on board the *Samson*. Thus the Negro monarch entered into his inheritance, tailored and valeted by English and American capitalists, supported on the one side by the King of England and on the other by the President of the United States. (*Black Jacobins*, 370)[99]

Even as it presages the way in which the birth of every postcolonial nation-state involves it in a new relation of domination, one marking a shift from territorial or administrative colonialism to indirect forms of rule with varying degrees of economic, cultural, and political penetration,[100] this passage also clarifies how the emerging global system can accommodate a regime, and leader, so culturally and ideologically hostile to the reigning order that recognizes it as an independent, constituent unit. In this chapter, what I attempt to highlight, among other things, is that this accommodating process, even when the economic (inter)dependence declined (e.g. when impoverished Haiti is no longer as important a trading partner as it used to be), is made possible by rendering the postcolonial phenomenon a *spectacle*—whether it be the spectacular political fail-

---

99 As James mentions in the following pages, what the British and the Americans wanted was a monopoly of trade wrested from the hands of the defeated French. To this end, they even played a role in instigating Dessalines, known for his hatred of the whites, to exterminate the remaining French in the colony, so as to permanently sever Haiti's French connection, and thereby any possibility of the French regaining control of the colonial interests in the region (370–373).

100 Among these new, potentially varied forms of rule, the most discreet, dispersed, yet no less effective or oppressive form of domination would be what Hardt and Negri call "Empire." Cf. Loomba, *Colonialism* 7.

ures and enduring economic destitution of the postcolonial state, the recurrent violence and catastrophes within its bounds, the mass migration of its people, or the presence of heterogeneous cultures in the metropole.

Toussaint and the Lure of Globalization

In the aftermath of his publication of the Constitution that solidified his rule in San Domingo, Toussaint had in mind a vision that was veritably *global*, as he set his sights on "the forms of liberty and equality newly made available in the increasingly interconnected world" (Hardt and Negri, 118). The ideas/ideals of the French Revolution also epistemologically transformed the world-view of this slave turned Jacobin, who saw this "new form of freedom" as connected to "the expansive networks of global exchange" (120). "The revolution under Toussaint," writes Eugene Genovese, "did not aspire to restore some lost African world or build an isolated Afro-American enclave." Rather, economically at least, "Toussaint, and after his death Dessalines and Henri Christophe, tried to forge a modern black state, based on an economy with a vital export sector oriented to the world market" (88).[101] Though undoubtedly a revolutionary in his thinking and actions, Toussaint firmly believed in *order and prosperity*, since he repeatedly preached the importance of hard work to those ex-slaves who had just gained their freedom, and implemented rigid regulations on plantations to ensure that these laborers wouldn't become free idlers (cf. James, 224–268).[102] Toussaint reminds the belligerent Dessalines, who swears to "again take up the rifle": "The rifle and the hoe; don't forget the hoe" (Glissant, *Monsieur Toussaint*, 64).

---

101 Though Dessalines was noted for his anti-modern and anti-white sentiments, he "took great care to protect the British and the American whites, and spared also the priests, the skilled workmen, and the officers of health" (James, 373). Such developmentalist, mercantile policies gave way to a self-contained system of small peasant proprietorship in Haiti after the presidencies of Pétion and Boyer (Genovese, 88–89).

102 Or, rather, it is precisely Toussaint's preoccupation with order, discipline, and prosperity that makes him a revolutionary in his time, especially when compared with the numerous bands of maroons who fight only guerilla wars and want nothing more than an isolated, self-contained existence. As Glissant describes it in his play, Toussaint tells his soldiers, "Let's wage war methodically.... *When we march, even the dust will be disciplined*. If you win amidst disorder and folly, you will still be slaves" (32; emphasis mine). One can also say that the key to the success of Napoleon's Revolutionary Army lies mainly in his genius for organization.

Toussaint's globalist outlook, once again, was not only in the product of merely economic consideration or the necessity of survival; it also had its cultural, emancipatory, universalist, or even phantasmatic, utopian overtones. In Glissant's play *Monsieur Toussaint*, Toussaint, in a prophetic tone, tells his "shadows"—the atavist Mama Dio, the isolationist maroon Macaïa ("the man of the forest"), etc., who represent his "internal conflicts": "My friends, the land grows, fertile, all the way to the sea! The sea opens upon the entire world. . . . Am I to blame for having discovered the universal faith?" (43). What drives this movement of "opening up" to "the entire world"—a vision which is nothing other than what the thinking and rhetoric of globalization postulates[103]—is, I argue, the "new form of freedom" in the Idea of the Revolution which enables a *freedom of movement* unimaginable to yet craved by the slaves. Yet what is most extraordinary about Toussaint's globalist vision is that he intends to extend this freedom of movement to *all* in that imagined global community, never losing sight of those most excluded in the euphemism and optimism of a now interconnected world. As James describes:

> Firm as was his grasp of reality, old Toussaint looked beyond San Domingo with a boldness of imagination surpassed by no contemporary. In the Constitution he authorised the slave-trade because the island needed people to cultivate it. When the Africans landed, however, they would be free men. But while loaded with the cares of government, he cherished a project of sailing to African with arms, ammunition and a thousand of his best soldiers, and there conquering vast tracks of country, putting an end to the slave-trade, and making millions of blacks "free and French," as his Constitution had made the blacks of San Domingo. It was no dream. He had sent millions of francs to America to wait for the day when he would be ready. (265)

Toussaint's ambitious project of ending the slave trade *at the source*, paradoxically, had to begin, as he certainly recognized, with San Domingo's active participation (or, more bluntly, complicity) in the slave trade, and by extension, in a global economy thriving on colonial slavery. This recognition, however, already foretold that his projected exploration/emancipation of Africa was destined to be mission impossible. For, as he conceded and endorsed, if only unwillingly and strategically, the prosperity he pursued hinged on the exploitation of both the cheap labor of (a) certain group(s) of people and the natural resources in (a) certain part(s) of the

---

103 Here I am not suggesting that Toussaint's conception of globalization is in all ways compatible with that of contemporary globalization theory. I will tackle the latter and other possible positions on globalization later in this chapter.

world *by* other groups of people or other parts of the globe.[104] Had Toussaint been successful in ending colonial slavery "from the source," it would have entailed a *total restructuring* of global economy as well as culture, terminating the one he was taking part in and presumably profiting from. Needless to say, that didn't happen in history.[105] The unevenness of development and relations, the underlying logic at the core of the *structural exploitation* of the economy of colonial slavery (indeed, of capitalism at large), survived the final abolition of slavery in the Western world and, at a much later time, the cessation of formal colonization throughout the globe. What Toussaint misrecognized in this *phantasmagoria* of an interconnected globe is that everyone was *equal*—the logical outcome of the inevitable triumph of the idea of *égaliberté*, which had profound impacts on both San Domingo and France. He failed to see that revolutionary ideology and/or culture hadn't penetrated as pervasively and deeply into the fabric of the societies on either side of the Atlantic. As in his fatal blindness to the "constitutive exclusion" or disavowal of the "colonial question" *by* the post-Bastille discourse in the metropole, Toussaint, in his faithful identification with everything French, mistook the French Republic and its revolutionary culture for the universal agent to carry out its ideas/ideals throughout the world, counting on French support—at least ideologically—to make millions of Africans "free and French."[106]

In other words, what Toussaint failed to perceive was that in this phantasmatic global picture, he and San Domingo were to be at once fundamentally separated and included in some way so that a global field of equal opportunities, even development, and seemingly unbounded, free

---

104 This uneven relation is even more characteristic of a globalizing context, since, economically at least, the colonialist expansion is prompted by a relentless overseas search for cheaper labor and raw materials, besides markets abroad, when those at home no longer suffice. A whole literature of Marxist analysis, despite its economic determinism, has rightly pointed out "the economic imbalance that was necessary for the growth of European capitalism and industry" (Loomba, *Colonialism*, 4).

105 This doesn't mean that what Toussaint envisaged was no more than a wild dream. It seems to me, especially under the rubric of our discussions of universality, that his "plan" would have been the only means imaginable, at that point in time, to combat capitalist/colonialist universality—by the radical following-through of its universalist logic.

106 In Glissant's play, Toussaint speaks to Dessalines about this ambitious project: "For Robespierre would have aided us. Think of that! Africa free and San Domingo out of danger!" (63).

movement for "all" could come together. They were "internally excluded" (Balibar, 55) in the sense that they were never seriously considered an *equal* player within this emerging global system, except as a *spectacle*, exceptionally spectacular given the context of that age-old racist regime of dehumanization. Established alongside European—that is, modern—colonialism, capitalism, which was made possible only through colonial expansion (cf. Loomba, 4), found a way to move on without slavery, and eventually without formal colonization; more importantly, in the process of solidifying the liberal-democratic order on a domestic as well as global scale, it liquidated, first, the memory of its dependence on slavery, and, later on, of its colonialist past (cf. Hesse). This accommodating process of a constitutive heterogeneity, together with the liquidation of its role as a constitutive exclusion, as I will argue in this chapter, crystallized in the spectacle which nevertheless adumbrated, if not obliterated, that memory. For example, at the height of his power in San Domingo, Toussaint was almost unanimously lauded as the supreme, irreplaceable leader of the island, including the white colonials, who saluted him on public occasions, while their women presented him with wreaths. Some French officers heartily admired his genius (e.g. Vincent and Laveaux), and one woman even told Toussaint, "my husband loves you, all the whites are attached to you" (James, 260). However, as James reminds us, Toussaint's exceptionally elevated status didn't really change the white prejudice against the rest of his race (259–261), aside from alleviating the whites' guilt for the horrific crimes and cruelties inflicted on the slaves in the immediate past, crimes regarding which no serious investigations had been opened, let alone any reparations or even reprisals. Last but not least, the basic structure of colonial society—with its plantations, hierarchies, and uneven economic relations—remained relatively intact.

Before I turn to more recent, "properly postcolonial" instances of such rendering of the spectacle, or spectacularization of a founding exception, I'd like to reflect momentarily on some issues related to "globalization," a term we've referred to from time to time, in light of our earlier explorations of universality (in Chapter 1).[107]

---

107 The vagueness or definitional inconsistency of the term "globalization" makes it no less multivalent and confusing than "postcolonial" or "postmodern." Fredric Jameson, for instance, calls "globalization" the "most ambiguous ideological concept [with] its alter-

Globalization and Its Limit(s)

We should make clear that the globalizing vision that confronted Toussaint was actually twofold, which could be read, in Étienne Balibar's terms, as "universality as reality" and "universality as ideal": the former the planetary, well-developed economic system (and socio-political organization), with necessary links and units already in place; the latter the potential promised by the existing global order or the ideals one postulates as its founding gestures—which will inevitably mean a *utopian* transcendence of the status quo. In the case of Toussaint, it appears that "the lure of globalization" lies in the latter, the utopian picture of global equity and exchange. However, Toussaint's white adversaries seemed to know better. In Édouard Glissant's *Monsieur Toussaint*, Toussaint's white secretary Granville offers a piece of advice to the plantation owners who conspire against Toussaint: "He has only one flaw, gentlemen, and it is by this flaw that we will destroy him: he believes in order and prosperity.... Make him Grand Protector of the Plantations.... Only Toussaint Abréda will triumph over Toussaint Louverture" (43; Abréda is the name of the homestead of Toussaint's former owner).[108] In addition to being a forward-thinking revolutionary, Toussaint was also known as a remarkably able administrator—hence the lure, too, lies in the maintenance and management of a given order that suffices to present itself as de facto, quotidian universality. I argue that Toussaint's ambivalent, dual vision of globalization somehow epitomizes the *alternating moments or facets of globalization*—Janus-faced

---

nating contents," comparing it, allegorically, to "that elephant we are here blindly attempting to characterize" (*Globalization*, 58, 66). He then proposes four positions on globalization, two of which have conflicting, contradictory tendencies yet are "twin positions" that "are however themselves reversible" (56–57). Timothy Brennan, a Marxist scholar, recognizes the myriad of positions available on globalization and delineates them in five categories, while singling out a position, globalization theory in a "restricted sense" (represented by Anthony Giddens), as one that dismisses other positions as "no longer tenable" and "already outside" globalization theory ("Development," 123–124). Acknowledging the contestations and ambiguities of the term/concept, I do not attempt to marshal all the possible positions here, but focus on those that are particularly germane to our discussion. This inevitably involves some position-taking—as any engaging approach to a contested issue would have to.

108 This is a flaw that insightful historians such as James have pointed out. Before joining the slave revolt, Toussaint was his master's coachman and had been entrusted to take care of much business on the plantation. He had done his best to ensure the safety of his master and his family before committing himself to the revolution.

globalization—in much globalization theory or thinking. As Fredric Jameson—among others—observes, the main strains of globalization theory tend to have a certain utopian tinge. For instance, Roland Robertson intends to offer "something like a utopian vision of 'globality'" (*Globalization*, xii) which could be said to be universalized and unified under the aegis of "global consciousness" and "compression of the world" (Hoogvelt, 117). On the other hand, certain strains of globalization thinking also consists in an emphatic, celebratory confirmation of the *existing* global order—perceived as postmodernity, an unprecedented, out-of-joint point in time that would itself hold "infinite possibilities" for the future (cf. Jameson, 65–66). Timothy Brennan wryly characterizes this line of globalization thinking as follows: "The 'now' is the new, and the new is rapturously and exuberantly embraced" ("Development," 122). While it is conceivable that the postulation of globalization as unconditional universalization may be the force that furnishes globalizing movements with a "progressive" character, it is plausible to contend that it may be a misrecognition of the now and susceptible to endorsing the existing order.

Recasting globalization in terms of universality, I'd like to draw on Balibar's notion of "universality as reality," which he unequivocally equates with "globalization," before we advance our arguments on globalization. In his conception of "real universality" (or universality as reality), Balibar proposes a well-rounded, perhaps rote, definition of globalization:

> I take it in the sense of an actual interdependency between the various "units" which together build what we call the World: institutions, groups, individuals, but also, more profoundly, the various *processes* which involve institutions, groups, and individuals: the circulation of products and persons, the political negotiations, the juridical contracts, the communication of news and cultural patterns, etc. (48; emphasis in original)

This ostensibly all-encompassing definition of globalization seems to consist of nothing more than what Benedict Anderson calls "quotidian universals" (*Spectre*, 33). It is only reasonable, then, to ask, "What's new?" Balibar's point, however, is that globalization is a *fait accompli*: "There have been stages in the extension and intensification of real universality [globalization], till, 'in the end,' a decisive *threshold* was crossed, which made it irreversible . . . to achieve any proper 'delinking'" (50; emphasis in original). One corollary of this pronouncement, or realization of the attainment of globalization, is that the utopian dimension, the "universalistic values" (ibid.) inherent in globalization thinking would be consequently rendered *impossible*: we are all globalized already—so what?[109] "This impossibility," argues Balibar, "did not arise because it proved impossible to connect the world as a single space, but exactly for the opposite reason: because this connection of humankind with itself was already achieved, because it was *behind us*" (ibid.; emphasis in original).

I take this proposal of the passé status of globalization as a heuristic, thought-provoking point of departure, rather than a definite marker of the temporality of globalization (to determine when globalization ends or ended would be as difficult as to agree on when it started). For, as mentioned before, there is always this forward-thinking, destabilizing facet or moment of globalization which is premised on the "unconditional," the universalization of its utopian ideals. There might exist—who knows?—a certain means of communication or transportation unthinkable at this point in history (just as internet instant messaging was unthinkable, say, twenty years ago). Nevertheless, it may be useful to reconsider the current state of globalization—and globalization theory—by adding "a dose of negativity" (Jameson, xii) to the acquiescence to the status quo (globalization as 'real universality') as well as to the optimism for the future (globalization as 'ideal universality')—that is, by asking, "What if globalization is already behind us?" The task ahead, I propose, is therefore twofold: In the *spatial* dimension, we need to rethink who or what is left behind in this presumably interconnected global network which may be behind us. In other words, under the rubric of our earlier theoretical elaborations (in Chapter 1), what is the "internal exclusion" (Balibar, 55), the constitutive exclusion, or the internal limit of this seemingly borderless, limitless, all-inclusive global field? *Temporally*, we need to examine the historicity of globalization, not to reconstruct its historical continuity, but to explore how the discontinuities or ruptures in history (and in the history of globalization theory) constitute the indissoluble "remainders" of history that,

---

109 One can, of course, counter that the utopian vision doesn't have to revolve on a universalist logic or homogenizing movements, as in the postmodernist, or Deleuzian envisaging of a globe characterized by decentering movements and a proliferation of differences. I will register my reservations about such a global picture in my arguments, later in the chapter, regarding the tendency to unwittingly homogenization of heterogeneous elements.

in variegated ways, shape and return to haunt the globalizing present. This is what I attempt to do, in a less than straightforward way, with my reflections on the postcolonial spectacle in the following pages.

Globalization and the Postcolonial Spectacle

Globalization, whose processes were first made possible by colonial slavery, is conceived in this book as a homogeneous system presupposing yet foreclosing some radically heterogeneous element as *spectacle*. In fact, globalization is characterized by uneven development and more refined demarcations within and beyond national borders, feeding on and perpetuating the uneven relations of domination at both inter- and intra-national levels. The case of Haiti, from its status as the richest colony in the world to the poorest country in the western hemisphere, tragically exemplifies what Ankie Hoogvelt calls the shift "from structural exploitation to structural irrelevance" as a result of the "implosion" of globalization (84). The globalizing system is adept at, or has adapted to, accommodating and regulating differences by incorporating what is otherwise heterogeneous to it into its fold, as is evidenced by the capacity of multinational corporations to put on a variety of "local" faces in their marketing efforts. A similar move of accommodating, demarcating, and regulating the heterogeneous element under the rubric of globalization, as we shall see, can be found in the case of the historical trajectories and cultural and academic productions of the postcolonial.

What I call "the postcolonial spectacle" takes shape in the historical trajectories and cultural as well as academic productions wherein the postcolonial serves as a heterogeneous element that is eventually "domesticated" into the metropole or the globalizing system which presupposes its heterogeneity and recognizes it only as *spectacle*. If the word "postcolonial" itself is fraught with definitional inconsistency,[110] the term "postcolonial spectacle" would have to be at least potentially multivalent. First of all, there has been the rapid expansion of the academic territory of postcolonial studies and the latter's eventual ascent to a paradigmatic status in at

---

110 This appears to be the only possible consensus of the definition of "postcolonial." For general polemics about the definition, see the special issue of the journal *Social Text* 31/32 (1992). For specific mentions and recountings of such "definitional inconsistencies," see, for example, Hallward (xi), Huggan (1) and Williams (179).

least English-speaking academia. Such a "meteoric rise of postcolonial theory [and literatures] in 1990's America" and beyond (Huggan, xv) has itself become a spectacle, which more and more people, whether identifying themselves as inside or outside postcolonial studies, feel obliged to address or respond to. This academic production or institutionalization of the postcolonial spectacle, of course, cannot be detached from, though neither can it be completely subsumed to, another sense—or level—of the postcolonial spectacle: the broader phenomenon of "cultural commodification" of the postcolonial exotic in the context of metropolitan consumption (Huggan, ix).[111] In addition to these two, I'd like to examine two other facets of this multivalent term which are not unrelated to the aforementioned meanings: 1) the oppositionalist, anti-imperialist rhetoric and ideology of postcolonialism and the varying degrees of complicity of this postcolonial rhetoric of resistance under the rubric of metropolitan multiculturalisms; 2) the Third World postcolonial "failure" or predicament as spectacle against the backdrop of a new world order of accelerating globalization.

Before we deal with contemporary instances of the postcolonial spectacle, specifically the case of Hanif Kureishi, I'd like to, first, reflect on a few historical antecedents of the postcolonial that illustrate the same formative process of the spectacle, and second, explore the theoretical underpinning and political efficacy of rendering postcolonial heterogeneity as spectacle.

The lumpenproletariat as spectacle

As Peter Stallybrass points out, nineteenth century novelists, painters, journalists, and social analysts tended to portray the street people of London and Paris as "a spectacle of heterogeneity" (70). The most dispossessed, marginal, or unclassifiable strata of society were represented in *racial* terms before the contemporary influx of immigrants of various races

---

111 Huggan's book, *The Postcolonial Exotic*, gives a detailed account of such a process of commodification, linking it to the exoticist consumption and representations in earlier colonial/imperial eras while acknowledging the peculiarity and unprecedented modes of production, distribution, and consumption under the rubric of contemporary postcoloniality and globalization (15–16, 243). Similarly, Carla Gallini characterizes the present-day massification of exotic commodities as a new generic form of exoticism, "suitable for all markets" (quoted. in Huggan, 15).

converged in the metropoles of the former empires, even when those thus portrayed were in fact of the same race as those depicting them. One such representations of heterogeneity as spectacle can be found in Marx's use of the term "lumpenproletariat," by which he sometimes echoes the commonplace bourgeois perception of the poor as "a nomadic tribe, innately depraved" or as "a distinct race" (Stallybrass, 70, 74). The name *lumpenproletariat*, however, suggests less the (political) emergence of a new, specific class or subclass than the problematization or unfixing of all class differentiations—in other words, a name Marx affixes to "the nameless thing" or unnamable phenomenon he, among others, witnessed and sought to represent (72, 79).[112]

In *The Eighteenth Brumaire*, Marx's description of the lumpenproletariat of Paris features a proliferation of (heterogeneous) categories:

> Alongside decayed *roués* with dubious means of subsistence and of dubious origin, alongside ruined and adventurous offshoots of the bourgeoisie, were vagabonds, discharged soldiers, discharged jailbirds, escaped galley slaves, swindlers, mountebanks, *lazzaroni*, pickpockets, tricksters, gamblers, *marquereaus*, brothel keepers, porters, *literati*, organ-grinders, ragpickers, knife grinders, tinkers, beggars—in short, the whole indefinite, disintegrated mass, thrown hither and thither, which the French term *la bohème*. (75)

The difficulty in naming this social heterogeneity signals a *crisis* in (the means of) representation as well as an impending disintegration or rupture of the existing socio-political order; furthermore, it generates, as Stallybrass remarks, a "veritable hysteria of naming," to the extent that Marx has to ransack other languages and cultures to construct "a spectacle of multiplicity" (72). Such a marshalling of miscellaneous elements on the fringe of metropolitan society reveals an "ambivalent celebration of the exotic" (*lazzaroni, marquereaus,* etc.)[113] and is characterized by its "striking juxtapositions of the homely and the grotesque" (ibid.). Meanwhile, in Arthur Conan Doyle's story "The Man with the Twisted Lip," London is depicted as "the space of a degradation imagined as foreign" (Stallybrass 75), with the drug culture of the opium den, which, housing "the dregs of the docks"

---

112 The foremost definition of "lumpen" in the OED is "rags and tatters." When using "lumpenproletariat" as a category, Marx is referring "*not* just to the 'lowest strata'" of society but to "'the refuse *of all classes*'" (Stallybrass, 85; emphasis in original). That's why the lumpenproletariat is not a subclass, or the same as the proletariat (83).

113 "Lazzaroni" denotes, originally, the lowest class in Naples before acquiring other, more romantic associations. "Marquereau" means "pimps" in French. See Stallybrass, 83.

(Doyle, 230), is run by a "lascar [Indian sailor] scoundrel" and his "sallow Malay attendant" (235, 231). Holmes, a drug taker and orientalist himself, is curiously placed amidst such a scene of oriental depravity, braving, and perhaps also enjoying, the fantasized corruption of the orient.

Fast-forwarding to the twentieth century, I'd like to highlight a contemporary counterpart of such a "spectacle of heterogeneity"—Hanif Kureishi's novel *The Buddha of Suburbia*, which can be read in light of the lumpenproletariat. For the question of class—with its "great tradition" in the British context—is problematized in this novel by a proliferation of new categories: race, ethnicity, gender, sexual orientation, and even more marginal, particularistic categories, such as disability and appearance. The novel features an Indian immigrant (Haroon Amir) of aristocratic origin working as the lowest ranking civil servant and marrying a lower-middle class English woman who has working class relatives; we see a poster boy (Charlie Kay) from a suburban upper-middle class family posing himself as a punk kid from a rundown urban neighborhood; there is a circle of petit-bourgeois intellectuals (especially Eleanor) who claim to represent the working class in their theatrical productions and who indeed have an off-stage, personal relationship with a street sweeper; there is an ugly, disabled Indian immigrant with a noble background (Changez) who, in wooing the love of a radical activist, protests that he'd fight for the right of the unattractive "to be kissed" (277–278); last, but not least problematic is the character Karim Amir, the bisexual son of Haroon, who, in the spirit of the bourgeois narrator of the nineteenth century, describes the emerging urban phenomenon of punk teenagers as "another race" (129) against the backdrop of the horrifying London night (131).[114] All these seem to exemplify what Marx calls the "unfixing of class differentiation," posing a new crisis parallel to the one Marx addresses, with perhaps some new twist in the question of race/ethnicity now that the "immigrant is the Everyman of the twentieth century" (141).

---

114 The irony here, of course, is that the punk kids are literally of "another race" for Karim, who, though half English, is almost exclusively identified as Indian. But here the question of ethnicity may be outweighed by that of class, since Karim's oscillating social roles may swing back to an unwitting identification with the British bourgeois subject, above all when he represents the punks in racial terms, because the social antagonism of the punk counterculture doesn't seem to spare ethnic minorities.

The "crisis" invoked by the name "lumpenproletariat"—a crisis in both of the means of representation and the social structure—is, however, accommodated or neutralized when the threat posed by the dangerous underclasses is figured by the image of the alien. I'd like to point out that, more often than not, rendering the alien in the spectacle of heterogeneity, under the scrutinizing gaze of the spectator, does little more than decontextualize the foreign—if anything, the racial and/or colonialist stereotyping is reinforced. The alien, therefore, functions literally, strictly as a *trope* while the colonial context/situation is effectively obscured or even consigned to oblivion after being invoked in the spectacle of multiplicity. In nineteenth-century London and Paris, where the presence and political leverage of non-white subjects from the colonies were still relatively minuscule, the seemingly more imminent crisis of the metropolitan society was represented—and displaced at the same time—by what Stallybrass calls "the conjunction of theatricality and racial fear" (75). This racial fear signals the positing of a radical otherness or heterogeneity that, I argue, is constitutive of both the lumpenproletariat spectacle and the crisis of society, but is itself foreclosed in their representation, or subject to institutional forgetting.

Such obliteration of constitutive heterogeneity can be illuminated by the representation of the question of the slaves—the lowest of the low who, in a sense, were not even part of the system of socio-political representations in slave-holding societies (in the same sense that property such as livestock was not). In the post-Bastille French Republic, the issue of slavery, as mentioned in Chapter 2, underwent what we might call an "institutionalized forgetting" and emerged as a *constituent exception* of the new socio-political order. For it was at once what made the Revolution possible, financially at least (it was the wealth the bourgeoisie accumulated in the highly profitable trade opportunities opened up by the colonialist exploitation of cheap slave labor and fertile lands overseas that gave the bourgeoisie the economic means and political status to challenge the *ancien régime*), and what would render the Revolutionary ideals constitutively unrealizable. That's why in the early years after the fall of Bastille, "everybody," as C. L. R. James puts it bluntly, "conspired to forget the slaves," except for the halfhearted attempts by the Friends of the Negro (70). We've pointed out that such an effacement of the question of slavery, quite paradoxically, coincided with a popularization of the term "slavery" as *trope* in post-Revolutionary social and literary discourses.

Apart from the French Romantic writers, William Wordsworth also sees in Toussaint the prototypical Romantic heroic figure who breaks loose from previous human bondage and opens up a new epoch for all. With his passion and sympathy for the French Revolution (at least in his early years), Wordsworth pays homage to Toussaint in the poem "To Toussaint L'Ouverture," which we quoted in full in the Introduction:

> Though fallen thyself, never to rise again,
> Live, and take comfort. Thou hast left behind
> Powers that will work for thee; air, earth, and skies;
> There is not a breathing of the common wind
> That will forget thee; thou hast great allies. (*Poems*, 577)

As Grant Farred comments, this poem is a "radical document in its time," since it "brings to bear critiques on race, colonialism, and revolution." In the end, however, it amounts to little more than a Romantic euphemism, according "'honor simply by celebration'" ("Victorian," 23). In the lexicon of our discussion, it elevates the figure of Toussaint to a spectacle, just like the white colonialists' tributes to him—though certainly less specious ideologically. What is obfuscated, in this spectacularization, are "the ideological and political imperatives that motivated the San Domingo slaves" (24). As Farred observes, Toussaint, contrary to Wordsworth's assertion, had been literally forgotten in the West for a long period of time before James's resuscitation of this history; however, perhaps an equally important question is how Toussaint is remembered, not just how he was forgotten. In similar fashion one can see the neutralization, incorporation or domestication of the metaphor of the slave (or Toussaintian figures) into the relatively innocuous representations of the memory of colonial slavery in many a Romantic writer, as well as those of the European colonial pasts in latter-day writings.[115]

---

115 Such a relentless process of domestication is most telling in the onslaught of globalization: Toussaint's reluctance or blindness to the option of independence was partly due to his prescient view of an impending prospect of economic (inter)dependence after the end of colonial slavery, as he insisted on hard work and repeatedly told his generals of the importance of prosperity ("don't forget the hoe"). It is a domestication into a hegemony, in Gramsci's terms, by both coercion and consent.

Heterogeneity on stage and the performativity of the spectator

In *The Prelude*, Wordsworth provides his version of the "lumpenproletariat" in his depiction of the heterogeneous mass at a fair—a carnival scene filled with monsters, freaks, and "perverted things." Against this backdrop of "anarchy and din" that causes nausea in him, the poet evokes the figure of the slave, as he attempts to regain his spectator subjectivity by rising, metaphorically, "above the press and danger of the crowd," who appear as "slaves ... of low pursuits" and "trivial objects":

> Living amid the same perpetual flow
> Of trivial objects, melted and reduced
> To one identity, by differences
> That have no law, no meaning, and no end.
> (7.700–704)

Here it is precisely the spectacle of heterogeneity, of proliferating differences, that constitutes "the homogeneity of the bourgeois subject" (Stallybrass, 73). The spectator's identity and epistemological well-being are secured when the profusion of heterogeneous elements is itself "melted and reduced" to the "one identity" of lawlessness and meaninglessness, at the expense of *the invocation of the slave as trope* that serves to unify them and interestingly, turns the proliferation of categories into the collapse of all categories, which amounts to "one identity."[116]

Although the low, the depraved are often grouped together with the alien or the exotic (with more or less racial connotations) in these writings, the uncanny is also somehow domesticated, assimilated in the juxtaposition with the homely. One of the ways in which such domestication is achieved is to foreground the heterogeneity of this "indefinite, disintegrated mass," thus rendering it a spectacle, whether as the object of disgust, fascination, or pity (the multiplicity of the spectacle seems to ensure all of these sentiments). The objectification or theatricalization of what is to be represented consists in "the distance between spectator and spectacle"

---

116 As for the issue of the slaves, it wasn't until 1806, one year after the publication of *The Prelude*, that the British Parliament first passed a law ending the British slave trade to other countries and to its colonies (which is not the same as the abolition of slavery). Yet, in 1807, a proposal by Earl Percy for the gradual emancipation of slaves in the colonies was defeated and disavowed by the *abolitionists*. For detailed historical accounts of this topic, see Blackburn and Davis.

(Stallybrass, 74), yet this distance assumes more than the form of a detached (bourgeois) subject rising above the heterogeneous throng, observing from his supposedly secure point of view, and making a drama out of the inherently theatrical phenomenon. As Stallybrass argues, this social distance can be rewritten and reinforced by an alternative, strategic move that seems to abolish it: the masquerade or theatrical impersonation of the privileged subject. In this "controlled theatrical performance," "social differentiation was no more than the ability of the bourgeois subject to assume an endless multiplicity of roles" (73).

One prime example of the privileged bourgeois subject masquerading as an underclass, antisocial outcast of the counterculture can be found in the character Charlie in Kureishi's *The Buddha of Suburbia*. Charlie is a born Adonis who grew up in the comfort (and boredom, as the narrator emphasizes) of a bourgeois suburb of London and had unsuccessfully pursued fame and a career in music with a band featuring less talent than his pretty face. One night, Charlie and the narrator Karim inadvertently stumble into a live performance of a (then underground) punk band. After being showered with abuse, saliva and cacophony (from the stage as well as the audience) at the concert, Charlie, shaken up but suddenly realizing something, hooked himself up, in a most dramatic but straightforward fashion, with this bunch of obscenity-mouthing, spiky-haired kids in ripped black clothes who come from the rundown urban neighborhoods and whose main rituals of initiation include spitting and yelling at each other, at their fans, and regularly taunting and being beaten up by the police. As the punk kids were piling into a car after the concert, Charlie sprinted through the traffic toward them, ripped off his shirt, "bundled it up and threw it at a police car. Seconds later, he'd leapt into car with the kids, his bare torso on someone's lap on the front seat" (132). Before long, Charlie rises to stardom, now dubbed "Charlie Hero," with his beautiful but angry face appearing continually in the national papers, magazines, and TV shows—a veritable spectacle of heterogeneity.

Throughout his career, Charlie often seeks his "inspiration" or "inner self" by knowing, experiencing, and getting something—"a temporary, borrowed persona" (246)—out of a diverse bunch of interesting persons he invites to his place and sometimes sleeps with. His success hinges on the fact that "he'd assembled the right elements" to conjure up "a wonderful trick and disguise," as Karim puts it (154). An extreme and more comical case of experiencing, or literally "entering," a heterogeneous group of characters in life is Pyke, a self-described radical and reputed director of an "alternative theater" for whom Karim works. Pyke once confides to Karim that when he was nineteen he swore to dedicate himself to two things: "to becoming a brilliant director and to sleeping with as many women as [he] could." His hobbies include "attending orgies and New York fuck-clubs; and of the pleasure of finding unusual locations for the usual act, and unusual people to *perform* it with" (190; emphasis mine). So Pyke manages to combine his two ambitions in one bid—he is, in real life as well as in the theater, doing the directorial job of assembling characters and arranging acts and locations to live out his fantasies. This leads to his adventure with a policewoman, who recounts to Pyke her first-hand dealings with the street people of London, the lumpenproletariat. Yet he never tires of further expanding his repository of life experience, as he concludes his boasting by announcing that "I'm on the look-out for a scientist—an astronomer or nuclear physicist. I feel too arts-based intellectually" (190). Viewed under the rubric of contemporary multiculturalist glamorization of the proliferation of somewhat free-floating "subject positions" ready to be assumed, or as the celebration of the fashioning or performativity of identity as a subversive act, it seems necessary to question, in a novel such as this, which features characters who happen to be performers attempting to practice some sort of radical politics through apparently staged heterogeneity, whether it is the performance, the "free play" of multiple, heterogeneous "subject positions" that ends up containing, obfuscating, or even precluding the allegedly subversive force of the heterogeneous mass, of the lumpenproletariat.[117]

Hanif Kureishi and the postcolonial spectacle

We have seen that in the historical and literary instances examined above heterogeneity does not disrupt homogeneity, as it seems prone to doing,

---

117 Slavoj Žižek cautions us that "the much-celebrated playing with multiple, shifting personas (freely constructed identities) tends to obfuscate (and thus falsely liberate us from) the constraints of social space in which our existence is trapped." Such is the "space of *false disidentification*," where "the very distance towards the symbolic feature that determines my social place guarantees the efficiency of this determination" (*Contingency*, 103).

but can ensure homogenization or serves as its precondition when the existing socio-political structure is confronted with (or posits) a certain radical otherness, a nameless or unnamable thing that poses *a crisis of representation*. This peculiar phenomenon prompts Marx to rethink his class theory. In *The Eighteenth Brumaire*, Marx begins to explore the "contingencies of class": the notion that class can be considered "an unstable yoking together," through political rhetoric or state processes, of heterogeneous elements (Stallybrass, 70). The "lumpemproletariat" is the name Marx gives to a crisis in class representation (and differentiation); it exemplifies the formative (or even transformative) process that fashions classes out of radically heterogeneous groups, while testifying that they are nonetheless vulnerable to further homogenizing operations.[118] What is noteworthy is that the proletariat, before Marx's formulation and legitimization, was once "the lumpenproletariat" in the eyes of the bourgeois subject, a threatening, heterogeneous multitude that has to be excluded from the socio-political representations of the benign bourgeois order. This shift of the trope for heterogeneity *from the proletariat to the lumpenproletariat* is curiously parallel to the tropological mutation of heterogeneity *from the alien as a radical outside of the metropole to the postcolonial (alien) as a fetishized exotic or otherness* in the context of contemporary metropolitan multiculturalism.

In many ways, Kureishi's *The Buddha of Suburbia* is primarily concerned with such postcolonial exoticism, provoking the question of the theatricality of this latest brand of heterogeneity—of its rendering as spectacle—in the British context not only by (literally) putting on stage the spectacle of postcolonial heterogeneity itself, but also by thematizing a political radicalism that seems to inevitably surround this staging of the postcolonial spectacle (as response, a critique, or accomplice). To begin with, "the Buddha of suburbia," as highlighted in the title, refers to Haroon Amir, father of the protagonist Karim. Cashing in on fashionable bourgeois curiosity with the exotic mysticism of the Orient in a quest for alternative spiritual experiences, Haroon, with the brokerage of Eva Kay, who later becomes his mistress, offers yoga and meditation sessions in middle-

---

118 The main case in point in *The Eighteenth Brumaire* is Napoleon III, whose rise to power counted on the support of an extraordinarily diverse constituency of radically heterogeneous groups. In terms of the challenge it poses to Marx's theory of the state, Bonapartism signals a state that represented no one but itself (cf. Stallybrass, 79).

class homes in the London suburbs, where everyone "looked keenly and expectantly at him" (13). His "gigs" in a sense epitomize the spectacle of postcolonial exoticism, evoking the performance of a "magician," as one of the spectators puts it (31). Although his guru-like antics reveal the inner emptiness of his credulous audience, Haroon, as Graham Huggan contends, "has arguably succeeded only in exchanging one form of mimicry for another" (96). For, as Karim muses, his dad has "spent years trying to be more of an Englishman, to be less risibly conspicuous, and now he was putting it back in spadeloads" (21). Toward the beginning of the novel, Kureishi foregrounds, as he does repeatedly throughout the text, an ironic distance from the growing fetishistic exoticism that appears to relish, and at the same time objectify, the colonial products which now seem to be more readily available close to home. When Karim, a teenager at the time, arrived at a party with his father, the hostess Eva gave Karim a typically Orientalist greeting, as Karim recalls: "holding me at arm's length as if I were a coat she was about to try on, she looked at me all over and said, 'Karim Amir, you are so exotic, so original! It's such a contribution! It's so you!'" (9).

To be exact, Karim is not as authentic as advertised, since he is the son of an Indian father and an English mother, but later on, the question of "authenticity" crops up again in a truly dramatic fashion, when Karim, as a novice actor, is asked by the director Jeremy Shadwell to perform an Indian accent during a rehearsal of Kipling's children's classic *The Jungle Book*:

> Shadwell took me aside and said, 'A word about the accent, Karim. I think it should be an authentic accent.'
> 'What d'you mean authentic?'
> 'Where was our Mowgli [Karim's part] born?'
> 'India.'
> 'Yes. Not Orpington [Karim's birthplace]. What accent do they have in India?'
> 'Indian accents.'
> 'Ten out of ten.'
> 'No, Jeremy. Please, no.'
> 'Karim, you have been cast for authenticity and not for experience.' (147)

Just why exactly he pleads to decline this request is never defined, but under no circumstance could Karim win this fight: he would betray himself by doing the accent because it isn't his own and he has never been to India; he would risk losing his job if he refuses to pander to racist/colonialist stereotyping (later on that accent proves amusing to the white audience at the preview.) Or, rather, it is possible that Karim resists putting on the accent, and making a fool of himself, simply because he has internalized white prejudices against Indian accents, costumes, and the other alleged markers of authenticity of which he presumably should have been proud. But if this were the case, then it would also bring to the fore the dilemma facing the call for the self-affirmation, for legitimate reasons, of stigmatized or marginalized group identities, which, in the context of metropolitan centers of the former empires, emerge in the form of a proliferation of authentic, particularistic identities.

While assimilation can be damaging to endangered minority cultures and perpetuates relations of domination, the "real thing" can be a prized commodity in the market of cultural consumption (in which the valorization of its authenticity may further raise the bidding price). The postcolonial exotic, whether truly authentic or not, also tends to be "museumized," securely displayed on (the margins of) the metropolitan cultural scene without undermining or disturbing the existing structure of cultural, political, and economic domination. What follows Karim's disagreement with Shadwell seems to illustrate the way the fetishistic, domesticating logic of the spectacle works. In the end, Karim relents and gives in to Shadwell's demand for the accent, along with the uncomfortable costumes and brown make-up. But no sooner has he pandered to the stereotypes than he starts to relish "being the pivot of the production" (150) and the benefits that come with it: asking for favors or even privileges at the theater, during rehearsals, sometimes at the expense of the other actors. He moves, self-consciously or cynically perhaps, from a position of resistance to one of complicity in the construction of the postcolonial exotic. Similarly, though Haroon's gigs can be seen as a way of exposing "the self-serving enthusiasms of his captive audience," they are nonetheless caught up in the fetishistic logic of the "post-1960s commodification of Eastern spirituality," since for the bourgeois subject "Eastern philosophizing is little more than the latest temporary panacea to their middle-class suburban boredom" (Huggan, 96).

Though ostensibly well-meaning and sympathetic to their racial Other (compared with the brute colonialist/imperialist putdowns of an earlier era), the white audience's enthusiasm for the authenticity of cultural otherness drives a fetishistic logic of spectacularization that turns on, and is coextensive with, a relentless commodificaiton of the alleged "authenticity." Such "passion for the Real," paradoxically, ends up culminating "in its apparent opposite, in a *theatrical spectacle*" (Žižek, *Welcome*, 9).[119] For what is really appealing (though unacknowledged) to the metropolitan eye is the theatricality of the Other, not the "real thing" itself, which is decontextualized—out of its "authentic" context—the moment it is rendered a spectacle. Yet if the white spectator is in a sense duped by his/her own expectations of a staged heterogeneity, which is securely encoded in, rather than hazardously decoding, an elaborate set of racial/colonialist representations of the Other, the culturally dominated (and consumed) performer does not fare better in this regard, since Karim is also implicated in this logic of spectacle which demands, however speciously, the authentic. Knowing that he is by no means authentic, Karim, who was born in England, racially and culturally hybrid, and sexually ambiguous, attempts in his next play to search for what he calls "the additional personality bonus of an Indian past" (213) by basing his character on the more "authentic" Indians he knows (since in this particular production, the actors, as well as the playwright, were invited to create characters out of their life experiences before the script was sent through workshops where the actors interact).

Karim's attempt to play Uncle Anwar the way he was in real life—as someone who staged a hunger-strike in order to force his politically progressive daughter, Jamila, to agree to an arranged marriage—may have been spawned by an innocent, well-intentioned adherence to truth—"A higher value," as Karim puts it (181); however, this radical following through of the demand for authenticity (as the "true story" not of a typical Indian, but of this particular Indian immigrant) cannot be immune to the logic of spectacle and the stereotyped, derogatory portrayals normally associated with it. This problematic is acutely foregrounded in the dialogue between Karim and the black girl Tracey—the other "minority" member of the theater—during a workshop:

> 'I'm afraid it shows black people—'
> 'Indian people—'
> 'Black and Asian people—'
> 'One old Indian man—'
> 'As being irrational, ridiculous, as being hysterical. And as being fanatical.' (180)

---

119 Make no mistake: the "Real" here is not the Lacanian real; rather, it is, as Žižek puts it, "a fake passion whose ruthless pursuit of the Real behind appearances [is] *the ultimate stratagem to avoid confronting the Real* [the Lacanian one]" (*Welcome*, 24).

The white members of this self-described radical theater company responded to this conversation with uneasy silence, until the director Pyke overrules, political-correctly, Karim's representation of the Indian character. After being spurned by the group, Karim moves on to base his character on Changez, but he is still caught up in the pursuit of authenticity, acting more as a native informer, a broker, an agent who *mediates or figures a radical otherness* than as the "real thing," the Other who is supposed to know—when Changez vehemently rejects being used in his performance, Karim panics because he "didn't know any other 'black' people" (185). Though defiant against what he alleges to be "censorship" (inappropriate or unauthorized portrayal of the minority), Karim goes on to play Changez (now called Tariq in the play) anyway, breaking his promise to a friend. His pursuit of authenticity, like "the passion for the Real," also winds up succumbing, even though self-consciously, to the white expectations of theatrical spectacle and stereotype, as he admits: "At night, at home, I was working on Changez's shambolic walk and crippled hand, and on the accent, which I knew would sound, to white ears, bizarre, funny and *characteristic of India*" (188–189; emphasis mine).

Commodity fetishism and resistance as spectacle

I'd like to approach the volatile issues of political radicalism inevitably teased out by the novel by a more theoretical exploration of the exotic and the spectacle under the rubric of present-day postcolonial discourses, with reference to our earlier discussion of heterogeneity. Exoticism, in its variegated (historical) forms, is characterized mainly by "the *aesthetics of decontextualisation* and *commodity fetishism*" (Huggan, 16; emphasis in original).[120] Originating from a radical otherness, a threatening heterogeneity, the exotic is to be kept at a safe distance, preferably purged of its more unappetizing aspects (brutality inflicted on the colonized, menial living conditions in the colonies, etc.). Concurrent with the contemporary influx of immigrants from former colonies to the metropolitan centers and the ensuing cultural diversification, the appeal of the postcolonial exotic lies precisely in the status that it comes from far-off places yet remains

---

120 Huggan gives a quite comprehensive yet succinct review of the significant scholarship on exoticism in the Introduction to his book (13–20).

within reach at the same time. The celebration of allegedly dissolving borders and an increasing sense of interconnectedness under the rubric of globalization usher in a new generic form of exoticism "suitable for all markets" (Gallini, 219), and this appears to enhance, more than anything else, the "availability of society's other as a source of commercial spectacle" (Huggan, xiv). As Huggan insightfully argues, "the exoticist rhetoric of fetishised otherness and sympathetic identification masks the inequality of power relations without which the discourse could not function" (14). Such masking involves the displacement and/or transformation of a pivotal yet less visible power-political structure into *spectacle* (Arac and Ritvo, 3). It is this structure, with its elaborate set of relations, from which the exotic is to be decontextualized en route to its aestheticization as spectacle.

Talk of commodity fetishism—with its attention on commercial spectacle—is, of course, hardly new, as it dates back to Marx. Yet the Marxian analysis of commodity fetishism is more than the covering up of the processes and material conditions under which commodities are produced, disseminated, and consumed. As Giorgio Agamben comments on the chapter of *Capital* on commodity fetishism, one of Marx's insights (or one of the insights he inspired) is that the "disclosure of the commodity's 'secret' was the key that revealed capital's enchanted realm to our thought—*a secret that capital always tried to hide by exposing it in full view*" (*Means without End*, 75; emphasis mine).[121] Aptly citing the example of the Crystal Palace exhibited in the first Universal Exposition in Hyde Park in 1851, Agamben contends that "the first great triumph of the commodity thus takes place under the sign of both transparency and phantasmagoria" (74–75). This logic of the spectacle, of concealment by exposure, further illuminates the literary and historical examples discussed earlier in which the spectacle masks or eclipses some constitutive heterogeneity the moment the latter is spectacularized (we shall return shortly to this point by examining another case). These two characteristics of the spectacle—transparency and phantasmagoria—need to be underscored here because

---

121 Agamben recounts that in the 1960s, Marx's reflections on commodity fetishism were "foolishly abandoned" by Marxist circles (and dismissed, in the spirit of the times, by some circles of contemporary radical intellectuals) (75). Against this intellectual backdrop, the prescience of Debord's analysis of the spectacle, as the vantage point from which to look back at the developments of historical events, appears even more remarkable (80).

contemporary commodity spectacle, phantasmatic as ever, has taken an increasingly abstract form—abstract in the sense that it's rendered substance-less, depth-less, rooted in nothing but its appearance. For, as Fredric Jameson famously argues, postmodernism is characterized mainly by the consumption of "sheer commodificaiton as a process," rather than that of commodities themselves (x). In other words, the spectacle invokes phantasmagoria beyond the individual image/commodity itself, and if what's appealing is the process of fetishization and not the "thing" itself, then the substance-less, mere appearance of the spectacle, its appearing transparent, is also its best disguise.

The commodity spectacle therefore constitutes a "reign of abstraction" based on what Marx calls the "power of real abstraction" of capital (qtd. in Žižek, *Totalitarianism*, 2). That is why Guy Debord, who extends Marx's idea of commodity fetishism and provides perhaps the most comprehensive, penetrating, and enduringly provocative (or provocatively enduring) study of the spectacle, envisions a ubiquitous spectacle which operates in a highly abstract fashion:

> The spectacle is not a collection of images; rather, it is a social relationship between people that is mediated by images.
> The spectacle cannot be understood either as a deliberate distortion of the visual world or as a product of the technology of the mass dissemination of images. It is far better viewed as a weltanschauung that has been actualized, translated into the material world—a world view transformed into an objective force. (12-13)

What Debord conceives as "the society of the spectacle" is, as Agamben puts it, "a capitalism that has reached its extreme figure," where "the commodity's last metamorphosis" results in the phenomenon in which "exchange value has completely eclipsed use value and can now achieve the status of absolute and irresponsible sovereignty over life in its entirety" (76). In all its manifestations in different areas of the social field, the fetishistic logic of the spectacle, it would seem, spares no one, even those who profess to challenge its airtight, omnipresent rule: threatening heterogeneous elements can become equivalent to commodities and the proliferation of differences usually accompanying them turns out to be a spectacle of commodification.

In a more specifically postcolonial context, the spectacle consists in a dazzling array of heterogeneous elements (in terms of geography, race, ethnicity, nationality, class, culture, sexuality, etc.) fraught with the rhetoric of resistance, antagonism, cultural embattlement, and, as in the case of Kureishi, "fashionable provocation" (Huggan, 94). Critics have pointed out varying degrees of the complicity of postcolonial cultural and literary discourses—despite their anti-imperialist, and more generally, anti-establishment, or anti-foundationalist gestures—with the global market of cultural commodification (which in the context of our discussion, may be termed the logic of the commodity spectacle).[122] How, then, does what might be dubbed "syndicated oppositionality" of the postcolonial (Dirlik, 356) become a (hot) commodity? Here Huggan's formulation of "the constitutive split within the postcolonial" (ix) appears to grasp the heart of the matter: "the global concerns of postcolonialism meet . . . with a different kind of globalism—the postcoloniality of the universal market. The well-intentioned desire for 'adversarial internationalization'—for the fashioning of global solidarities in the continuing anti-imperial struggle—must contend with the power of a market that seeks, in part, to contain such oppositional gestures" (10–11).

This susceptibility, or even complicity of radical politics (of postcolonialism) with the spectacle of postcolonial commodification is fittingly epitomized in the scene where Pyke, as the director of a self-designated radical theater, approves and unabashedly announces the synopsis of their upcoming production after Karim briefs the group about his work on the Changez character (now called Tariq): "'Tariq comes to England, meets an English journalist on the plane . . . . This is real quality, upper-class crumpet. He is briefly among the upper classes because of her, which gives us another area to examine! Girls fall for him all over the place because of his weakness and need to be mothered. So. *We have class, race, fucking and farce. What more could you want as an evening's entertainment?*'" (189; emphasis mine). Ethnic minorities or the culturally dominated, for more than economic reasons, are likely to be susceptible to this logic of the spectacle, to accommodate to expected "authenticity"—the theatrical effect of the spectacle, even as they are self-consciously aware of such expectation,

---

122 The most notable and fierce critiques of this sort are levied by Aijaz Ahmad, Timothy Brennan, Arif Dirlik, E. San Juan, Jr., and Stuart Hall, though Hall is adamantly critical of what he perceives as reductionist dismissals by more orthodox Marxists, particularly Dirlik. See Hall, 258–259.

or strategically use it as a means of resistance, as Kureishi apparently does in much of his work.[123]

It is not hard to discern the inherently contradictory tendencies within postcolonial theory itself: on the one hand, it is characterized by a celebration of the proliferation of differences and its insistence on increasingly marginal and particularistic identities; on the other hand, its glorification of the effacement of boundaries of all kinds, of a borderless globality, of indeterminacy and in-between hybridity, appears to amount to the obliteration, and even overcoming of all difference. For instance, Peter Hallward remarks that "postcolonial theory often seems to present itself as a sort of general theory of the non-generalisable as such" (xi). Self-consciously or unwittingly, the postcolonial spectacle of heterogeneity, as a putatively particularizing tendency and rhetoric of resistance, ends up sustaining a seemingly totalizing or universalizing force of the global commodification of the spectacle, much like the literary and historical examples examined earlier, where heterogeneous elements, instead of undermining homogeneity, are mobilized to stabilize an emerging or existing socio-political order and are subject to further homogenization when they are rendered as spectacle. The eventual surrender of the allegedly thriving multiplicity of the contemporary lumpenproletariat to the homogenizing force of the spectacle is also ominously anticipated in Debord's vision, as Agamben, with today's new global order in mind, points out: "It is clear that the society of the spectacle is also one in which all social identities have dissolved . . . . The different identities that have marked the tragicomedy of universal history are exposed and gathered with a phantasmagorical vacuity in the global petite bourgeoisie—a petite bourgeoisie that constitutes the form in which the spectacle has realized parodistically the Marxian project of a classless society" (87-88).

---

123 One way to trump the relentless entrapment of being commodified is to stage this problematic—that is, foregrounding or bracketing it in a theatrical framework. As Kureishi demonstrates in the novel, the minority is represented as a commodity spectacle in the play produced by a supposedly sympathetic, politically progressive group. This, however, doesn't mean Kureishi's novel, and his work in general, can escape being a marketable commodity; it just gains some self-reflexive perspective, critiquing such commodification by laying bare its machinery.

Revisiting the postcolonial problematic

That the unprecedented mass migration of postcolonial subjects brings to the fore a sense of social crisis in the former colonial metropoles, whether in the form of xenophobia or white guilt, hardly needs to be stated, but this immigrant/alien figure also engenders a new crisis of representation in the metropolitan centers in the postcolonial era (if it can ever be periodized). The tired, irresolvable, and sometimes unproductive disputes regarding the ever elusive definition(s) of the "postcolonial" allow this term to function as some sort of catch-all metaphor for, among other things, "cultural embattlement" (Suleri, 759). This difficulty in naming an existing (or emerging) set of conditions, coupled with the felt need to urgently respond to the hitherto marginalized or excluded, may have given rise to the speciously wide range of parameters of postcolonial studies—a symptom most visibly evidenced by recent postcolonial readers or anthologies. Citing a recent example, Hallward observes:

> The recent *Companion to Postcolonial Studies* (eds. Schwarz and Ray, 2000), for instance, in addition to theoretical reviews of imperialism, colonialism, hybridity, postmodernism, multiculturalism, transnationalism, feminism, queer theory, and English studies, includes more empirically focused surveys of topics ranging from patriotic literature in South Asia, Arabic literature in the 'middle east', the handover of Hong Kong, 'Japan and East Asia' and 'failed narratives of the nation in late colonial Java', to studies of 'settler colonies', 'Ireland after history', orality in the Caribbean, and 'Africa: varied colonial legacies'. (336)

This grouping or proliferation of heterogeneous categories, this academic production of the postcolonial, is no doubt part of the postcolonial spectacle of heterogeneity.

As illustrated earlier, in moments of crisis, an ostensibly radical outside (which is not really outside but a constitutive exclusion)[124] is mobilized to bring about an emergent hegemony, or stabilize, reinforce an existing or emerging force of domination or homogenization.[125] Once the

---

124 A theoretical homology of such a "constitutive exception" is offered by Agamben's conception of "bare life" (*zoē*) vis-à-vis the political life (*bios politikos*) in his book *Homo Sacer: Sovereign Power and Bare LIfe*. According to Agamben, *zoē*, "which expressed the simple fact of living common to all living beings" (1), serves as "an inclusive exclusion" in the *polis* (7). Bare life, with its "natural sweetness," "remains included in politics in the form of the exception, that is, as something that is included solely through an exclusion" (11).

125 This homogenizing force or operation is *not* necessarily reactionary, but can also be revolutionary/progressive. See Fanon's interpretation of the lumpenproletariat in decolonizing nationalism (*Wretched*, 135).

heterogeneous is invoked and rendered as spectacle, it becomes part of the representational system, in the form of an *internal* or already integrated element of the system, however marginal it appears in that socio-symbolic order: The alien figure is summoned to be *radically excluded* from the social order that has hitherto included the proletariat and now attempts to accommodate the crisis posed by the lumpenproletariat; in the same way, in an earlier era the once unrepresentable "lumpenproletariat" (not yet a word) had been invoked, under the name "proletariat" (still a dirty word at the time), to guard the bourgeois order against the threat of a growing working-class. In addition to the historical instances and literary instances mentioned above, we draw on the theoretical insight that a constitutive heterogeneity is the precondition, the founding exception of a homogeneous system, one that has to be presupposed yet foreclosed.[126] Such heterogeneity, however, seems always destined to be recognized as spectacle. If the spectacle of heterogeneity, as our earlier examples show, functions strictly as trope, obliterating a certain constitutive heterogeneity, what does the postcolonial spectacle mask, or more precisely, foreclose?

I propose that the multicultural, liberal-democratic postcolonial metropoles that constitute the globalizing new world order are made possible only on the basis of the former colonizer's forgetting their colonialist past and the continuing economic exploitation and cultural domination which serve as the foundation of this new order. Barnor Hesse points out what might be called the traumatic kernel of postcolonial memory—"the West's liberal-democratic culture of de/colonial fantasy," by which Hesse means:

> Those Western attitudes, practices, and discourses that *imagine against the evidence, against counter-interrogation*, the comprehensive undertaking and successful completion of decolonization, both within the metropolis and the former colonies

---

126 Here a nuanced distinction has to be made between the radically heterogeneous and the particular. The heterogeneous, in the context of our discussion, is that which is not (yet) representable, or a radical difference not yet integrated in any perceptible way into a given socio-political-symbolic order (but we are not talking about any absolute or perpetual incommensurability). On the other hand, the particular is one term of the representational system, as a difference already integrated or internal to it. In terms of social antagonism (as we're dealing with political radicalism here), heterogeneity signals radical antagonism, which, as Laclau and Mouffe conceive it, is irreducible to antagonistic relations *between* particular sectors in a given social order but can only be represented through the *particular differences* internal to that order. See Chapter 1 for similar lines of argument.

or sites of racial segregation. At the same time, the notion of decolonization must be wrested from the provenance of a Western liberal-democratic tradition that disavows how it was bitterly fought and grudgingly conceded every step of the way. (159; emphasis in original)

Interestingly, this "de/colonial fantasy" isn't lived out in the postcolonial spectacle itself, which is usually presented as something quite different. For the most riveting yet misleading view of the potentially multivalent postcolonial spectacle revolves on postcolonial failure or predicament as spectacle, with the TV screen bombarding the Western spectator with images of Third World catastrophe, atrocity, or misery. Once again, the staging and restaging of the spectacle of heterogeneity, paradoxically, winds up ensuring the obliteration or disavowal of what is constitutive of the spectacle. It is perceived as *a radical outside*, not only because of the great physical distance but also because of the "time lag" linked to the very designation of the "*post*colonial" that renders colonialism a thing of the past, having nothing to do with present-day metropoles. Yet this spectacle is at the same time *intimately at home* not only due to the proximity of the TV screen, but also thanks to the fact that it allows for the reinscription of (post)colonial memory in the "minority" or "ethnic" cultures readily available in the metropolis.

If, as the historical and literary representations of the proletariat and the lumpenproletariat exemplify, the success of the dominating force to defuse social crisis or consolidate its dominance lies in "the availability of society's other as . . . spectacle" (Huggan, xiv), then the danger of the proverbially antagonistic rhetoric of the postcolonial lurks on two fronts which are often entangled with each other: 1) spatially, it reveals a presumed domestication of the Third World in the former (or new) metropolitan centers, a presumption that has become so pervasive and quotidian that postcoloniality is often presented in terms of the cosmopolitan postcolonial's valorization of his/her marginality in, and preoccupation with, the metropoles; 2) temporally, it implies a premature celebration of the end of colonialism, in its variegated forms, or the jettisoning of an allegedly outdated mode of resistance (namely, decolonization), while disavowing the legacies or lingering effects of colonization persisting within and beyond the borders of both the Western and the postcolonial nation-states.

This false sense of "domesticated postcoloniality" has, of course, its consequences. Some postcolonial critics situated in US academia even flirt with duplicating the typical American-centric worldview by suggesting that the recent boom of Third World literatures is the natural outgrowth of American minority discourses: "the political context for the study of postcolonial literature was created in the American academy by feminist and Afro-American critiques of the literary canon, critiques *that were echoed in the international scene* by writers such as Chinua Achebe and Ngugi wa Thiong'o" (Mohan, 30; qtd. in Huggan, 242; Huggan's emphasis). Yet even if we rectify the historical trajectories and give credit to the transnational postcolonial writers, this "international scene" covers little more than the metropolitan centers of former empires, since the word "postcolonial" appears to resonate quite differently in different parts of the globe. R. Radhakrishnan, for instance, asks a question that is probably on the mind of many Third World intellectuals not trained in Western academic institutions: "Why is it that the term 'postcoloniality' has found such urgent currency in the First World but is in fact hardly ever used within the excolonized worlds of South Asia and Africa?" (750)

In the postcolonial context, the exotic immigrant tends to figure, or evoke, an *authentic alien*, someone who is really "out there," some radical otherness that is, however, securely displayed "on the screen" or on stage (hence Karim is cast as a "real Indian"). The postcolonial, therefore, *points to* a "real thing" not yet named or not yet namable—an unthinkable monstrosity, an inassimilable heterogeneity. But when the alien becomes a domesticated figure of the postcolonial Third World, that radical outside of the global metropolis, both as an actual existence and a postulated "otherworld," it evaporates from metropolitan memory in tandem with the purportedly disappearing borders concurrent with an expanding globality. Or rather, what remains is the spectacle of the "postcolonial failure" of the world of post-independence ex-colonies, a spectacle in which the perennial failure to establish democracy, the cycles of dictatorial rule, the violent ethnic conflict, corruption, economic dependency, and mass poverty amount to sheer theatrical effects—to such an extent that metropolitan spectators seem not to hesitate to absolve themselves of the kind of economic exploitation and cultural domination characteristic of colonial relations and that still characterize, though in a less conspicuous way, contemporary relationships between the ex-colonizer and the ex-colonized.

Such misperception of the cessation of formal colonization brings us to the temporal dimension of the postcolonial problematic. Linking the postcolonial phenomenon to earlier discourses of exoticism, Huggan contends that "the postcolonial exotic, like postcolonial criticism itself, registers continuities with the earlier historical paradigms it believes itself to have outgrown. The exotic, we might then say, is the *ghost* that comes back to haunt the corridors of postcolonial critical history" (243; emphasis mine). If the exotic is the ghost that returns to haunt the institutional or disciplinary history of the postcolonial, what is the unappeased or implacable phantom lurking in the "actual" history of the postcolonial? I would argue that the parallel I've drawn between literary and historical examples of different eras represents less historical continuities than variegated forms of the *specter* of the historical trauma of colonialism. Such "undead colonialism" returns to undermine any rigid periodization of (post)colonial histories by showing, for instance, "how decolonized situations are marked by the trace of imperial pasts they try to disavow" (Gikandi, 15), or by disrupting the former empire's fantasy in which the memory of colonialism is constructed as the memory of its *fait accompli* decolonization. I draw on Hesse's argument that the de/colonial fantasy of the West results in its "memory of slavery as *the memory of its abolition*" (149; emphasis in original). If the spectacle, as Agamben contends, "still contains something like a positive possibility—and it is our task to use this possibility against it," then that possibility, I argue, would be the spectrality constitutive of the spectacle. Our task, in the context of our discussion, would be to invoke this spectrality by confronting and remembering properly the historical trauma of colonialism.

Epilogue

> What does a man want?
> What does the black man want? . . . .
> The black is a black man; that is, as the result of a series of aberrations of affect, he is rooted *at the core of a universe from which he must be extricated.*
>
> Frantz Fanon[127]

This book took shape as an attempt to address a central question that preoccupies the terrain of postcolonial studies as well as contemporary theory of radical politics in general: In the ambiance of the increasing celebration of marginalized, particularistic positions or identities, coupled with a growing dismissal of or discontent with universalist categories, *how do the particulars articulate themselves*? Do the particulars valorize themselves simply by virtue of being particular and without recourse to the universal, or have they already reinscribed themselves in the universal en route to a contestatory articulation against or "negotiation" with the universal? The model of negotiation or reinscription may be a rote, if not unsatisfactory, one, depending on where you stand in the postcolonial world. As argued in this book (Chapter 1), it is not enough to stand up against the dominant order as a particular, which can be grasped, delineated, compartmentalized in terms of difference and can be readily incorporated into a system of differential relations—as part of the system. We've pointed to, rather, a "part of no part," a radical exclusion on which an antagonistic universal is to be based. It is, however, a constitutive exclusion, an *internal limit* "rooted at the core of a universe from which [it] must be extricated." The postulation of such a radically excluded element from the socio-symbolic field of (post)colonial struggles, is, however, what makes possible the grounds of contestatory articulations and opens up the possibility for the particulars to find empowerment in the (another) universal, rather than contending

---

127 These lines are quoted from Fanon's *Black Skin, White Masks*, 8; emphasis mine. If Fanon is to be credited as a precursor of postcolonial studies, then this dual question, "What does a man want?/What does the black man want?" seems to presage postcolonialism's sometimes unacknowledged, yet inescapable struggle between the universal and the particular.

to be (and being content with being) identified as "particulars." The latter, at least, is not what I gathered from reading Fanon.[128] The emancipation from power lies, paradoxically, in power (Laclau *Contingency*, 208).

Post-Revolutionary Haiti prefigured and heralded the spectacle of postcolonial failure that serves as an "inclusive exclusion," a disavowed precondition of a thriving capitalist-democratic world order going by the name of globalization, where the harsh realities in the former colonies are perceived as otherworldly spectacle, staged as a potential threat to the spectator so as to justify the latter's continuing dominance. In the metropoles, the "postcolonial" is often used to market an innocuous exoticism, or prematurely celebrate the pastness of colonialism, thereby conveniently supporting the former's colonizer's "de/colonial fantasy" as well as its disavowal of ongoing economic exploitation and cultural domination.

As in all systems, a borderless or non-differential globality is theoretically possible only when confronted with or positing a radical otherness as a threat whose unannounced, unaccounted-for exclusion enables the constitution of the system in the first place. This radically heterogeneous element, which has no place in the reigning representational system, hence poses a spectral existence vis-à-vis capitalist globalization, since it's at once inside and outside the system; however, it can only be articulated through some homogenizing, domesticating force and is thus constantly subject to the logic of the spectacle. Any attempt to break free of a systematic domination (of globalization, for example) can only resort to a certain homogenizing force that invokes and mobilizes the most heterogeneous elements, a collective struggle based on equivalential logic, and a universalist ground that brings to the fore the internal limit of the existing system. As we've mentioned in Chapter 4, the potential overcoming of such an inclination to spectacularization lies precisely in a recourse to the irreducible spectrality of the spectacle itself—not by making it even more particularized, marginal, or inaccessible, but, on the contrary, by connecting to the internal limit of *all*. In the context of the predicament presented by the postcolonial spectacle, I would venture to say that it can only be overcome by shifting the postcolonial preoccupation with the metropoles, which is symbiotic

---

128 I am well aware of the divergent interpretations and appropriations of Fanon—one poststructuralist, the other humanist/activist. See Gordon, Sharpley-Whiting, and White's Introduction to *Fanon: A Critical Reader*, and Alessandrini's Introduction to *Frantz Fanon: Critical Perspectives*.

with rendering postcolonial misery as insulated spectacle, and by effecting a change in the peripheries the postcolonial critic left behind, a change that would have definitive repercussions in the metropoles where he/she resides, just like the Haitian Revolution on its French counterpart, or Toussaint's Africa project, had he been fortunate enough to begin to undertake it.

About the Author

Dr. Li-Chun Hsiao studied Comparative Literature in University at Buffalo (State University of New York), specializing in Postcolonial Studies, Literary and Cultural Theories, and Caribbean Literatures. Having taught at National Chiao Tung University and National Taiwan University, Hsiao is currently Associate Professor at Waseda University in Tokyo, teaching at its School of International Liberal Studies as well as Graduate School of International Culture and Communication Studies. Previously, he was the Editor-in-Chief of *Chung Wai Literary Quarterly* (2015–2017), served on the Editorial Board of *Concentric: Literary and Cultural Studies*, and has been a Visiting Scholar at Hitotsubashi University in Tokyo and at UCLA. Hsiao edits, introduces, and contributes a chapter to the book *"This Shipwreck of Fragments": Historical Memory, Imaginary Identities, and Postcolonial Geography in Caribbean Culture and Literature* (Cambridge Scholars Publishing 2009), and has book chapters collected in the edited volumes *Representing Humanity in an Age of Terror* (Purdue UP 2010), *Comparatizing Taiwan* (Routledge 2015), and *Keywords of Taiwan Theory* (Unitas 2019). His papers have been published by, among other journals, *Critical Arts* (2020), *Chungwai Literary Quarterly* (2014), *Concentric: Literary and Cultural Studies* (2010), *CLCWeb: Comparative Literature and Culture* (2009), and *M/MLA Journal* (2008).

Bibliography

Agamben, Giorgio. *Homo Sacer: Sovereign Power and Bare Life.* Trans. Daniel Heller-Roazen. Stanford, California: Stanford UP, 1998.

---. *Means without End: Notes on Politics.* Trans. Vincenzo Binetti and Cesare Casarino. Minneapolis: U of Minnesota P, 2000.

Ahmad, Aijaz. *In Theory: Classes, Nations, Literatures.* London: Verso, 1992.

---. "The Politics of Literary Postcoloniality." *Race & Class.* 36.3 (1995): 1–20.

Alessandrini, Anthony C., ed. *Frantz Fanon: Critical Perspectives.* New York: Routledge, 1999.

Anderson, Benedict. *Imagined Communities: Reflections on the Origin and Spread of Nationalism.* Rev. ed. London: Verso, 1991.

---. *The Spectre of Comparison: Nationalism, Southeast Asia and the World.* London: Verso, 2000.

Ansell-Pearson, Keith, Benita Parry, and Judith Squires. *Cultural Readings of Imperialism: Edward Said and the Gravity of History.* New York: St. Martin's Press, 1997.

Appiah, Kwame Anthony. *In My Father's House: Africa in the Philosophy of Culture.* New York: Oxford UP, 1992.

---. "Is the Post- in Postmodernism the Post- in Postcolonial?" *Contemporary Postcolonial Theory: A Reader.* Ed. Padmini Mongia. London: Arnold, 1996. 55–71.

Ashcroft, Bill, Gareth Griffiths, and Helen Tiffin. *The Empire Writes Back.* London: Routledge, 1989.

Badie, Bertrand. *The Imported State: The Westernization of the Political Order.* Trans. Claudia Royal. Stanford, California: Stanford UP, 2000.

Badiou, Alain. *Ethics: An Essay on the Understanding of Evil.* Trans. Peter Hallward. London: Verso, 2001.

---. *Saint Paul: The Foundation of Universalism.* Trans. Ray Brassier. Stanford, California: Stanford UP, 2003.

Balibar, Etienne. "Ambiguous Universality." *differences.* 7.1 (Spring 1995): 48–73.

Balibar, Etienne, and Immanuel Wallerstein. *Race, Nation, Class: Ambiguous Identities.* Trans. Chris Turner. London: Verso, 1991.

Bataille, Georges. *Visions of Excess.* Ed. and trans. Allan Stoekl. Minneapolis: University of Minnesota Press, 1985.

Bhabha, Homi K. "DissemiNation." *Nation and Narration.* Ed. Homi Bhabha. London: Routledge, 1990. 291–322.

---. "Minority Maneuvers and Unsettled Negotiations." *Critical Inquiries.* 23.3 (Spring 1997): 431–59.

---. *The Location of Culture.* London: Routledge, 1994.

---. "The Third Space." Interview with Jonathan Rutherford. *Identity: Community, Culture, Difference.* Ed. Jonathan Rutherford. London: Lawrence & Wishart, 1990. 207–21.

---. "Postcolonial Criticism." *Redrawing the Boundaries: The Transformation of English and American Literary Studies.* Eds. Stephan Greenblatt and Giles Gunn. NY: Modern Language Association, 1992. 437–466.

Blackburn, Robin. *The Overthrow of Colonial Slavery, 1776–1848.* London: Verso, 1988.

Brennan, Timothy. "From Development to Globalization: Postcolonial Studies and Globalization Theory." *The Cambridge Companion to Postcolonial Literary Studies.* Ed. Neil Lazarus. Cambridge, UK: Cambridge UP, 2004.

---. *At Home in the World: Cosmopolitanism Now.* Cambridge, Massachusetts: Harvard UP, 1997.

Breslin, Paul. *Nobody's Nation: Reading Derek Walcott.* Chicago: U of Chicago P, 2001.

Buell, Frederic. *National culture and the New Global System.* Baltimore: The John Hopkins UP, 1994.

Butler, Judith. *Gender Trouble: Feminism and the Subversion of Identity.* New York: Routledge, 1990.

Butler, Judith, and Ernesto Laclau. "Uses of Equality." *Diacritics.* 27.1 (1997): 3–12.

---, Ernesto Laclau, and Slavoj Žižek. *Contingency, Hegemony, and Universality: Contemporary Dialogues on the Left.* London: Verso, 2000.

Caruth, Cathy. *Unclaimed Experience: Trauma, Narrative, and History.* Baltimore: John Hopkins UP, 1996.

Césaire, Aimé. *Discourse on Colonialism.* New York: Monthly Review Press, 1972.

---. *Toussaint Louverture: la Revolution francaise et le probleme colonial.* Paris: Presence africaine, 1962.

---. *The Tragedy of King Christophe: a Play.* Trans. Ralph Manheim. New York: Grove Press, 1970.

Chambers, Iain. "Signs of Silence, Lines of Listening." *The Post-Colonial Question: Common Skies, Divided Horizons.* Eds. Iain Chambers and Lidia Curi. London: Routledge, 1996.

Chatterjee, Partha. *The Nation and Its Fragments: Colonial and Postcolonial Histories*. Princeton, New Jersey: Princeton UP, 1993.

Cheah, Pheng, and Bruce Robbins, eds. *Cosmopolitics: Thinking and Feeling beyond the Nation*. Minneapolis: U of Minnesota P, 1998.

Cheah, Pheng. "Grounds of Comparisons." *Diacritics*. 29. 4 (1999): 3–18.

---. "Spectral Nationality: The Living On [*sur-vie*] of the Postcolonial Nation in Neocolonial Globalization." *boundary 2*. 26.3 (Fall 1999): 225–53.

Chrisman, Laura. "Inventing Post-colonial Theory: Polemical Observations." *Pretexts* 5.1–2 (1995): 205–12.

Chrisman, Laura, and Benita Parry, eds. *Postcolonial Theory and Criticism*. Woodbridge, UK: D. S. Brewer, 2000.

Clifford, James. *The Predicament of Culture: Twentieth Century Ethnography, Literature and Art*. Cambridge: Harvard UP, 1988.

Cooppan, Vilashini. "W(h)ither Post-colonial Studies?: Towards the Transnational Study of Race and Nation." *Postcolonial Theory and Criticism*. Ed. Laura Chrisman and Benita Parry. Woodbridge, UK: D. S. Brewer, 2000. 1–35.

Copjec, Joan. *Imagine There Is No Woman: Ethics and Sublimation*. Cambridge, Massachusetts: The MIT Press, 2002.

---. *Read My Desire: Lacan Against the Historicists*. Cambridge, Massachusetts: The MIT Press, 1994.

Davis, David Brion. *The Problem of Slavery in the Age of Revolution 1770–1823*. New York: Oxford UP, 1999.

Dash, J. Michael. Introduction. *Caribbean Discourse: Selected Essays*. By Édouard Glissant. Charlottesville: UP of Virginia, 1989. xi–xlv.

Debord, Guy. *The Society of the Spectacle*. Trans. Donald Nicholson-Smith. New York: Zone Books, 1994.

Desai, Gaurav. *Subject to Colonialism: African Self-Fashioning and the Colonial Library*. Durham: Duke UP, 2001.

Dirlik, Arif. "The Postcolonial Aura: Third World Criticism in the Age of Global Capitalism." *Critical Inquiry* 20 (Winter 1994): 328–56.

Eagleton, Terry, Fredric Jameson, and Edward W. Said. *Nationalism, Colonialism, and Literature*. Minneapolis: U of Minnesota P, 1990.

Fanon, Frantz. *Black Skin, White Mask*. Trans. Charles Lam Markmann. New York: Grove Press, 1967.

---. *The Wretched of the Earth*. Preface by Jean-Paul Sartre. Trans. Constance Farrington. New York: Grove Press, 1963.

Farred, Grant. "First Stop, Port-au-Prince: Mapping Postcolonial Africa through Toussaint L'Ouverture and His Black Jacobins." *The Politics of Culture in the Shadow of the Capital*. Ed. David Lloyd and Lisa Lowe. Durham, NC: Duke, 1997.

---. "New Faces, Old Places: Re-Centering the Periphery." Lecture given at State University of New York at Buffalo. Buffalo, New York. February 2001.

---. "A Thriving Postcolonialism: Toward an Anti-Postcolonial Discourse." *Nepantla: Views from South* 2.2 (2001): 229–246.

---. "'Victorian with the Rebel Seed': C. L. R. James, Postcolonial Intellectual." *Social Text* 38 (Spring 1994): 21–38.

Featherstone, Mike. *Global Culture*. London: Sage Publications, 1990.

---. *Undoing Culture: Globalization, Postmodernism, and Identity*. London: Sage Publications, 1995.

Freud, Sigmund. *The Standard Edition of the Complete Psychological Works of Sigmund Freud*. Ed. and trans. James Strachey et al. 24 vols. London: Hogarth Press, 1958 [SE].

---. *Moses and Monotheism*. SE XXIII, 1–137.

---. *Totem and Taboo*. SE XIII, 1–161.

Furet, François. *Revolutionary France 1770–1880*. Trans. Antonio Nevill. Oxford, UK: Blackwell, 1992.

Genovese, Eugene D. *From Rebellion to Revolution*. Baton Rouge: Louisiana State UP, 1979.

Gikandi, Simon. *Maps of Englishness: Writing Identity in the Culture of Colonialism*. New York: Columbia University Press, 1996.

Gilroy, Paul. *The Black Atlantic: Modernity and Double Consciousness*. Cambridge, Massachusetts: Harvard UP, 1993.

Glissant, Édouard. *Caribbean Discourse: Selected Essays*. Trans. and ed. J. Michael Dash. Charlottesville: UP of Virginia, 1989.

---. *Le discourse antillais*. Paris: Seuil, 1981.

---. *Monsieur Toussaint*. Trans. Joseph G. Foster and Barbara A. Franklin. Washington D. C.: Three Continents Press, 1981.

---. *The Ripening*. Trans. and ed. J. Michael Dash. London: Heinemann, 1985.

Goldberg, David Theo and Ato Quayson, eds. *Relocating Postcolonialism*. Oxford: Blackwell, 2002.

Gordon, Lewis R., T. Denean Sharpley-Whiting, Renee T. White, eds. *Fanon: A Critical Reader*. Intro and Trans. by Gordon, Sharpley-Whiting, and White. Oxford: Blackwell, 1996.

Gourgouris, Stathis. *Dream Nation: Enlightenment, Colonization and the Institution of Modern Greece*. Stanford, California: Stanford UP, 1996.

Griffiths, Gareth. "Critical Approaches and Problems." *New National and Postcolonial Literatures*. Ed. Bruce King. Oxford: Oxford UP, 1996. 164–77.

Hall, Stuart. "When Was 'the Post-colonial'?: Thinking at the Limit." *The Postcolonial Question: Common Skies, Divided Horizons*. Ed. Iain Chambers and Lidia Curti. London: Routledge, 1996. 242–59.

Hallward, Peter. *Absolutely Postcolonial: Writing between the Singular and the Specific*. Manchester: Manchester University Press, 2001.

---. *Badiou: A Subject to Truth*. Minneapolis: University of Minnesota Press, 2003.

Hardt, Michael, and Antonio Negri. *Empire*. Cambridge, Massachusetts: Harvard UP, 2000.

Harootunian, H. D. "Ghostly Comparisons: Anderson's Telescope." *Diacritics* 29.4 (1999): 135–49.

Harvey, David. *The Condition of Postmodernity: An Enquiry into the Origins of Cultural Change*. Cambridge: Blackwell, 1989.

Heinl, Robert Debs, Jr., and Nancy Gordon Heinl. *Written in Blood: The Story of the Haitian People, 1492–1971*. Boston: Houghton Mifflin Company, 1978.

Hesse, Barnor. "Forgotten Like a Bad Dream: Atlantic Slavery and the Ethics of Postcolonial Memory." *Relocating Postcolonialism*. Ed. David Theo Goldberg and Ato Quayson. Oxford, UK: Blackwell Publishers, 2002. 143–73.

Hill, Pinckney Leslie. *Toussaint L'Ouverture: A Dramatic History*. Boston: The Christopher Publishing House, 1928.

Hoogvelt, Ankie M. *Globalization and the Postcolonial World: The New Political Economy of Development*. Basingstoke: Macmillan, 1997.

Huggan, Graham. *The Postcolonial Exotic: Marketing the Margins*. London: Routledge, 2001.

James, C. L. R. *The Black Jacobins: Toussaint L'Ouverture and the San Domingo Revolution*. Second ed., revised. New York: Vintage Books, 1989.

---. *The C. L. R. James Reader*. Ed. Anna Grimshaw. Oxford: Blackwell, 1992.

---. *At the Rendezvous of Victory: Selected Writings*. London: Allison & Busby, 1984.

Jameson, Fredric. *Postmodernism, or, the Cultural Logic of Late Capitalism*. Durham, NC: Duke UP, 1991.

---. "Third-World Literature in the Era of Multinational Capitalism." *Social Text* 15 (Fall 1986): 65–88.

Jameson, Fredric, and Masao Miyoshi. *The Cultures of Globalization.* Durham: Duke UP, 1998.

JanMohamed, Abdul R. "The Economy of Manichean Allegory: The Function of Racial Difference in Colonialist Literature". *Critical Inquiry* 12 (1985), 59–87.

---, and Lloyd, David. *Nature and Context of Minority Discourse.* Oxford: Oxford University Press, 1990.

Jenson, Deborah. *Trauma and Its Representations.* Baltimore: The John Hopkins UP, 2001.

King, Anthony D. "Introduction: Spaces of Culture, Spaces of Knowledge." *Culture, Globalization, and the World-System: Contemporary Conditions for the Representation of Identity.* Ed. Anthony D. King. Minneapolis: U of Minnesota Press, 1997. 1–18.

---. "The Global, the Urban, and the World." *Culture, Globalization, and the World-System.* Ed. Anthony D. King. Minneapolis: U of Minnesota Press, 1991. 149–154.

King, Bruce, ed. *New National and Postcolonial Literatures.* Oxford: Oxford UP, 1996.

Lacan, Jacques. *Écrits: A Selection.* Trans. Alan Sheridan. New York: Norton, 1977.

---. *The Four Fundamental* Concepts *of Psychoanalysis.* Ed. Jacques-Alain Miller. Trans. John Forrester. New York: Norton, 1981.

---. *The Seminar of Jacques Lacan, Book 1: Freud's Papers on Technique.* Ed. Jacques-Alain Miller. Trans. John Forrester. New York: Norton, 1988.

---. *The Seminar of Jacques* Lacan, *Book 7: The Ethics of Psychoanalysis.* Ed. Jacques-Alain Miller. Trans. Dennis Porter. New York: Norton, 1992.

---. *The Seminar of Jacques Lacan, Book 20: On Feminine Sexuality, the Limits of Love and Knowledge, 1972-1973.* Trans. Bruce Fink. Ed. Jacques-Alain Miller. New York: Norton, 1999.

Laclau, Ernesto. *Emancipation(s).* London: Verso, 1996.

---. *New Reflections on the Revolution of Our Time.* London: Verso, 1990.

Laclau, Ernesto, and Chantal Mouffe. *Hegemony and Socialist Strategy: Towards a Radical Democratic Politics.* London: Verso, 1985.

Lane, Christopher, ed. *The Psychoanalysis of Race.* New York: Conlumbia UP, 1998.

Laplanche, J., and J. B. Pontalis. *The Language of Psycho-analysis*. Trans. Donald Nicholson-Smith. Intro. Daniel Lagache. New York: Norton, 1973.

Larsen, Neil. "Marxism, Postcolonialism, and *The Eighteen Brumaire.*" *Marxism, Modernity, and Postcolonial Studies*. Ed. Crystal Bartolovich and Neil Lazarus. Cambridge, UK: Cambridge UP, 2002.

Lazarus, Neil, ed. *The Cambridge Companion to Postcolonial Literary Studies*. Cambridge, UK: Cambridge UP, 2004.

---. *Nationalism and Cultural Practice in the Postcolonial World*. Cambridge, UK: Cambridge UP, 1999.

---, et al. "The Necessity of Universalism." *differences* 7.1 (Spring 1995): 75–146.

Lefort, Claude. *Democracy and Political Theory*. Trans. David Macey. Cambridge, UK: Polity Press, 1988.

---. *The Political Forms of Modern Society*. Ed. and Intro. John B. Thompson. Cambridge: The MIT Press, 1986.

Loomba, Ania. *Colonialism/Postcolonialism*. London: Routledge, 1998.

---. "Overworlding the 'Third World'." *Oxford Literary Review* 13 (1991): 164–91.

MacCannell, Juliet Flower. *The Regime of the Brother: After the Patriarchy*. London: Routledge, 1991.

---. "Stage Left: A Review of *Contingency, Hegemony, and Universality: Contemporary Dialogues on the Left.*" *Umbr(a): A Journal of the Unconscious* (2001): 29–50.

MacClintock, Anne. "The Angel of Progress: Pitfalls of the Term 'Postcolonialism'." *Social Text* 31/32 (1992): 84–98.

---. *The Imperial Leather*. New York: Routledge, 1992.

Mamdani, Mahmood. *Citizen and Subject: Contemporary Africa and the Legacy of Late Colonialism*. Princeton, New Jersey: Princeton UP, 1996.

Marx, Karl. *The Eighteenth Brumaire of Louis Bonaparte*. With explanatory notes. New York, International Publishers, 1963.

Mbembe, Achille. *On the Postcolony*. Berkeley, CA: University of California Press, 2001.

Miller, Paul B. "Enlightened Hesitations: Black Masses and Tragic Heroes in C. L. R. James's *The Black Jacobins*." *MLN* 116 (2001): 1069–90.

Miyoshi, Masao. "A Borderless World?: From Colonialism to Transnationalism and the Decline of the Nation-State." *Critical Inquiry* 19.4 (Summer 1993): 726–51.

Moore-Gilbert, Bart. *Postcolonial Theory: Contexts, Practices, Politics.* London: Verso, 1997.

Morley, David. "EurAm, Modernity, Reason and Alterity or, Postmodernism, the Highest Stage of Cultural Imperialism?" *Stuart Hall: Critical Dialogues in Cultural Studies.* Eds. David Morley and Kuan-Hsing Chen. London: Routledge, 1996. 326–360.

Morrison, Toni. *Beloved.* New York: Plume, 1987.

---. "Unspeakable Things Unspoken: The Afro-American Presence in American Literature." *Michigan Quarterly Review* 28 (Winter 1989): 1–34.

Olaniyan, Tejumola. "On 'Postcolonial Discourse': An Introduction." *Callaloo* 16.4 (1993): 743–49.

Parry, Benita. "Problems in Current Theories of Colonial Discourse." *Oxford Literary Review* 9 (1987): 27–58.

---. "The Postcolonial: Conceptual Category or Chimera?" *The Yearbook of English Studies* 27 (1997): 3–21.

Porter, Dennis. "Orientalism and Its Problems." *Colonial Discourse and Postcolonial Theory.* Eds. Patrick Williams and Laura Chrisman. New York: Columbia UP, 1994.

Prakash, Gyan. "Postcolonial Criticism and Indian Historiography." *Social Text* 31/32 (1992): 8–19.

Radhakrishnan, R. "Postcoloniality and the Boundaries of Identities." *Callaloo* 16.4 (Fall 1993): 750–772.

Rancière, Jacques. *On the Shores of Politics.* Trans. Liz Heron. London: Verso, 1995.

Renan, Ernest. "What is a Nation?" *Nation and Narration.* Ed. Homi K. Bhabha. London: Routledge, 1990. 8–22.

Robertson, Roland. *Globalization: Social Theory and Global Culture.* London: Sage Publications, 1992.

Said, Edward. "Criticism, Culture, and Performance: An Interview with Edward Said." *Performing Arts Journal* 37 (January 1991): 21–43.

---. *Culture and Imperialism.* London: Chatto & Windus, 1993.

---. Interview with Jennifer Wicke and Michael Sprinker. [1989]. *Edward Said: A Critical Reader.* Ed. Sprinker. Oxford: Blackwell, 1992.

---. *After the Last Skies: Palestinians Lives.* New York: Pantheon, 1986.

---. *Orientalism.* New York: Vintage, 1979.

---. "Orientalism Reconsidered." *Cultural Critique* 1 (1985): 89–107.

Sassen, Saskia. *Globalization and Its Discontents.* New York: The New Press, 1998.

Schor, Naomi. "French Feminism Is a Universalism." *differences*. 7.1 (Spring 1995): 15–48.

Schwarz, Henry, and Sangeeta Ray, eds. *A Companion to Postcolonial Studies*. Oxford: Blackwell, 2000.

Scott, Joan. "Universalism and the History of Feminism." *differences*. 7.1 (Spring 1995): 1–14.

Seshadri-Crooks, Kalpana. "At the Margins of Postcolonial Studies." *Ariel*. 26.3 (July 1995): 47–71.

Shohat, Ella. "Notes on the 'Post-Colonial'." *Social Text* 31/32 (1992): 99–113.

Silenieks, Juris. Introduction. *Monsieur Toussaint*. By Édouard Glissant. Trans. Joseph G. Foster and Barbara A. Franklin. Washington D. C.: Three Continents Press, 1981. 5–15.

Slemon, Stephen, and Helen Tiffin, eds. *After Europe: Critical Theory and Postcolonial Writing*. Mundelstrup, DK: Dangaroo, 1989.

Spivak, Gayatri Chakravorty. "Can the Subaltern Speak?" *Marxism and the Interpretation of Culture*. Ed. Cary Nelson and Lawrence Grossberg. Urbana: U of Illinois P, 1988. 271–313.

---. *A Critique of Postcolonial Reason: Toward a History of the Vanishing Present*. Cambridge, Massachusetts: Harvard UP, 1999.

---. *In Other Worlds: Essays in Cultural Politics*. London: Routledge, 1988.

---. *Outside in the Teaching Machine*. London: Routledge, 1993.

---. *The Post-Colonial Critic*. London: Routledge, 1990.

---. *The Spivak Reader*. Ed. Landry, Donna and Gerald MacLean. New York: Routledge, 1996.

Springer, Hugh W. *Reflections on the Failure of the First West Indian Federation*. New York: AMP Press, 1962.

Sprinker, Michael, ed. *Edward Said: A Critical Reader*. Oxford: Blackwell, 1992.

Stavrakakis, Yannis. *Lacan and the Political*. London: Routledge, 1999.

Srivastava, Sanjay. "Postcoloniality, National Identity, Globalization, and the Simulacra of the Real." *The Australian Journal of Anthropology*. 7.2 (August 1996): 166–191.

Stallybrass, Peter. "Marx and Heterogeneity: Thinking the Lumpenproletariat." *Representations*. 31 (Summer 1990): 69–95.

Suleri, Sara. "Woman Skin Deep: Feminism and the Postcolonial Condition." *Critical Inquiry*. 18 (Summer 1992): 756–69.

Taussig, Michael. *Mimesis and Alterity: A Particular History of the Senses.* New York: Routledge, 1993.

Terada, Rei. *Derek Walcott's Poetry: American Mimicry.* Boston: Northeastern UP, 1992.

Torfing, Jacob. *New Theories of Discourse: Laclau, Mouffe and Žižek.* Oxford: Blackwell, 1999.

Trouillot, Michel-Rolph. *Haiti: State against Nation.* New York: Monthly Review Press, 1990.

Walcott, Derek. "The Caribbean: Mimicry or Culture?" *Critical Perspectives on Derek Walcott.* Ed. Robert D. Hamner. Washington, D.C.: Three Continents Press, 1993. 51–57.

---. *The Haitian Trilogy.* New York: Farrar, Straus, and Giroux, 2002.

---. *What the Twilight Says.* New York: Farrar, Straus, and Giroux, 1998.

Wallerstein, Immanuel. "The National and the Universal: Can There be Such a Thing as World Culture?" *Culture, Globalization, and the World-System.* Ed. Anthony D. King. Minneapolis: U of Minnesota Press, 1991. 91–105.

---. *The Politics of the World Economy.* Cambridge: Cambridge UP, 1984.

---. "Revolution as Strategy and Tactics of Transformation." *Marxism in the Postmodern Age.* Ed. Antonio Callari. New York: Guilford Press, 1994. 225–32.

West, Cornel. *Keeping Faith: Philosophy and Race in America.* London: Routledge, 1993.

White, Stephen. *Political Theory and Postmodernism.* Cambridge: Cambridge UP, 1991.

Williams, Adebayo. "The Postcolony as Trope: Searching for a Lost Continent in a Borderless World." *Research in African Literatures.* 31.2 (Summer 2000): 179–193.

Williams, Patrick, and Laura Chrisman, eds. *Colonial Discourse and Postcolonial Theory: A Reader.* New York: Columbia UP, 1994.

Wordsworth, William. *The Poems/William Wordsworth.* Vol. 1. Ed. John O. Hayden. London: Penguin, 1990.

---. *The Prelude (1805).* Ed. Ernest de Selincourt. London: Oxford UP, 1970.

Young, Robert J. C. *Colonial Desire: Hybridity in Theory, Culture, and Race.* London: Routledge, 1995.

---. *White Mythologies: Writing History and the West.* London: Routledge, 1990.

Zerilli, Linda M. G. "This Universalism Which Is Not One." *Diacritics*. 28.2 (1998): 3–20.

Žižek, Slavoj. "Beyond Discourse-Analysis." *New Reflections on the Revolution of Our Time*. London: Verso, 1990. 249–60.

---. *Did Somebody Say Totalitarianism?: Five Interventions in the (mis)use of a Notion*. London: Verso, 2002.

---. *Enjoy Your Symptom!: Jacques Lacan in Hollywood and out*. London: Routledge, 1992.

---. *For They Know Not What They Do*. London: Verso, 1991.

---. *The Plague of Fantasies*. London: Verso, 1999.

---. *The Sublime Object of Ideology*. London: Verso, 1989.

---. *Tarrying with the Negative: Kant and the Critique of Ideology*. Durham, NC: Duke UP, 1993.

---. *The Ticklish Subject: The Absent Centre of Political Ontology*. London: Verso, 2000.

---. *Welcome to the Desert of the Real*. London: Verso, 2002.

ibidem.eu